TOWARD HUMAN DIGNITY

TOWARD HUMAN DIGNITY:
SOCIAL WORK IN PRACTICE:

Fifth NASW Symposium

Selected Papers
Fifth NASW Professional Symposium on Social Work
November 19–22, 1977, San Diego, California

JOHN W. HANKS, Editor

NATIONAL ASSOCIATION OF SOCIAL WORKERS, INC.

1425 H STREET, N.W.

WASHINGTON, D.C. 20005

Designed by Gloria Gentile

International Standard Book No.: 0-87101-079-8
Library of Congress Catalog Card No.: 78-65076
NASW Publications No.: CBO-079-C
Printed in U.S.A.

Tip in, please.

Professional Symposium Planning Committee

Positions are those held at the time of the symposium (November 1977)

FLORENCE MOORE, MS *(chairperson)*, Executive Director, National Council for Homemaker–Home Health Aide Services, New York, New York

DONNA JO ABERNETHY, MSW, Family Counselor III, Family Services, Inc., Winston-Salem, North Carolina

HOBART A. BURCH, Ph.D., Director, School of Social Work, University of Nebraska, Omaha

DONALD L. FELDSTEIN, DSW, Executive Director, Federation of Jewish Philanthropies, New York, New York

JOHN W. HANKS, Ph.D., Director, Social Work Program, University of Wyoming, Laramie

SHANTI K. KHINDUKA, Ph.D., Dean, George Warren Brown School of Social Work, Washington University, Saint Louis, Missouri

ALICE C. McKINNON, MSW, Acting Director, Blue Water Mental Health Clinic, Port Huron, Michigan

M. TRUEHEART TITZL, Ph.D., Director, Social Work Program, Spalding College, Louisville, Kentucky

DORIS M. WILLIAMS, Ph.D., Associate Dean and MSW Program Director, School of Social Work, University of Alabama, University

RICHARD L. EDWARDS, MA *(staff)*, National Association of Social Workers, Washington, D.C.

Professional Symposium Book Committee

JOHN W. HANKS, *(chairperson)*, Ph.D., Director, Social Work Program, University of Wyoming, Laramie

SARAH CONNELL, MSW, Deputy Regional Director, New York State Department of Mental Hygiene, New York, New York

SHANTI K. KHINDUKA, Ph.D., Dean, George Warren Brown School of Social Work, Washington University, Saint Louis, Missouri

DOLORES G. NORTON, Ph.D., Associate Professor, School of Social Service Administration, University of Chicago, Chicago, Illinois

DONALD C. WILLIAMS, MSW, Program Administrator, State of Alabama Department of Pensions and Security, Montgomery

BEATRICE N. SAUNDERS *(staff)*, Director, Department of Publications, National Association of Social Workers, New York, New York

Contributors

Positions are those held at the time of the symposium (November 1977)

BERTRAM M. BECK, MSW, General Director, Community Service Society of New York, New York, New York

LOIS BRAVERMAN, MSW, Social Worker, Polk County Mental Health Center, Des Moines, Iowa

SCOTT BRIAR, DSW, Dean, School of Social Work, University of Washington, Seattle

JUDITH ANNE BRIDGEMAN, MSW, Director of Consultation-Education, Johnson County Mental Health Center, Olathe, Kansas

MARVIN E. BRYCE, Ph.D., Project Coordinator, National Clearinghouse for Home-Based Services to Children, University of Iowa, Oakdale

GENEVIEVE BURCH, Ph.D., Senior Research Associate, Center for Applied Urban Research, University of Nebraska, Omaha

HOBART A. BURCH, Ph.D., Director, School of Social Work, University of Nebraska, Omaha

LEON W. CHESTANG, Ph.D., Associate Professor, School of Social Service Administration, University of Chicago, Chicago, Illinois

JOYCE De CHRISTOPHER, MSW, School Social Worker, Bedford Central Schools, Mount Kisco, New York

JO ENSMINGER, MSW, Senior Social Worker, Center for Rape Concern, Philadelphia, Pennsylvania

SUE A. FERGUSON, BA, Graduate Student in Social Work, University of Pennsylvania, Philadelphia

LINDA K. FISHMAN, MSW, Social Work Consultant, Jarrett Associates, Van Nuys, California

DOROTHY N. GAMBLE, MSW, Research Assistant, School of Nursing, and Lecturer, Department of City and Regional Planning, University of North Carolina, Chapel Hill

MORLEY D. GLICKEN, DSW, Associate Professor, School of Social Welfare, University of Kansas, Lawrence

CECILY GREEN, Staff Associate, Center for Social and Sensory Learning, Los Angeles, California

DONNA L. JOHNSON, RN, MSW, Mental Health Therapist, Larimer County Mental Health Center, Fort Collins, Colorado

ROSALIE A. KANE, DSW, Research Consultant, Rand Corporation, Santa Monica, California

OSCAR KURREN, Ph.D., Professor, School of Social Work, University of Hawaii, Honolulu

MARILYN La CELLE, MSW, Mental Health Therapist, Larimer County Mental Health Center, Fort Collins, Colorado

E. VIRGINIA SHEPPARD LAPHAM, M.Ed., MSW, Senior Social Worker–Legislative Specialist, New York Institute for the Education of the Blind, Bronx, New York

JOANNE E. MANTELL, MS, MSPH, Doctoral Student, School of Public Health, University of California at Los Angeles

Part 3 Services to Individuals and Groups

Editor's Preface

Toward Human Dignity: Social Work in Practice expresses two major complementary professional values within the National Association of Social Workers (NASW). One concern is for the enhancement of professional practice through the dissemination of practice wisdom. The second related concern addresses the responsibility of a professional association to provide its members with opportunities for continuing education, as exemplified by the Fifth Professional Symposium, held in San Diego, California, November 19–22, 1977.

This book, together with the new NASW periodical that began publication in 1978, *Practice Digest,* epitomizes the continuing—now deepening—NASW emphasis on addressing the needs of social workers in all practice settings and modalities. These publications respond not only to the desire of some social workers to focus on clinical practice, sometimes too narrowly conceived, but to a much broader spectrum of practice. That unifying breadth—with its cross-fertilization among settings, target groups, and modalities—serves well to counterbalance the emerging centrifugal forces of social work specializations.

The growth of legal regulation, in force in nearly half the 50 states in 1978, has also become a catalyst for NASW to assume greater responsibility for continuing education programs. Clauses in licensing acts that require professionals to receive continuing education to renew their licenses reflect the dynamism of a rapidly changing practice (if not also knowledge) base, combined with the ever growing need for greater competence. The foundations of professional practice are laid in degree-granting curricula, but lifelong professional growth must come through continuing education. The NASW Professional Symposium, with this book as one specific outcome, addresses that educational continuum and is a mark of the maturity of the social work profession.

The Professional Symposium Planning Committee clearly attempted, in its call for papers, to have authors focus on practice skills. Similarly, the Book Committee responsible for this volume attempted to stress content about skills as one major criterion for the acceptance of papers for publication. Readers, however, will find that the emphasis on skills is uneven and, especially in three papers solicited and accepted from the plenary sessions, is deliberately nonexistent.

Harold Lewis, in his article "The Structure of Professional Skill," professional articles, can also help offset the current disadvantages of practitioners.

That this book came to fruition has been through the efforts of many individuals, but special recognition is due broadly to the members of the Professional Symposium Planning Committee, listed elsewhere, and more specifically to the members of the Book Committee: Sarah Connell, Shanti Khinduka, Dolores Norton, and Donald C. Williams.

The diligence and dedicated volunteer efforts of the Book Committee members, whose good humor was frequent and noteworthy, made the work of the editor both easier and more rewarding than would otherwise have been possible. The committee's careful review of all submitted articles was marked by the highest professional commitment and competence. The Book Committee members—and the editor in particular—recognize with esteem and affection the outstanding staff consultation and support from Beatrice Saunders, director, NASW Department of Publications, and her staff members. Similarly, we are deeply indebted to Dick Edwards, then staff associate, NASW, who provided incomparable staff consultation and administrative management for all the preliminary efforts, including the symposium itself, without which this book would not have been possible.

On a closing note, I call your attention to the fact that for the first time in the issuance of five symposium volumes, an undergraduate faculty member, in contrast with the graduate deans and faculty members who edited the first four symposium volumes, was chosen to edit this book. I regard my selection as a measure of the growing professional stature of the BSW social worker. This status reaffirms NASW's own concern that BSW members are fully perceived as entry-level professionals and as an important constituency with special needs within NASW itself. The implied accolade, then, comes to that constituency. In the same tenor it is also significant that in this symposium, for the first time, abstracts were solicited from students, and one of those accepted for the symposium itself was from a BSW student. Although no student paper was accepted for publication, even with anonymity being assured, it is to be hoped that future symposia will receive not only more participation from practitioners (especially those at the BSW level) but more involvement by students, both graduates and undergraduates, as well.

Laramie, Wyoming
November 1978   —JOHN W. HANKS

PART 1
ISSUES
FOR TODAY

EDITOR'S COMMENT

Policy issues, program innovations, humanistic professional values, and research related to social work practice and education come within the purview of the three invitational papers selected for this book. Despite the rich diversity in content, the papers collectively and individually are pertinent to social work practice and skills.

Beck's "Humanizing the Human Services" discusses critical, albeit controversial, issues about what he purports to be protective self-interest directions in the social work profession. Beck also reports an innovative Family Union program that exemplifies the management function of social work he stresses as a professional role for coordinating social service delivery systems in a large urban setting. Readers may well contrast and compare this program with the traditional functions for case management and interagency cooperation of the case conference and community services council.

Briar's "Research and Practice: Partners in Social Work Knowledge Development" addresses the continuing goal of forging a stronger linkage between practice and research. That need is amply demonstrated by the innumerable implications for untested research hypotheses in the papers in this book and in the rest of the social work literature. Briar describes a practitioner-scientist model, stressing competence in the single-subject design, to help bridge the chasm still too prevalent between practice and scientific evaluation.

Chestang's article, "Increasing the Effectiveness of Social Work Intervention with Minority Group Families," reminds us of the ever present struggle for human dignity of individuals and families suffering from racial discrimination. Chestang's research, reported peripherally, suggests a healthy corrective to early analyses stressing the weaknesses in black family life. Although realistically cognizant of the threats to human dignity in racism, Chestang emphasizes the strengths of survival and achievement in black families. He focuses on the crucial need for social intervention—supported by commitment, knowledge, and skills—to utilize and maximize these essential strengths for the enhancement of human dignity threatened by prejudice.

The authors of each of the three invitational papers functioned independently in addressing the theme of the 1977 symposium: "Humanizing the Human Services." Their unique responses are a stimulating "trialogue" that expresses the creativity of leaders in the social work profession. Each article, too, exemplifies anew the close-knit interrelationships of knowledge, values, skills, and program activities.

Humanizing the Human Services

BERTRAM M. BECK

As we approach the end of the seventies, those of us with a concern for the human services must acknowledge a growing sense of dissatisfaction that the promise of the sixties has not been fulfilled. During the sixties, in response to a variety of pressures, there was a significant expansion in the amount of government funds flowing into social programs.[1] As we reach the end of the seventies, there is much skepticism concerning the value of the programs launched in the sixties, pervasive doubt that governmental programs can solve social problems, and a growing lack of respect for the professions—including social work.

EXPERIENCES OF THE PAST

The response of the social work profession to this threat is to try harder to make progress on the road professions have traditionally traveled to gain economic security for their members. Legal and administrative measures are sought that favor those with full credentials. This is always done, of course, under the banner of public interest, not self-interest.[2] That road, if pursued as a major avenue, leads to disaster not because it is self-serving, but because it is out of tune with the times and ignores the sense of direction derived from the experiences of the last two decades.

Dominance of Program Maintenance over Customer Service

One such experience brought the awareness that while it is difficult to prove that increased social expenditures result in a commensurate decrease in human misery, we can with certainty prove that they result in a vast multiplication of public and voluntary agencies on a federal, state, and local level, each concerned with a different aspect of the human condition.[3]

5

Congress tends to act on the basis of perceived needs or problems. Therefore, during times of welfare expansion, programs are established to deal with persons of a specific age; or to deal with a given social problem, such as mental retardation, juvenile delinquency, child abuse, alcoholism, or drug addiction; or to make social provision for mental health, public health, education, and the like. Each time the president signs into law bills aimed at dealing with such problems, a new federal bureaucracy is established that then has its counterpart on the regional, state, city, and often neighborhood levels.

Once congressional action establishes public bureaucracies and sends money flowing into the nonprofit sector—or sometimes the proprietary sector—everybody who holds a job becomes a partisan of a given program. In that fashion, program maintenance rather than customer service achieves dominance. Medicare and Medicaid are prime examples of the way in which reimbursement to providers of care—not patient welfare—determines the nature of the care given and its intensity.[4] Coming closer to home, it seems likely that the incidence with which foster care is provided has a higher correlation to the availability of funds for providing foster care than to fluctuations in family functioning. When providers lead, consumers may follow so that alliances can be created between the persons who benefit from programs and the persons whose jobs and livelihood depend on the existence of such programs. Most who advocate social measures have a need to see themselves as concerned not with their personal welfare but with the general welfare. However beguiling such notions may be, it is well that we at least recognize the possibility that self-interest is as important a motive force in social workers' behavior as it is in the behavior of others.

This is not to denigrate the real benefits that have accrued to consumers and communities as a consequence of the social programs of the sixties and seventies. Millions of people have received health care, housing, welfare funds, jobs, education, and the like. The basic approach to problems associated with poverty, however, has been to provide services, not to reform the economic system. Given the nature of our economy, there is a reluctance on the part of any national administration—Republican or Democrat—to do anything that will cause it to lose the confidence of the business community. Nevertheless, the business community has difficulty providing sufficient job opportunities in times of peace. The alternative to jobs as an answer to poverty is the redistribution of wealth through income maintenance programs. Neither Republicans nor Democrats have found a path to the kind of welfare reform that will make a substantial dent in the problem of poverty and still pass Congress. Therefore, tax money derived from an inequitable tax structure is used to support an admittedly miserable public assistance program and to purchase programs and services primarily for the poor as America's major address to those trapped in poverty.

The New Careers Movement

Recognition that government-sponsored programs and services are a form of income transfer abetted the new careers movement in the human services. Because the Great Society's programs had no real economic base, its greatest economic impact was the provision of jobs.[5] The availability of jobs, plus consumer governance, plus the shaky status of the case for human service jobs as requiring professional training, combined to give rise to the new careers movement. At its most sophisticated, this movement held that skills attained through life experience, plus special training, would qualify masses of unemployed or underemployed people for jobs in the human services. At its least sophisticated, new careers was and is the single statement that anyone with a big heart and the right personal attributes can perform the helping task. The concern with the declassification of social work jobs that one sees in the seventies had its roots in these developments of the sixties.

Although budgetary constraints and ignorance concerning the relationship of education to quality practice are the major factors in downgrading requirements for social work jobs, there are other elements. Not only is there the aftermath of the new careers movement, there is a restlessness with structural impediments to participation that are historically related to the civil rights movement. Increasingly, persons of diverse physical capacities, sexual orientation, ethnicity, and the like proclaim their right to participate. This makes supine acceptance of the legal barriers to employment less likely than was the case in past decades. The human potential movement, with its focus on various avenues of self- and group exploration to the goal of self-actualization, is another development that deemphasizes professional credentials.[6] In addition there is the retardation of the United States' economic growth and its decline as a world power. Edging toward a less expansive economy, there may be diminished interest in aggressive economic competition and heightened interest in finding satisfying work in the service of others.

To the extent that declassification is a manifestation of these trends—which may be characterized as the human service movement—the social work profession cannot stem the tide by utilizing the traditional means—social and political power—by which professions create monopolies. Rather, it is necessary to relate tasks to education systematically, as has been done in California and elsewhere.[7] Also—and even more important—it is necessary to motivate schools, students, and practicing social workers to move away from the preoccupation with status and clinical practice, focusing instead on the role of social worker as social manager. Such managers are needed to give leadership to the organization of all human service personnel out of a chaotic provider-oriented service system into one that is more responsive to human need.

a substitution for income has been a major obstacle facing the development of social provisions. Persons with extensive education and experience in specialized areas of health, economics, education, and ecology are certainly needed. But it is the social worker of tomorrow as social planner whose role it is to deal with the interrelationships of social provisions and the heightening of community consciousness concerning the difference between social provisions and rehabilitative services.

Just as necessary social provisions need to be articulated, so it is also necessary to define problem-solving services focused on the family or individual that cut across health, welfare, education, and housing. These time-limited problem-solving services can be successfully provided by many different kinds of people with different types of training. Such people need to be deployed so as to be accessible to neighborhood groups. These people provide what have come to be called information and referral services (or more recently, access services), and they do something close to what is generally termed advocacy. Computer technology provides a way of giving such personnel access to information they require and of ensuring that there is systematic feedback from those who seek services. The job of the social worker is to envision the network of problem-solving services, assist in the training of the staff, manage the system, get customer feedback, and make necessary adjustments. It is also the social worker's job to help the community make the crucial decision as to how much of the resources available should flow to social provisions and how much to the problem-solving services that restore function so that consumer is once again dependent only on social provisions.

The third dimension of the social worker's job deals with the rehabilitation of those whose function is so impaired that massive intervention is required before they can use problem-solving services or social provisions effectively. Here are included all manner of individuals and families with physical and psychological impairments, many of which can be traced to the impact of poverty. Whatever the source, restoration of maximum function demands skills of all types of helping persons that can be brought together by social workers.

MOVING INTO THE EIGHTIES

The experience of the sixties and seventies sets the stage for the eighties. Becoming arises out of being. In stimulating development of an organization, an individual, or a profession, one cannot ignore forces arising out of past history. An immediate task before the social work profession is to find ways to weld together in a coherent whole the fragmented pattern of health, welfare, education, and community development services that have resulted from our past. This cannot be done merely by shifting boxes around and bringing together under the human services rubric all types of programs at a federal, state, or city level. Such reorganization can only be helpful insofar as it facilitates integration of services around the needs of the client in the neighborhood.

In the course of this paper, the author has sought to show how the civil rights movement of the sixties was related to the rise of interest in consumer participation in delivering and managing services. At least by inference, a relationship has been suggested between such phenomena and the increasing interest not in the abolition of centralized government, but in some forms of decentralization that will make the public structures more responsive to human need. The misuse of management technology has been cited as dehumanizing, with an emphasis on regulatory control mechanisms that do not address impact and make no provision for consumer feedback. The author has suggested that program growth must be organic, proceeding from one stage to another, and any effort at evaluation that denies this fundamental evolutionary process cannot help build knowledge that is truly useful. The emphasis on self-actualizing exercises and therapies, the interest in intuitive ways of knowing, and the entrance into human services of persons of many different backgrounds is seen not as a threat to the social work profession but as an opportunity at long last to bring to fruition the promise inherent in the many different strands that formed this profession, advancing the idea of the role of the social worker as a social leader.

Despite all the ugly and negative things that could truthfully be said about the world in which we have lived, the world in which we now live, and the world in which we will live, there is a new world struggling to be born. It is a world characterized by exchange of human feelings and human sympathy. It is a world in which artificial barriers are demolished but true differences are respected. It is a world in which social work can finally take its rightful place as the integrater and maximizer of human services. It is a world in which what has long been seen as social work's deficits—its inability to define its own knowledge and its own boundaries—become its assets. It is a world that is not alien to our past but is full of promise for our future.

NOTES AND REFERENCES

1. **Charles L. Schultz**, "The Public Use of the Private Interest," *Harpers Magazine* (May 1977), p. 43.

2. *See* **Arthur Katz**, "From the President," *NASW News,* 22 (November 1977).

3. **Schultz**, op. cit., pp. 56–57.

4. The Medicare program—officially Title XVIII of the Social Security Amendments of 1965—is a federal health-insurance program for persons 65 and over. These amendments also carry Title XIX, providing federal assistance to state medical-aid programs, known as Medicaid. Most disabled people under 65 who have been entitled to social security disability benefits also have Medicare protection. Medicaid programs cover persons receiving Aid to Families with Dependent Children and Supplemental Security Income benefits, as well as others determined by the states to be medically needy.

5. The name Great Society became the slogan of President Lyndon B. Johnson's domestic program when he said in May 1964 ". . . we have the opportunity to move not only toward the rich society, but upward to the Great Society." The Great Society's programs included the creation of new jobs, improving the nation's educational system, providing for the elderly, and aiding urban areas.

6. The human potential movement refers to programs (such as EST), places (such as Esalen in California), and practices (such as transcendental meditation) that are designed with the objective of enhancing personal development.

7. "Validation Studies Regarding Declassification Trend," *NASW News,* 22 (November 1977), p. 8.

8. *See,* for example, "Human Service Development Programs in Sixteen Allied Services (SITO) Projects" (Wellesley, Mass.: The Human Ecology Institute, 1974). (Duplicated.)

9. "Regulatory Control Models vs. Feedback Control Models in Human Services Management" (Wellesley, Mass.: Organization for Services in the Public Interest, Inc., July 1977). (Mimeographed.)

10. Laetrile, a chemical derived from apricot pits, has been widely touted as a cure for cancer and the subject of several court suits by cancer victims who wanted access to the drug. Because of such pressures, several states have authorized its use after all other means of treating the disease have failed.

Research and Practice: Partners in Social Work Knowledge Development

SCOTT BRIAR

Social work, like all professions, has its paradoxes. One—an especially unfortunate one—has to do with the relationship between practice and research. On the one hand the social work profession is publicly committed to basing its practice on a foundation of scientific knowledge. And society expects social workers to demonstrate that commitment—the concern with accountability is only one expression of that expectation. On the other hand —and here is the paradox—most social workers do not value research, and most practitioners rarely if ever look to research for solutions to their practice problems. However, not all social workers are afflicted with this ambivalence, and these exceptions are instructive.

Social workers engaged in the practice of management and administration, advocacy, planning, and policy analysis and developments tend to regard research as an integral and indispensable part of their work. They need and value the information that relevant research can provide, and, they constantly yearn for more and better information and suffer when they do not have it. Until recently, however, the kind of research needed by such practitioners was not valued by researchers because of *their* ambivalence about applied research as contrasted to what they call "basic" research. This distinction, which carries the implication that applied research as compared with basic research is less important, less difficult, more mundane, and therefore to be assigned a lesser value and status, is fading rapidly. Questions such as the long-term consequences of a substantial expansion of day care or the effects of specific policies on families are now regarded as legitimate, valued, and complex questions requiring the best that research-

15

ers can offer, and some of the most prestigious social and behavioral scientists are rushing into the applied field.

As a result, the information needs of social work administrators, planners, advocates, and policy analysts are considered respectable subjects for research, and these practitioners, at least, need have no ambivalence about their symbiotic relationship to research. Thus the research paradox and the ambivalence associated with it apply now primarily to direct service, or clinical, social work practitioners.

This leads to a second paradox, closely related to the first. The paradox is that although social work has long claimed to be one of the scientifically based professions, the field has not produced more than a handful of clinical scientists. Social work stands in sharp contrast, in that respect, to psychiatry and clinical psychology, both of which have significant numbers of clinical scientists. Social work has produced a number of gifted practice theorists, but that is not the same thing.

SOURCES OF AMBIVALENCE TOWARD RESEARCH

What are the sources of ambivalence about research among clinical practitioners? One source that has been rationalized most frequently and extensively probably should be addressed first.

Humanism versus Science

It is alleged that clinical practice is a humanistic art, and since science is not humanistic, research cannot inform art and may even be destructive of it. To put it another way, art, and therefore practice, include many unique and inherently unmeasurable phenomena that cannot be comprehended by the methods of science; to force practice into the mold of science would distort and screen out of practice its most essential ingredients. This myth —and it *is* a myth—is extremely persistent.

It is a myth because it severely distorts the realities of both practice and research. Practice is not wholly an art, if by that it is meant that the most important thing practitioners do is unique. On the contrary, practitioners engage in a constant search—from consultants, from colleagues, and from conferences—for better methods and techniques that they can use to increase their effectiveness. Methods and techniques that can be learned, transferred, and used with effective results in other practice situations are quite obviously not unique phenomena. We should be grateful for that, because if practitioners truly believed that the most essential things they do to help others are existentially unique and singular, then the social work profession would have to dispense with any aspirations to professionalism as a delusion and a sham, since social workers would have nothing to learn from each other or from the past.

It is true that the practitioner must weave together a combination of methods and techniques to suit the specific circumstances of given clients. But to liken that exercise of professional judgment and skill to the work of an artist—in the sense of a Michelangelo or a Bach—is presumptuous in the extreme. Social workers have not been commissioned to produce aesthetic masterpieces, nor would they want to be judged by such an aesthetic standard. Instead social workers are expected to solve or ameliorate human and social problems, and those outcomes are capable of measurement. A better analogy than art to what the practitioner does—if one is needed—is the engineer who applies human principles to the design of a bridge tailored to a specific set of conditions or, if you prefer, the physician who brings to bear the available knowledge about theraputics on the patient's problems. This is not to say that the exercise of professional judgment and skill does not involve creativity, or may not even be beautiful—in fact, considerable creativity and ingenuity are frequently required—but only that the purpose of the activity is not primarily aesthetic.

The function of science in a profession such as social work is to validate —or invalidate, as the case may be—the intervention principles that the practitioner uses to guide interventions, not to challenge or invalidate the reality that the practitioner must apply these principles selectively according to the particular circumstances of a specific practice situation. The latter is the essence of professional judgment.

Irrelevant Research Model

Research instruction in schools of social work—which is where the primary socialization of social workers to research occurs—has presented a model of research—the project model—that practitioners correctly perceive to be irrelevant to their own professional careers. This model depicts research ideally, as an activity that is conducted in large-scale projects; directed by professional specialists in research, involving the use of control groups, complex sampling, and statistical procedures; and in which the role of the practitioner is to provide data or to be the object of evaluation. Moreover, the examples that are presented to students for study as models of this kind of research (*Girls at Vocational High* would be a prime example) are not good examples of how research might help practitioners.[1] After all, of what use is it to be told that what you are doing is not effective? How should a practitioner apply that research?

This is not intended to be a criticism of research faculty. They taught the research models that were consistent with the highest standards of research. They were correct in teaching clinical practitioners that traditional case studies and uncontrolled group studies could not provide a valid base for drawing definitive conclusions about their effectiveness.

THE CLINICAL SCIENTIST

In the past five to six years, a major methodological breakthrough has been occurring that makes it possible to conduct rigorous research with single cases and series of single cases, and that makes it possible to conduct developmental research in practice (by developmental is meant research designed to discover and test more effective methods of practice). Moreover, these methodologies can be incorporated into the practitioner's normal practice routine. In short, these methodologies, called single-subject designs, make possible the development of the missing clinical scientists mentioned earlier.

Since the creation of more clinical scientists in social work is necessary if a scientifically based and validated profession is to be developed, and since the methodology for vigorous clinical science now is available, it is time to describe what is meant by clinical scientists: Who are they, what do they do, and what skills do they need?

What Is a Clinical Scientist?

What is meant by clinical scientist in this paper is a direct service practitioner who

1. Uses with his or her clients the practice methods and techniques that are known empirically to be most effective

2. Evaluates continuously and rigorously his or her own practice

3. Participates in the discovery, testing, and reporting of more effective ways of helping clients

4. Uses untested, unvalidated practice methods and techniques cautiously and only with adequate control, evaluation, and attention to client's rights

5. Communicates the results of his or her evaluations of practice to others

Many practitioners do not regard the concept of the clinical scientist as alien to their own image of social work practice (even though many practitioners tend to be ambivalent about research). On the contrary, the initial reaction of many practitioners is that social workers already do or at least are committed to doing the things listed as the distinctive attributes of clinical scientists. Such reactions are hardly surprising, since the characteristics of the clinical scientist are not unlike what social workers are taught should be their commitment to a scientific approach. However, any belief that social workers already do these things, or are even prepared to do them, quickly evaporates when these attributes are compared more closely with the actual behavior of social work practitioners. A few examples of such comparisons for each of the attributes will suffice to illustrate the operational meaning of the concept.

To begin with the first characteristic of the clinical scientist, to what extent do social work practitioners make an effort to use practice methods and techniques of empirically tested effectiveness? The indications are that relatively few practitioners make such efforts. For example, in order to know what tested results have been reported, it obviously is necessary to follow the research literature on practice, but it has been shown that most practitioners regard research literature as the last place they would look for answers to practice questions, and many say they would never look there. Another example is the continued refusal of many practitioners even to consider using some of the highly successful, carefully tested methods and techniques that have been reported by behaviorally oriented practitioners, even in those instances when the superior effectiveness of some of these procedures has been replicated repeatedly.

Second, to what extent do social work practitioners engage in continuous, rigorous evaluation of their own practice? For example, one of the elementary components of evaluation is posttreatment follow-up. Although the author is not aware of any systematic surveys on the subject, it is likely that most social work practitioners do not routinely follow up the progress of their cases. Moreover, when a few years ago direct-service students began to use clinical research methods in their field practice, it was found that some agencies did not want to allow the students to follow up their cases.

Third, to what extent do social work practitioners participate in the discovery and testing of more effective practice methods and techniques? Perhaps the most telling illustration is the persistent lament from researchers about the difficulties they encounter in obtaining the participation of practitioners in research projects. Of course, many practitioners do participate to the extent of generating data for studies, but their responses often are less than enthusiastic.

Fourth, to what extent do social work practitioners use untested methods and techniques only with appropriate control, evaluation, and attention to client's rights? The author's impression is that few social workers ever say to a client, "What I will do to try to help you is an untested and therefore still experimental approach—I believe it will be helpful, but there is no scientific evidence to indicate that it is, and I do not know whether there are any undesirable side effects." On the contrary, many social work practitioners make constant use of methods that have not been tested and, moreover, often act as if the validity of these methods were well established. One example, among an awesome number that could be mentioned, is the approach of Virginia Satir to family therapy that has been in widespread use for over 15 years although systematic, empirical evidence about its effectiveness still remains to be presented.

Fifth, to what extent do social work practitioners communicate the results of their work to others? *Social Work* (a professional journal published by NASW) has often been accused of being biased in favor of articles submitted by academicians. The real reason for the high proportion of academicians among the published authors in that journal is the lack of articles submitted by practitioners.

These illustrations—which could be elaborated extensively—indicate that the number of social work practitioners who possess these attributes —in other words, the number of clinical scientists in social work—is extremely small, despite the apparently widespread belief in the desirability of these qualities for practitioners.

There is no intention here to suggest or even imply that all social work practitioners should be clinical scientists—only that some should be. Specifically, any agency that employs more than a few social workers engaged in direct practice should have one clinical scientist. There should be concentrations of clinical scientists in, or connected with, schools of social work, and some students should be trained for this role.

Benefits of Clinical Scientists

What would be the expected benefits of more clinical scientists in social work? Or, to put it more bluntly, who needs them?

First, the clients of social workers need them. Clients have a right to expect that the social workers from whom they seek help will be knowledgeable about the relative effectiveness of the available methods and techniques for helping them, will use the most effective methods, and will accurately inform them (the clients) about what can be expected from the worker's interventions.

Second, clinical scientists need to meet the demands from the public for proof of social workers' effectiveness or, at least, indications that efforts are being made to increase social workers' effectiveness. The emergence of practitioner-scientists in social work would, in itself, be a strong, positive demonstration of the profession's commitment to develop more effective methods.

The development of clinical scientists also could be expected to have a number of more specific benefits for the profession. Two of these benefits are especially pertinent to this discussion. First, establishment of systematic clinical research activity in social work—even on a small scale—would accelerate the development of tested knowledge that can be applied directly in practice. The kinds of studies that thus far have dominated research on social work practice—perhaps exemplified best by *Girls at Vocational High* —have been relatively large-scale projects requiring a substantial investment of professional research staff and related resources.[2] Such studies take a long time, can be conducted only infrequently because of the heavy investment required, and—whatever other knowledge they generate—by virtue of their design tend not to generate findings that have immediate, direct utility for practitioners.

In contrast, programs of clinical research could be conducted with relatively small investment of resources by clinicians themselves. Moreover, the nature of clinical research is more likely to produce findings that are directly utilizable by practitioners. A second specific benefit is that encouragement of clinical scientists in social work is likely to lead to the development of models and methods for the continuous, empirical evaluation of practice that can be incorporated into the routine practice of social work clinicians generally. This benefit is suggested by the author's experience in teaching clinical research methods to students.

PREPARATION OF CLINICAL SCIENTISTS

Assuming that it may be desirable to have more clinical scientists in social work, a next question is: What is required to prepare and develop them? Before describing the approach taken at the University of Washington, it will be useful to identify the necessary conditions and requirements for clinical scientists, since these must be satisfied both in the educational preparation of clinical scientists and in their subsequent work.

Requirements for Clinical Scientists

1. Clinical scientists in social work need to be practitioners first. That is to say, practitioner-scientists should have adequate—and preferably superior—training and skill in direct practice. One obstacle to meeting this requirement is the still widespread but completely fallacious belief that it is impossible for the same person to be a good practitioner and a good researcher. There are a variety of reasons for this requirement—many of them obvious—but one especially important reason is that the credibility of a piece of clinical research, in the eyes of other practitioners, is affected by the perceived practice competence of the person who conducts it.

2. The practitioner-scientist should have a thorough knowledge of the literature and research on social work practice. It is important that such practitioners be familiar with what has been done before as well as with the current issues and questions.

3. Students preparing for the clinical scientist role must have the capacity to practice in the face of uncertainty. Absolute, unconditional faith in the efficacy of a given practice approach is not compatible with the attitude required to evaluate that method. There is, of course, a view held by some social workers that faith in the practice approach one is using is a necessary condition for effectiveness, and conversely that doubts about the

efficacy of the practice methods one uses increases the likelihood that outcomes will be unsuccessful. The author is unaware of any systematic evidence that supports this view, which suggests that it is not true.

4. The clinical scientist in social work needs to have an understanding of the logic and methodology of science and detailed knowledge and competence in the application of the developing methodology of single-subject designs.

5. One of the more difficult requirements for many practitioners to meet is skill in translating and expressing service objectives and interventions in observable, measurable terms. This skill can, however, be acquired and is a necessary condition for use of single-subject design methodologies.

6. Practitioner-scientists should acquire a reasonably clear sense of research practices, especially the centrality of outcome and effectiveness questions. The intervention process has many fascinating aspects, and it is easy to be drawn into the study of intrinsically interesting questions that, however, may have no bearing on effectiveness.

7. Clinical scientists also should assume a commitment to the development of research and evaluative methodologies and tools that can be incorporated into the routine practice of social workers. Some components of typical single-subject design methodologies, such as baselining and monitoring, have been incorporated into routine practice by some social workers who find them useful in their practice, apart from their usefulness for research purposes.

8. Another essential requirement is that clinical scientists disseminate the results of their work—negative as well as positive—as widely as possible.

9. Finally, the practice of clinical research imposes certain requirements on the practice environment, requirements that must be satisfied if clinical research is to develop. One of these requirements is time. A clinical researcher in an agency, for example, would need to carry a smaller case load than other workers, because the amount of time devoted to each case would be substantially greater. Second, the research practitioner would need greater freedom to select cases for research purposes, especially since replication is a frequently used tool in clinical research. And third, an environment that accepts and even encourages experimentation and research is essential. Some students at the University of Washington reported that agency colleagues viewed them with suspicion simply because they were making graphs of the behavior of their clients over time. Such practices are commonplace, of course, in medical settings, but the attitude toward research procedures in many social agencies is mixed and can inhibit clinical research.

As this example makes clear, this requirement, and the previous ones as well, are not the responsibility of schools and educators alone—they extend obviously into the profession and into agencies. In fact, it is the author's experience that unless these requirements are addressed, our best educational efforts to prepare and encourage students to engage in clinical research, even of the most modest kind, can be blunted following training because these requirements and conditions are not present where the former student is practicing. This problem may be more clear after the following brief overview of how the objective of training students for clinical research has been approached at the University of Washington.

A Case History

Four years ago, the author and a colleague took one section of a two-quarter required research course and, on an experimental basis, set out to teach the methods and techniques of clinical research within the clinical scientist model. Heavy reliance was placed on the single-subject design—which was just emerging in the field at the time—as the primary research model, which was elaborated into a research-practice model. By research-practice, is meant a model that can be incorporated into practice routinely without altering the social worker's normal or preferred mode of practice. Since we also wanted the students to conduct clinical research on their cases in the field, we were in communication with the students' field instructors. The students enrolled in our section of the course were self-selected volunteers.

Evaluated against general criteria, the course appeared to have been relatively successful, but one of the most important outcomes was unexpected. By about the sixth or seventh week of the class, it was found that a distinct and clear separation between research and practice could no longer be maintained. As students began to apply what they were learning in the field, they not only incorporated the research-practice model into their practice, but research and practice became fused, and we found that when we addressed research, we were also talking about practice and vice versa.

It is difficult to illustrate this point fully without lengthy examples. For instance, in order to consider how to measure a potential intervention target —either for baseline or monitoring purposes—it turns out to be necessary to examine how that or any target is selected, how it should be specified for a given client, how to measure it in the intervention process, what kind and direction of change in this target is desired, what interventions are to be used, and so on to a host of questions that are directly pertinent to the research task but also are simultaneously "practice" questions. Since both of us were qualified to teach practice courses, we responded to these realities as best we could, but we lacked the time to be as effective as would have been desirable.

A year later, some major changes were made in the course based on the first year's experience. First, we assumed responsibility for one section of a two-quarter direct-practice course and combined that with the section of the required research course to create a two-quarter practice-research course that was the equivalent, in time and credit, to two courses. Second, several field work sites were selected that (a) were supportive of the model we were teaching and (b) were agreeable to our plan that we would supervise one of the student's cases (the student's "research case") in the classroom. (This combination of practice, clinical research, and selected field sites into one unit has come to be called "educational units.") The seminar met twice a week for a total of four to five hours. For most of the two quarters, one of the weekly sessions was used as a continuous case conference to review and provide detailed consultation to the students on their research cases; the field instructors were invited to these conferences, as well as to any other part of the course they wanted to attend.

This course attracted the interest of other faculty members and of other students who requested an opportunity to have a similar educational experience. As a result, a few additional educational units were added the following year and still more the next year, so that by 1977 the educational unit format became standard for *all* first-year direct-service students. A number of faculty members at the university have the background to teach both practice and clinical research, but several sections are taught conjointly by two faculty members, one who brings in the practice component and the other of whom is responsible for clinical research materials and perspectives.

CONCLUSIONS

On the basis of these experiences at the University of Washington, a few generalizations can be drawn that are pertinent to the subject of integrating research into education for direct practice in social work.

1. The author is under no illusion that students trained in the university's educational units are thereby prepared to be clinical scientists. However, they now have the concept of what a clinical scientist is, they have learned some of the basic tools of clinical research—and many of them will continue to use some of these tools as part of their practice—and they see clinical research as something that can be of direct help to them as practitioners. In other words, there is no discontinuity between the practitioner and the practitioner-scientist; rather, the difference is only one of degree and emphasis.

2. That small number of students who complete the educational unit and want to develop careers as clinical scientists will need to acquire the additional training required to conduct more sophisticated clinical research. Plans are now being made to develop programs for

such students in the second year of the MSW program. Beyond that, of course, is doctoral study, where even more intensive preparation of clinical scientists is possible.

3. The emergence of single-subject design methodologies has played a critical, probably indispensable, part in the recent success of efforts in a number of schools to incorporate research into the education of direct-service social workers. Essentially these methodologies have made it possible to conduct fairly rigorous experimental and evaluative research on a small scale with limited resources. Potentially even more important, these methodologies are especially well suited for developmental research that seeks to discover new and better practice methods.

Unfortunately, a belief has emerged among some social workers that the single-subject methodologies are suitable only for behavioral approaches to intervention. This belief, which has impeded more extensive use of these methodologies, is without foundation. For example, at the time of this writing nine sections of the educational units described are being offered. In some of these the practice approach is based on ego psychology, others follow the task-centered approach, others teach an interpersonal orientation, and some are behaviorally oriented. What these instructors have in common is a commitment that the same questions should be raised about each approach, none of them has a superior a priori claim to truth, students should be taught the elements of clinical research, and in the long run the differences between approaches should be resolved or clarified through research findings.

The tools are now available with which to begin to build a systematic, empirical base for clinical practice in social work. Moreover, it has been demonstrated that these tools can be taught to students and that most students find this learning to be interesting, pertinent, and even exciting. However, it also seems clear that if graduates are asked to use these tools, ways will have to be found to help create in the profession and in social agencies the conditions that are necessary if clinical research is to take root and flourish in social work.

NOTES AND REFERENCES

1. **Henry J. Meyer, Edgar F. Borgatta, and Wyatt C. Jones**, *Girls at Vocational High: An Experiment in Social Work Intervention* (New York: Russell Sage Foundation, 1965).

2. Ibid.

Increasing the Effectiveness of Social Work Intervention with Minority Group Families

LEON W. CHESTANG

At the heart of social work values and at the center of the profession's mission is a belief in the dignity of all human beings. This belief has particular relevance for our concern with the social problems and the social functioning of blacks and other ethnic minorities because a major challenge facing ethnic minorities—especially blacks—is the assertion of their dignity in a society in which this is threatened.

It is a commonplace that the attainment and maintenance of a person's sense of value and worth is a function of the interaction of factors in the family and factors in the person's social environment. Both sets of factors can play a crucial role in fostering or restricting a person's sense of dignity as a human being.

Differences of opinion about the relative weight to be assigned to family factors as fostering or restricting the sense of dignity of blacks continue to exist. Some observers argue that social factors deserve primary attention in the effort to understand the social functioning of blacks. Others argue that the nature of family life is the crucial variable. Neither of these single-faceted perspectives, however, contributes to a meaningful understanding of or effective intervention with such families.

The thesis of this article is that consideration of both sets of factors as they interact promises to be the most fruitful path to a clearer understanding of and effective intervention with these families. An effort will be made to analyze the critical familial and environmental factors that threaten the dignity of and interfere with the achievement of goals by black and other minority group persons. A proposal thought to have potential for increasing the effectiveness of social work intervention with members of these groups will be presented and implications for practice will be discussed.

In spite of an abundance of evidence to the contrary, the popular view persists that deficits in the black family explain the failure of black people to achieve their goals.[1] Investigators, both black and white, have demonstrated the inaccuracy of that position and have argued instead that the black family is surprisingly adaptive, resilient, and effective in the face of unconscionable social assault.[2] It is unnecessary to repeat their arguments here. Interest in social and interpersonal factors as these affect dignity will be advanced, however, by a brief review of the context and content of black family socialization. Black families thought to epitomize the interaction of familial and environmental factors were selected for scrutiny.

This analysis is based on a study by the writer of the lives of 20 successful black Americans.[3] The study was done according to the constant comparative method of qualitative analysis described by Glaser and Strauss.[4] This method permits close interaction between the investigator and the data, but it requires that propositions and hypotheses generated from the study emerge from the data themselves, not from external sources. The 20 autobiographies were selected according to the subjects' region of residence, sex, and period in which the book was written. This selection served to identify appropriate sources of information for the study. The goal in gathering data, however, was to select from these sources incidents relevant to the question under study. These *incidents* comprised the data for the study. The method of analysis involved coding each relevant incident into a category, integrating the categories by comparing incidents with the accumulated knowledge on a category, and finally delineating the analysis by clarifying logic, taking out nonrelevant properties, and supplying elaborating details so that one ends up with a major outline of a set of interrelated categories.

Although the study sought to explain how blacks achieve success in American society, some of the findings shed light on the main concern of this article. The discussion that follows is anchored in selected formulations from that earlier analysis.

THE FAMILY: WHERE DIGNITY BEGINS

The subjects whose lives were analyzed in the study cited could be divided into two broad categories. The first of these was designated *achievement oriented* and the other, *survival oriented.*

Achievement-Oriented Families

Among achievement-oriented families, two factors seemed to account for the families' capacity to socialize their children toward success: the presence of the father and the family's capacity to support itself. Fathers in such families characteristically function effectively in their roles as provider for and protector of their families. They share with the mothers the responsibility for socialization of the children.

The central theme of socialization among these families is success, or "getting ahead in life." In keeping with this goal, children are instilled with the same values associated with achievement in society at large. Their socialization occurs in a supportive and benign relationship with their parents, and they are taught to aspire toward educational achievements and to have a strong religious orientation. Optimism is fostered by teaching hope for the future.

But these parents are not unaware of the barriers their children will face because of their race. Because they are acutely sensitive to the realities of racism, they consciously seek to shield their children from the most blatant expressions of racism while the children are young and impressionable. As the children inevitably move out into the wider world and encounter racism, their parents didactically affirm their worth and dignity. "You are no piece of dirt," one subject's mother said. "You are somebody." The experience of innumerable black youths parallels that of Angela Davis, Malcolm X, and Lena Horne in this regard.[5] What all of this suggests is that black children from achievement-oriented families typically enter the wider society with dignity intact and that belief in one's worth and dignity is begun in the family.

Survival-Oriented Families

Whereas socialization in achievement-oriented families focuses on success, or "getting ahead" in life, socialization in survival-oriented families focuses on fulfilling basic needs and maintaining self-esteem. Two conditions dispose these families toward a survival orientation: the absence of the father and the family's inability to support itself. As a result of these conditions, the mothers have to assume the roles of provider and protector. The effect of this situation is reflected in the context and the content of child socialization.

In survival-oriented families, a special relationship exists between the mothers and their children. As the child's sole nurturer, provider, and protector, the mother is idealized by the child as altruistic, powerful, and self-sacrificing—in effect, the child's savior. It is to be emphasized that the child's perception of the mother is not an illusion, nor is this designation of her fully explained by a childish tendency to idealize the parent on whom one is dependent. The mother's is an identity, to borrow Erikson's phrase, "won through action."[6] It is the mother, after all, who provides for the children's physical needs, who shows them affection, and who, even when the family is large, makes each child feel special. On this point, one of the subjects recalled:

> When my mother did my hair or washed my face, it was like I was a princess, because she made it so plain that I was important and how I looked was important too. My grandmother said it was wrong to be dirty, but Mama said it was beautiful to be clean. Looking back, I guess Mama treated all us kids the same, but somehow she made each one feel the most important.[7]

The ingenuity of these mothers in creating a sense of specialness in their children is revealed in a recollection by Dick Gregory:

> Garland and I'd be fighting and one of us would say, "Mama likes me better than you, look what she gave me," and we both found out that the other had a secret present too.[8]

In spite of valiant efforts by the survival-oriented mother to meet the needs of her children, her circumstances, the absence of male support, and her limited financial resources greatly restrict her capacity to do so. Work, necessitated by the absence of a husband, and fear, occasioned by preoccupation with her responsibilities, limit her physical and emotional availability to her children.

It is within this context that children from survival-oriented families are socialized, and their socialization is dominated by two themes: precocious independence and early assumption of responsibility. These children learn to meet many of their own needs, to care for themselves, to protect themselves. In short, they must assume, well before they are sufficiently mature, the responsibilities of adults. Space does not permit a detailed discussion of the processes involved in their socialization, but a brief comment on its effects may be helpful.

Forced to assume adult responsibilities but still a child, the survival-oriented child has an inner life pervaded by anxiety and fear. For all the mother's efforts to neutralize or nullify the child's anxiety, for all the benefits accruing to the child's coping with and adaptation to the racial and family situation, these processes are accompanied by fear. One subject gave the following account of his mother's attempt to direct him and his siblings on the course of survival:

> When she returned [from work] at evening she would be dispirited and would cry a lot. Sometimes, when she was in despair, she would call us to her and talk to us for hours, telling us that we had no father, that our

lives would be different from those of other children, *that we must learn as soon as possible to take care of ourselves, to dress ourselves, to prepare our own food; that we must take upon ourselves the responsibility of the flat while she worked. Half frightened we promised solemnly.* [Italics added][9]

Shame allies with fear to assault further the survival-oriented child's sense of dignity. Shame is felt most poignantly as the child grows older and moves beyond the family. This feeling is associated with having to depend on the largesse of others, with having fewer and more modest possessions than one's peers, and with living in less adequate housing than others. One subject tells of her embarrassment when some of her schoolmates happened on her younger brother and sister playing naked in the sand in front of her house. Seeing the subject's siblings, her friends laughed and made fun of them. The subject's response was revealing:

I was ashamed to go in the house or recognize Adline or Junior as my little sister and brother. I had never felt that way before. I got mad at mama because she had to work and couldn't take care of Adline and Junior herself. Everyday after that I hated the sand in front of the house.[10]

These and like experiences exact their toll on the coping and adaptation of survival-oriented children, and they also play an important role in rendering vulnerable their sense of dignity and self-esteem.

SUPPORTS OF AND THREATS TO DIGNITY

As black children move out from the family into their own community and beyond into the world of the larger society, they face powerful influences on their sense of dignity. These influences are the realities of ghetto life and of the wider society.

The Black Community

What was the nature of the experiences in their own community and in the wider society that supported or threatened the sense of dignity of survival-oriented children? Within the black community, it was the subjects' perception of and participation in a world that was at once impoverished and sordid, exciting and supportive. These seemingly paradoxical perceptions of the black community reflected the combination of realities these children encountered in their own neighborhoods. These realities, not unknown to achievement-oriented persons, represent, however, the crucial difference between the worlds of achievement- and survival-oriented subjects. The achievement-oriented subjects usually looked out from the secure realm of family protection and support upon the poverty about them; the survival-oriented subjects, at home and in the neighborhood, were surrounded by and lived in the midst of poverty.

Again, it is the effect of this condition that claims attention. Achievement-oriented persons saw the inadequacy and inferiority of their physical surroundings as a reflection of benefits denied them by the wider society. They were pushed by this to acquire the privileges of white society that they saw as the basic difference between the two communities. The urgency of the survival-oriented subjects' needs renders them less ambitious in this respect and willing to settle for the more limited goal of need satisfaction. This idea is epitomized in the aspiration of one subject's friend—almost an adult—who grew up in a family in which the children had to fight and scheme to get food before anyone else because the mother seldom bought food. His grand aspiration was "to get [my] own place so that I [can] have me a refrigerator that's always full of food."[11] This and like levels of aspiration show how consistent deprivation can cause survival-oriented persons to restrict their ambitions and restrain their hopes.

The pressures that poverty exerts on the lives of the poor must inevitably be coped with. How people cope has important implications for an understanding of the black poor. In this connection, subjects described fights in which people were cut, stabbed, or shot to death. One subject described the broad-scale use of drugs as a "big ghost haunting the community."[12]

Dealing with the pressures on their lives, however, was by no means limited to violence and drugs. Such benign activities as playing cards, throwing dice, or simply hanging about the streets talking and singing served to bring people together and to bind them in friendships. For the survival-oriented child, the neighborhood, its impoverishment notwithstanding, was interesting and exciting.

A dimension of life in poor black communities that cannot go unmentioned is its supportiveness. This encompasses sharing homes, food, conversation, and leisure-time activities with family and friends. It also includes the practice of extending acceptance and support to persons whose life styles differ from one's own. This means that the gambler, the prostitute, the numbers runner, and many other types are judged in the context of survival values rather than normative social values. This idea clarifies the nature of the bond existing among survival-oriented persons and their families, and it connects the discrepant and paradoxical perceptions of the black community just discussed.

There exists among survival-oriented subjects a network of relationships that evolves out of their common encounter with deprivation and discrimination. These relationships, based on understanding and sympathy, motivate those with little to help those with less. They may be expressed in taking an orphan into one's family or in contributing money for the education of a promising student. What all of this suggests is that in spite of the impoverishment, violence, and sordidness so frequently seen among survival-oriented subjects, coexisting with these are tenderness and caring.

The Wider Society

The black family (and the black community), as Billingsley has shown, does not function in a vacuum.[13] It functions in the context of the wider society, subject to impingements from it. These bear heavily on all black families but are experienced with even greater force by poor or survival-oriented families. The manner in which these impingements are experienced by poor black families deserves special mention.

For black people, the white world is alien, the white world is privileged, and the white world disparages their worth. Experiences associated with these three aspects of interaction with the wider society condition the black person's perception of and attitude toward that society.

Among survival-oriented persons, alienation leads to a feeling that whites and their world are strange. The feeling of fear figures prominently in these persons' perceptions of the strangeness of the white world. Both fear and strangeness originate in the process and the content of the black child's learning about the peculiar relationship existing between blacks and whites. As was the case with much of their earlier social learning, these children are left to discover the nature of this relationship for themselves. Thus, to paraphrase one subject, they stumbled upon the relations between blacks and whites, and what they learned frightened them. They learned, as did Malcolm X, that one's home could be destroyed by night riders; they learned, as did Anne Moody, that a black person could be killed for almost any reason; and they learned, as did Claude Brown, that the law did not necessarily guarantee them protection from these things.[14] They learned, in a word, that white persons held the power of life and death over them, and their fears, previously vague and uncertain, became concrete and specific. Equally important, their fears were compounded when they learned that usually their parents could neither protect their children nor themselves from harm.

The point has been made that poor black children tend to evaluate the world in terms of their poverty. Nowhere is this more striking than in the manner in which they evaluate what may be called the privileges of the white world. Like black children of greater means, these children were aware, as one subject put it, that white "schools, homes and streets were better than [theirs]," but they tended to evaluate these things from the vantage point of their poverty.[15] Thus, to the envy and ambivalence felt by achievement-oriented persons in response to observation of white advantage, survival-oriented persons add their unabashed desire to possess the material benefits enjoyed by whites.

White privilege is seen as extending to almost every realm of life—in the legal system that incarcerates blacks without provocation, in the welfare system whose social workers enter black homes freely, in the world of employment where whites always have the most authority and certainly hold the most desirable positions.

As concerns their exposure to social injustices, survival- and achievement-oriented blacks differ primarily in the extent to which they are exposed to these practices, not in the manner by which they accommodate to or resist them. In confronting social injustice, they differ only in their motivation: achievement-oriented blacks are motivated to succeed; survival-oriented blacks are motivated to survive.

Finally, confronting implications of inferiority and lack of worth is a common experience among survival-oriented blacks. While such experiences may occur in informal transactions with whites, such as in stores and shops, more frequently, because of limited contact with whites in other spheres, poor blacks encounter personal disparagement in the context of their employment. The importance of this lies in the contrast between the responses of these subjects and their counterparts.

Achievement-oriented blacks often speak of being refused some common courtesy or of being denied access to some social opportunity. Disparagement as experienced by survival-oriented subjects is more basic and blatant and has the effect of threatening self-esteem. Because they are in pursuit of fundamental survival needs, poor blacks often have no recourse but to accept the insults and indignities thrust at them. Thus, although they resent and are angered by implications of inferiority, poor blacks are more often compelled by their circumstances to suppress their feelings. Suppression of feelings and acceptance of indignities constitute a major adaptive technique for these people. It is used because through such behavior they see themselves as being able to meet their most pressing needs—food, clothing, and shelter.

One subject's response to being assigned to the furnace pit (the least desirable work area) by a bigoted employer acting on the stereotype that blacks are able to endure intense heat is illustrative:

Well the system wasn't going to beat me. I stood up next to that furnace, and I ate their goddamned salt tablets and just refused to pass out. They weren't going to make me quit, and I wasn't going to give them cause to fire me. I'd lean over that blazing pit until my face would sting, and

when the lunch whistle blew I'd fall on the floor and vomit blood for half
an hour and I'd clean it up myself.

It was all worth it. I could walk home at the end of the week and put
money in Mama's hand. We could go shopping with cash in hand instead
of the green tablet.[16]

THE PROCESS OF SOCIAL INTERVENTION

Examined next will be the factors that foster or inspire the dignity of
blacks regardless of family functional orientation. The focus will again be
on survival-oriented blacks, although process applies also to achievement-
oriented persons.

As black children seek to achieve their goals and to assert their dignity,
a critical factor in determining whether these goals are reached—and indeed, whether the desire to reach them is sustained—is the presence and the
active involvement of other people, black and white, who provide various
forms of emotional support, guidance and direction, and concrete help.
Such persons may be referred to as *social intervenors.* While the interaction
between these persons and blacks fits well the familiar concept of "significant others," they are designated here as social intervenors because this term
seems to capture more specifically the nature and the process of their
relationships with blacks.

Intervenor as Provider of Emotional Support

Social and sometimes family conditions can threaten the black child's
sense of dignity and self-esteem. Parents who are harsh or unavailable to
their children, insensitive teachers who criticize unnecessarily, neighborhood influences that militate against achievement, and discrimination that
limits social opportunity threaten self-confidence, singly but most often in
combination. If the black child is to maintain self-esteem, a response that
will be effective against the threatening condition is called for. Thus, one
of the central needs of the black child is for emotional support. Encouragement that strengthened belief in oneself; acknowledgment of talents, abilities, and skills; and demonstration of interest and concern are among the
ways in which emotional support was given to the subjects in the study.
Emotional support also became the mode for other forms of social intervention. Emotional support, then, describes both something the social intervenor does and how she or he does it.

The aspect of interaction with social intervenors that had a profound impact on survival-oriented subjects was the intervenors' consistency and fairness, because this was in such sharp contrast to the subjects' previous experience and hence to their expectations. Being treated
equally was important to these subjects because of the unfairness and

disparagement they had encountered from persons in authority or from more advantaged peers as well as from the wider society. The subjects' identification with the social intervenors gave these persons a special significance for the subjects, opening the way for provision and acceptance of help in other ways.

Intervenor as Mentor

The role of the social intervenor as mentor involves teaching specific knowledge and skills, giving guidance and direction, and exposing the person to new experiences. Such help is required by black children from both achievement- and survival-oriented families, except that for the survival-oriented child, this help needs to be more basic in its content.

For example, many survival-oriented parents are unable to help their children with schoolwork or are not available for this activity. Uneducated themselves and focused on meeting survival needs, these parents cannot serve as models for their children in regard to education. To be sure, many of these parents are highly aware of the value and importance of education, and they admonish their children to "get a good education." Beyond such admonitions, however, these parents can do little to aid their children with schoolwork, so the major task of inspiring and helping children in relation to school is left to teachers and other mentors.

Encountering new experiences is an important extension of the learning process just discussed. Social intervenors often introduce the person to such experiences through books. Through books, many of the subjects in the study were acquainted for the first time with black history and the contributions made by outstanding black persons to various fields of endeavor. Their introduction to books came in various contexts and through persons of both races. It was typical of survival-oriented subjects to be impressed with the power of the written word and, after an initial introduction to books, to pursue further reading on their own. After Claude Brown read the autobiography of Mary McLeod Bethune, for example, he became fascinated with reading and began asking his mentor for books. "I started reading more and more," he said, "and liking it more and more."[17] Malcolm X's response to the suggestion of Bimbi, a fellow prisoner, that he should take advantage of the prison library and correspondence courses is still another example: "When the mimeographed listing of available books passed from cell to cell, I would put my number next to titles that appealed to me which weren't already taken."[18]

A person might also be introduced to new experiences by simply being told about places to which someone had traveled. The experience of one of the subjects in the study is a good example:

> Miss Clairborne would tell me about places she had traveled and people she met while traveling. I was learning so much from them. Sick or well,

I went to work. I was afraid if I stayed home I would miss out on something.[19]

Intervenor as Role Model

Social intervenors also represented models to be emulated. What made
them attractive to so many subjects was their ability to use language to
communicate, to persuade, and to achieve their goals. For the black child,
this is a novelty because of the uncommonness of encounters with such
persons among their immediate associates. Here is one subject's description
of his reaction to talking with a minister:

> I sat down and talked to him. I didn't know anybody with such a gigantic
> intellect existed in Harlem. When I first met him, I wanted to talk for
> hours to the guy . . . Somehow I had the feeling that talking to him that
> night was more profitable than sitting in the library and reading for
> weeks.[20]

Social intervenors provide children with new identifications. And as
models they help children broaden their horizons, heighten their aspirations, and stimulate interest in learning. It is important to point out that
in doing this, these social intervenors begin the process of these children's
socialization toward an achievement orientation.

Intervenor as Provider of Concrete Help

The survival-oriented child's need for concrete resources has been
stressed throughout this article. This need is of special importance in changing the person's orientation. Emotional support, knowledge, and skill are
not sufficient to give substance to these children's emerging hope that their
lives can be fuller and more meaningful. If their awakening hopes are to be
transformed into realities, they need in addition to have access to material
means. These means include such things as money and other material goods
and opportunities to exercise their abilities. By providing concrete help,
social intervenors demonstrated their real concern for the person, and they
facilitated the transition from a survival to an achievement orientation.

IMPLICATIONS FOR SOCIAL WORK

Implementing the social work profession's belief in the value of human
dignity and achieving its goal of effective service to blacks and other minorities requires a fresh look at some of the profession's traditional beliefs. As
a first step, social work's own behavior and practice theorists, in combination with practitioners, should seek to specify further the nature of the
interaction between family and neighborhood and impingements from the

wider society as these affect the social functioning of blacks and other minorities. The evidence presented here and in many other places amply demonstrates the existence and the erosive impact of discrimination and prejudice in the lives of black and other minority persons. But there is also evidence for the powerful influence exerted by family and neighborhood.

It is time, therefore, to cease the polemics about what and who is to blame. It is necessary instead to develop the knowledge, skills, and commitment to intervene in any or all of these areas—family, neighborhood, and society—when this is called for.

In taking this stance, however, one need not forget the individual child, and the observations made here about the role of social intervenors are a good point of departure. These observations reaffirm the importance of emotional support and guidance as a foundation for providing help, and they highlight its importance to those for whom the twin evils of poverty and racism present additional barriers to the assertion of dignity.

In addition, the concept of the social intervenor has important implications for the development of practice principles. This idea of the social intervenor suggests that black and other minority families need someone who is willing to serve in a mentor relationship, who will teach and show the way, who will open doors of opportunity, and who can serve as a role model. Such a social intervenor is an active participant with the client in achieving goals. He or she may recognize the value of insight but will know also that for the person who has had little, for whom hope may be in short supply, and who has been victimized by prejudice and discrimination, efforts to help cannot be restricted to the office or the mind.

Finally, if social workers are to be truly effective social intervenors, they must be willing to get their hands dirty again. They must be willing to go into the ghettos and *barrios* and to work with families whose styles of communication, organization, and participation do not fit the social mold. More important, they must be willing to do this not with the goal of changing these families, but to help them fulfill a common human need —the assertion of dignity—and a basic human right—the right to service that is both human and effective. Social work, having a profound concern with human welfare, a tradition of service to those who stand at the fringe of society, and knowledge accumulated over years of involvement in the lives of such families, is uniquely qualified to rise to this challenge.

NOTES AND REFERENCES

1. **Daniel P. Moynihan**, *The Negro Family: The Case for National Action* (Washington, D.C.: United States Department of Labor, March 1965).

2. *See,* for example **Andrew Billingsley,** *Black Families in White America* (Englewood Cliffs, N.J.: Prentice-Hall Inc., 1968); **E. Liebow,** *Tally's Corner* (Boston: Little, Brown, 1967); and **J. A. Ladner,** *Tomorrow's Tomorrow: The Black Woman* (Garden City, N.Y.: Anchor, 1972).

3. **Leon W. Chestang,** *Achievement and Self-Esteem Among Black Americans: A Study of Twenty Lives.* Unpublished Ph.D. dissertation, University of Chicago, School of Social Service Administration, June 1977.

4. For a detailed explication of these procedures, *see* **B. Glaser** and **A. Strauss,** *The Discovery of Grounded Theory: Strategies for Qualitative Research* (Chicago: Aldine Publishing Co., 1967), pp. 101–115.

5. Examples of such parental teaching are seen in **Angela Davis,** *An Autobiography* (New York: Random House, 1974); and **Malcolm Little,** *The Autobiography of Malcolm X* (New York: Grove Press, Inc., 1964).

6. **E. H. Erikson,** *Childhood and Society* (2d ed.; New York: W. W. Norton & Co., 1963).

7. **Ossie Guffy,** *Ossie: The Autobiography of a Black Woman,* as told to Caryl Ledner (New York: Bantam, 1971), pp. 2–3.

8. **Dick Gregory,** *Nigger: An Autobiography,* with Robert Lipsyte (New York: Pocket Books, 1965), p. 5.

9. **Richard Wright,** *Black Boy: A Record of Childhood and Youth* (New York: Harper & Bros., 1966), p. 23.

10. **Anne Moody,** *Coming of Age in Mississippi* (New York: Dell, 1968), p. 33.

11. **Claude Brown,** *Manchild in the Promised Land* (New York: Signet Book, New American Library, 1965), p. 247.

12. Ibid., p. 188.

13. **Billingsley,** op. cit, p. 111.

14. **Little,** op. cit, pp. 3–4; **Moody,** op. cit, p. 121; **Brown,** op. cit, p. 142.

15. **Moody,** op. cit, p. 38.

16. **Gregory,** op. cit., p. 52.

17. **Brown,** op. cit, p. 155.

18. **Little,** op. cit, p. 66.

19. **Moody,** op. cit, p. 46.

20. **Brown,** op. cit, p. 395.

PART 2
COMMUNITY ORGANIZATION, PLANNING & ACTION

EDITOR'S COMMENT

Within the purview of macromethodologies and concerns, five articles range in rich diversity from the "grand design" in human service programs to interrelationships between research and programming, to information systems for program planners and direct-service practitioners, to the implementation of programs through effective legislative testimony.

Kurren's "Design of Human Service Programs" defines "human services" as a new and revolutionary concept that is beyond traditional social services. Some readers may challenge the degree to which this model is either "new" or "revolutionary," but Kurren's thesis is that new knowledge, values, and skills are required for his design in planning and implementing programs. The call for new skills is general rather than specific, and some elements of Kurren's model correspond to Alfred Kahn's "developmental" historical phase in the personal social services.[1] However, Kurren's is a unique design from which practitioners may derive insightful perspectives or contexts for their practice within contrasting program designs.

In "Coordinating Program Goals and Research Goals," Burch and Burch, one a program manager and one a researcher, continue a vein of thought

[1] Alfred J. Kahn, *Investments in People: A Social Work Perspective* (New Brunswick, N.J.: Urban Studies Center, Rutgers University, 1963), p. 6.

found earlier in Briar's dichotomy, if not polarization, between program managers (practitioners) and researchers, particularly in the evaluation of programs. With a focus on what they term "process" research, Burch and Burch delineate key differences in values found between program managers and researchers. They then address three conflict areas and suggest operational methods and skills for resolving or minimizing these differences.

For direct-service practitioners, this article adds dimensions at the program level that directly or indirectly affect service delivery. Both program managers and program evaluators may well differ about the typologies and interventive approaches to conflict resolution presented by Burch and Burch. However, they should be stimulated to evaluate this article within the context of their own practice experiences and conceptual assumptions.

Zimmerman and Sterne's "Use of Information and Referral Service Data" usefully underlines the reciprocal, perhaps too-often unrealized, potential for linking information and referral-service data to social planning. The authors test out this assumed reciprocal hypothesis with an exploratory survey that revealed some support for their assumption, but some significant gaps as well. Finally, they detail constraints on the use of "I and R" data for social planning as well as the requisite skills for the use of such data by program planners and administrators. This paper is unique among the articles on social planning, programming, and action in this book in that the authors report an empirical study directly apposite to the concepts proposed in the article. The authors link their concepts to the empirical data with a clear delineation of some of the skills directly needed for collaboration between information systems and planning.

In "Problems with Information Systems," Theisen and Braverman similarly are concerned with the utilization of data, but stress social workers' needs to master computer skills. Such mastery, they argue, should help social workers become both designers and users of information systems. In widening their perspectives beyond the skills needed in clinical practice, supervision, and administration, practitioners will perceive how vital information systems can become for obtaining resources that, in turn, are essential for providing high-quality services to clients. Whether the authors' eloquence will overcome the formidable psychological and educational barriers between the level of current social work skills and computer competence is arguable. However, the authors reiterate, although with a different emphasis, the need for sound data collection and research found in the articles by Briar, Zimmerman and Sterne, and Burch and Burch.

"How To Testify Before a Legislative Committee," by Sharwell, stresses how-to skills in legislative advocacy. This article well illustrates the needed convergence of both theory and skills from another discipline—political science—with that of social work. Social action as a professional emphasis in social work tends to fluctuate, but historically there has been a core of social workers committed to social change through legislation. Articles about legislative action are sparse in the social work literature, probably reflecting the marginal competence of social workers as lobbyists in their own causes.

The first NASW conference on "Social Workers in Politics" in 1977 closely coincided in time with the 1977 Fifth Professional Symposium from which Sharwell's article emanated. Sharwell, then, makes a contribution to a subject, with its related skills, too little understood and practiced in the social work profession, despite our historical antecedents to the contrary and despite our proclaimed commitment to social change. This article also appropriately complements the article by Bell and Bell, "Lobbying as Advocacy," in the Fourth NASW Symposium book.[2]

[2] Budd Bell and William G. Bell, "Lobbying as Advocacy," in Bernard Ross and S. K. Khinduka, eds., *Social Work in Practice* (Washington, D.C.: National Association of Social Workers, 1976), pp. 154–167.

Design of Human Service Programs

OSCAR KURREN

Social work is in a watershed period, truly at a point of division between two fundamentally different phases in its policy-planning and delivery approaches to human services. Others perhaps might describe the present period in bleaker terms, feeling that a nadir has been reached in the general public's as well as the professional's belief in the efficacy and role of human services in a postindustrial society. Unquestionably the state of the art in human services programming is underdeveloped. Fragmentation, inaccessibility, discontinuity, inadequate response to presenting problems, and lack of accountability have become part of a litany of charges leveled at much of the social programming developed during the high period of activity of the War on Poverty. There is ample evidence that many of the social programs launched in the fifties and sixties failed to change in any measurable way the incidence and prevalence of major social problems—poverty and unemployment, substance abuse (including alcohol and drug use), school maladjustment and dropout, child and adult abuse (especially in long-term care facilities), delinquency, and adult crime.[1]

For a brief period extending from the mid-sixties through the early seventies, a number of experimental studies were initiated to test the effectiveness of social services. The social welfare community is well acquainted with many of these.[2] A number of professional nerve endings were pinched in the findings of these studies, and the controversy kindled over the implications of the findings continues to the present.[3]

The study findings have, as Warren noted, exposed a great deal of naiveté on the part of social programmers.[4] A cardinal principle in program planning and development had been violated. The complex etiology of the social problems addressed in the studies had been ignored. Programmers had relied in the main on micro intervention techniques in an effort to effect significant change in the total situation.

It is the thesis of this paper that a "quiet revolution" is gaining momentum, recasting substantially the traditional concepts, structures, and principles in the organization and delivery of human services. The revolution is quiet in the sense that fundamental changes in the basic fabric of the social welfare system are occurring without the fanfare or sloganeering that accompanied earlier social change efforts. A consequence of the changed context for human services is the demand for competence in program design. The major changes include the following:

1. Human services as a basic frame of reference replacing a traditional social services ideology

2. The human rights revolution establishing a new value and belief system

3. Sweeping changes in the organization and administration of human services and their relationship to the basic system of social provision

HUMAN SERVICE AS A BASIC FRAME OF REFERENCE

Use of the term *human services* instead of *social services* reflects a fundamental change in program ideology. The author agrees with Demone and Schulberg that a reference to human services reflects discontent with current structure and practice and a recognition of the common elements underlying the concerted helping actions of a diverse group of caregivers and consumers working in consort within a mutual support framework.[5]

The report of the Task Force on the Organization and Delivery of Human Services to the U.S. Department of Health, Education, and Welfare represented an opportunity to clarify the distinction among human services, social services, and the nation's basic system of social service provision.[6] For whatever reason, the task force failed to grasp the realities of human service developments in communities throughout the United States. They failed to perceive that human services cannot be equated with the basic system of social programs or social service provision—education, employment, health and medical care, justice/lay compliance (criminal justice and civil rights, including affirmative action programs), housing, and income maintenance, as defined in the report. Human services are in fact the alternative primary care-oriented service programs that serve in a boundary-spanning role. The mission of human service programs is to maintain the ability of individuals and families to cope with the social roles and requirements necessary for meaningful participation in society by providing services that the primary or extended family might have provided but is not now providing. Alternative primary care includes adoptive services, foster care, group homes, protective services, and day care. Human services also serve to facilitate the use of the basic social programs through outreach efforts and information and referral systems as well as in an alternative relationship to basic social programs, for example, neighborhood health centers, alternative schools for the school dropout, and halfway houses for the discharged mental patient.

Basic social provision systems and human services are defined in this paper as follows: *Basic social provision systems* are those interdependent institutionalized systems providing resources for living required by all people—employment, education, health and mental health, housing, justice/lay compliance, income maintenance, and human services. *Human services* in turn are those interdependent institution-based programs that meet the need for alternative primary care-oriented services required by all people for developing and maintaining the social roles necessary for meaningful participation in society. Human services are an integral element of the nation's network of basic social provision systems that are essential to the functioning of all individuals and families in modern society.

Human Service Themes

Replacing a prior preoccupation with social pathology, blaming the victim, remediation, and social control are the following human service themes, which place high value on achieving a more adequate fit between human needs and conditions with social policies and programs:

1. Human services as a right rather than a privilege extended to selected populations

2. Right of the individual to participate in the conditions of treatment provided by the caregiving system

3. Right of the person to community-based care rather than being institutionalized for indefinite periods in isolated custody-oriented facilities

4. Right of the individual to human services based on the criterion of need rather than income-tested criteria

5. Right of the individual to confidentiality and due process for equality of opportunity

Organizational and Administrative Patterns

Closely linked with the dramatic changes in the value and belief systems undergirding the human services has been the emergence of the organizational and administrative themes of decentralization, devolution, and decategorization. Vertically oriented policies and programs supporting a narrow, pyramid-shaped structure of federal-state programs is giving way to horizontally patterned approaches to human services programming. A major policy instrument spurring the development of locally administered public social programs has been the Social Security Title XX revenue-sharing program. Devolution—or the delegation to communities of authority for fundamental decision-making in policy formulation, program organization, and development—has been built into the system of basic social programs through federal-state rules and regulations mandating authentic citizen participation in all areas of human services programming.

A CONCEPTUAL FRAMEWORK

Program designers must avoid pitfalls in programming listed here that have made too many prior efforts "formulas for failure."[7] These six major dilemmas of program design are as follows:

1. Assessment of need for populations of concern have been superficial and without any coherent frame of reference.

2. Program intervention strategies are devoid of a conceptual framework that links the problem area with a rationale for mounting an effective change system.

3. Intervention systems lack creativity and do not have the technical capability to mount an adequate response to the presenting problem.

4. Organizational and administrative arrangements are underdeveloped. Guidelines and standards for organizing an action system are absent or ineptly applied.

5. Program linkages are nonexistent. Network-building as a systematic process has not been part of policy-planning.

6. Evaluation and accountability systems are primitive in design and execution.

Program design for the human services is a disciplined process guided by concepts and principles that demand of the practitioner a substantial command of social science knowledge and practice skill to accomplish the analytic, formulative, and prescriptive tasks entailed. Five basic components of program design form the foundation and building blocks for human service programs: defining the program mission, intervention system design, program network-building, program evaluation and accountability, and program funding base development. Each of these components consists of a cluster of concepts, principles, and methods. Binding in the total process are three basic design principles—program congruence, coherence, and capacity response.

Program congruence represents intersystem agreement on design component formulation among the service consumer population, sponsoring agency for the human services program, cooperating agencies that comprise the community network, and the funding authorities for the program. Intersystem agreement must be presented in regard to the following conditions: definition of the problem addressed, priority consensus, strategies for problem resolution, and resultant changes expected from program intervention. *Program coherence* involves intrasystem synchronization and agreement beginning with the goal through objective formulation, program conceptualization, intervention system design, organizational and administrative measures, and procedures for evaluation. With respect to *program capacity response,* resources must be adequate to undertake and effectively respond to presenting problems and needs addressed in the program.

Defining the Program Mission

Defining the program mission is an interrelated process consisting of the following stages:

1. Needs assessment of the population of concern through the use of the following criteria: attributed need (predetermined societal and professional standards for human well-being, expressed need (empirical evidence of service utilization patterns), and population-at-risk concept, as defined under current policies.

2. Policy problem analysis of the community service delivery system for the population of concern by means of these criteria: accessibility—personal accessiblity, comprehensive service, quantitative adequacy; continuity—person-centered care, central source of care-coordinated services; quality—professional competence, personal acceptability, qualitative efficiency, administrative adequacy; efficiency—equitable financing, adequate compensation.

3. Identifying the program functional classification. Kahn's program typology is especially useful in classifying programs in relation to their primary function or, stated another way, their essential purpose or mission:[8]

Socialization and Development (Partial Listing)
    Child day care
    Senior centers
    Nutrition programs for children and the elderly
    Camping and recreation for the elderly
Therapeutic, Rehabilitative, and Social Protection (Partial Listing)
    Child and family counseling service
    Transitional facilities—halfway houses, group homes, care homes, and the like
    Rehabilitation centers
    Vocational rehabilitation centers
    Child abuse and adult protective centers
    Sexual abuse centers
Access and Crisis Intervention (Partial Listing)
    Information and referral centers
    Suicide and crisis centers
    Ombudsman programs for the chronically ill and elderly residing in

long-term-care facilities
  Neighborhood service centers

Specifying the primary function for a human service program contributes significantly to sound program design in a number of ways:

1. *Clarity of purpose.* The test for clarity of purpose is whether the program demonstrates through its activities fulfillment of the primary function. Transitional programs should evidence transition for the population served from one setting to another. To illustrate, a halfway house for discharged patients from the state mental hospital cannot become another custodial long-term-care facility; it must be rehabilitative-transitional in function.

2. *Boundary determination.* Boundary in this instance refers to the limit or range of program responsibility accepted by the sponsoring agency. To illustrate, nutrition programs for the elderly are designed to supplement the nutritional needs of the elderly. The program is not designed to substitute for or supplant a basic income maintenance program that provides the resources for a basic diet.

3. *Program coherence.* Agreement on the primary function of a given program makes possible program coherence, defined as complementarity among the program's goals and objectives, the intervention system, and program outputs.

4. *Goal-objectives specification.* Program goals must identify the ultimate change for the population served that is expected to result after completion of the program services. Program objectives must be stated in terms that are measurable, attainable, and explicit about the changes that are expected to result for the population served.

5. *Intervention strategy design.* The strategic intervention model selected must correspond with the primary function selected for the program. To use the halfway house as an illustration again, the rationale for a transitional program, such as the halfway house, is that a person who has spent a considerable period of time in a total care institution needs help in the area of independent functioning when returning to the community. The structured, therapeutic environment of the halfway house can facilitate social recovery and autonomy in managing life's responsibilities. The strategic model is the concept of a halfway house that maximizes leadership and responsibility of action.

6. *Community service system determination.* Practice wisdom informs us that a human service program is imbedded in a matrix of community social programs. A mutually supportive network of relationships exists among programs that are members of a given service system. The transitional halfway house program is part of the community mental health care system and is at the same time an integral part of the community's transi-

tional care system. All of this makes extremely important the need for clarity about the population served, the problem(s) identified for service, and the limits of service responsibility.

Designing the Intervention System

Designing the intervention system must take into account elements, principles, and levels of intervention:

1. *System elements*
   a. Intervention subsystems and technology
   b. Structural plan: organizational and administrative arrangements essential to sustaining service delivery capacity
   c. Task environment: clarifying those parts of the program environment that are relevant to goal-setting or attainment
2. *Programming principles*
   a. Service sequencing: assuring the cumulative buildup of program impact through a planned phasing in of one intervention subunit with the succeeding unit and strengthening serial interdependence
   b. Service integration: developing a service delivery system that assures for the consumer a unified cohesive system of services in contrast to a splintering of services
   c. Matrix design: developing a framework for the planned interplay of allied service programs essential to fulfillment of the primary function of the program
3. *Levels of intervention*
   a. Macro: community-wide, statewide, or national level of intervention
   b. Mezzo: intervention bounded by corporate agreements established within a social welfare sector (for example, mental health, housing, and the like)
   c. Micro: intervention at the individual and family level within a limited geographic area or neighborhood

Program Network-Building

Design of the human service network is based on a body of knowledge, skills, and methods. At stake is the task of creating "systems serving people," to borrow the title of an excellent monograph by Rosenberg and Brody.[9] Knowledge areas include the following:

1. *Vertical and horizontal authority and community patterns*—differences that exist in organizations relative to differences in their authority structure and orientation
2. *Alternative auspice formation*—recognition that organizations over

time change in relation to their goal (goal displacement and succession) and nature of service or function provided to their constituency

3. *Exchange flow direction*—organizations will maintain unilateral, reciprocal, or joint exchange processes in their interorganizational relations.[10]

4. *Interorganizational contracting*—criteria, principles, and procedures undergirding purchase of service agreements or contracts between the public and community voluntary sector

5. *Consortium strategy in network-building*—the criteria and process of forming service coalitions and corporate structures in the interest of service integration

Network design concepts essential to organizing and maintaining effective human service networks include the following:

1. *Functional interdependence*—acknowledgment that a state of interdependence does exist and is essential to fulfillment of service goals and commitments

2. *Domain consensus*—clarification of organizational domains[11]

3. *Task environment*—identified earlier as the key elements in the environment of the total service system that are relevant or potentially relevant to goal-setting and goal attainment[12]

4. *Community institutional thought structure*—a concept developed by Warren, defined as the normative structure or climate present within a given service network[13]

5. *Diffusion and specificity of mission formulation*—recognition that diffusion or ambiguity in the definition of service mission is related to the degree of risk or precariousness in acceptance by the community of the service mission[14]

Program Evaluation and Accountability

Although well understood, at least cognitively, this is the least developed and least applied area in program design. Quite significant is the position program evaluation occupies in a project description. Usually it is at the end of the project narrative, and invariably it is inadequate in specifying the mission and tasks to be completed in the evaluation. It is also rather rare to find the adequate budget, personnel, and other resources essential to the conduct of the evaluation. Evaluation is by no means unrelated to program design or an end stage to it; rather it is a process by which relevant information is consistently gathered and fed back into the program to be used as the basis for enlightened decision-making, leading to improvements in the program.[15] Design concepts include these:

1. *Dimensions of evaluation.* This refers to the need to specify outcome

in terms of long-range versus short-term impact, broad versus focused impact, and cost effectiveness versus program effectiveness.

2. *Conceptualizing the objectives in evaluative criteria terms.* This is the process of converting program objectives to criteria that are measurable.

3. *Formulation of value hierarchy for evaluative criteria.* This refers to establishing a priority system for achieving program objectives and incorporating this plan into the evaluation design.

4. *Conceptualizing anticipated and unanticipated relevant outcomes.* A model based on the following criteria is recommended: programs in operation, extreme quantitative value of an intended effect, literature review, and anticipated unintended objective.[16]

5. *Comparative analysis designs.* This represents a discussion of the criteria and recommended stages for utilizing the following comparative analysis strategies: pre-post, time interval, matched sample, and experimental (classic control group design; use of the experimental group as its own control group over some time period other than the experimental period).

6. *Organizational and administrative criteria for conduct of the evaluation.* These include the following: structural adequacy, designated personnel, and funding base.

Designing the funding source information system entails the use of the following criteria in examining the potential support from a funding source: purpose, system relationship, procedures, normative system, conditions for participation, nature of communication, expectations, and performance demands. The technology of project proposal development is essentially an integral part of the total learning process in program design. The Project Critique Checklist is illustrative of the programmed learned materials used in the educational process to prepare the program designer.

7. *External and internal organizational constraints on program evaluation.* Constraining factors include examination of the "politics of evaluation," specifically the relationship among evaluation, policy formulation and the decision-making process, and the management of relations in the evaluation process; and methodological, bureaucratic, political, and organizational constraints.

8. *Models for effectiveness status monitoring.* Effectiveness status monitoring, defined as process-oriented evaluation, uses a variety of means: observation, critical collection of documents, and determination of the nature of institutional and individual change as the program is implemented.

Program Funding Base Development

This is an essential part of the program design process. For many, program funding means the art of grantsmanship and is erroneously re-

PROJECT CRITIQUE CHECKLIST

A. Criteria for Proposal Evaluation

1. Problem Definition
   a. Identification of change that has become problematic

   b. Authorities identified

   c. Magnitude of the problem

   d. Impact on target population

   e. Target population described

   f. History of problem area noted along with previous efforts reported
2. Background and Rationale

   a. Organizational Activities Preceding Proposal

   b. Need for funding from source identified

   c. Qualifications of sponsoring organization for involvement in problem area

   d. Theoretical framework for proposal

   e. Literature references identifying previous and/or related approaches
3. Goal and Objectives

   a. Goal: stated in performance terms

   b. Objectives: measurable, attainable, stated in programmatic terms
4. Methodology

   a. Sequential buildup of activity

   b. Organization of an intervention system

   c. Time frame

   d. Interorganizational network identified in system terms

   e. Conceptualization of function (primary strategy)

   f. Boundary definition made
5. Administration and Organization

   a. Determination of accountability for project

garded as the sum and substance of program design. Clearly, as the previous discussion demonstrates, program design entails the mastery of a wide range of knowledge and skill, including program funding as a design process.

A social systems perspective is essential to designing a base of funding support for the human service program. An operational level of consensus is essential among the principal parties that comprise the funding action system: the client group or consumers of the program services, the program developers or sponsors, and the program funders. The regions of consensus include definition of the problem addressed, agreement on priorities and strategies for problem resolution, and agreement on projected changes stemming from the program efforts.

The project funding process is guided by the following design concepts and strategies: (1) *concept of feasibility,* entailing consideration of criteria assessing the extent of influence on the program planner on the one hand and the amount of resistance to the proposed project on the other that can be expected, (2) *presentation of self* refers to examining the quality of the exchange between program staff and funding source, and (3) *legitimation* refers to the criteria for establishing and maintaining credibility among the groups concerned with supporting the program.

SUMMARY

Human service program design is a creative and analytic process for transforming an idea about a human need area into a functionally adequate service program. The design process is comprehensive and complex and provides for the following interrelated stages: defining the service mission, specifying the nature of intervention, structuring the network system of community agency supports, designing the evaluation and program monitoring system, and organizing the system of program funding supports. Each of the design components requires the mastery of concepts, principles and technologies that are integrally related to the core areas of knowledge and skill for professional practice.

NOTES AND REFERENCES

1. **Neil Gilbert and Harry Specht,** *Dimensions of Social Policy* (Englewood Cli ffs, N.J.: Prentice-Hall, 1974), p. 109; **Marvin Rosenberg and Ralph Brody,** "Systems Serving People: A Breakthrough in Service Delivery" (unpublished manuscript, School of Applied Social Sciences, Case Western Reserve University, Cleveland, Ohio, 1974); **Peter H. Rossi and Walter Williams,** *Evaluating Social Programs* (New York: Seminar Press, 1972); **Sheila B. Kamerman and Alfred J. Kahn,** *Social*

Services in the United States (Philadelphia: Temple University Press, 1976); **Edward J. Mullen, James R. Dumpson**, et al., *Evaluation of Social Intervention* (San Francisco: Jossey-Bass, 1972).

2. **H. J. Meyer and W. C. Jones**, *Girls at Vocational High: An Experiment in Social Work Intervention* (New York: Russell Sage Foundatioon, 1965); **G. E. Brown**, *The Multi-Problem Dilemma* (Metuchen, N.J.: The Scarecrow Press, 1968); **A. R. McCabe** et al., *The Pursuit of Promise: A Study of the Intellectually Superior Child in a Socially Deprived Area* (New York: Community Service Society, 1967); **Margaret Blenker, Julius Jahn, and Edna Wasser**, *Serving the Aging: An Experiment in Social Work and Public Health Nursing* (New York: Community Service Society, 1964); **J. S. Coleman**, *Equality of Educational Opportunity* (Washington, D.C.: U.S. Government Printing Office, 1966).

3. **Joel Fischer and Walter W. Hudson**, "An Effect of Casework? Back to the Drawing Board," *Social Work*, 21 (September 1976), pp. 347–349.

4. **Ronald L. Warren**, "The Social Context of Program Evaluation Research," in **William C. Sze and June G. Hopps**, eds., *Evaluation and Accountability in Human Service Programs* (Cambridge, Mass.: Schenkman Publishing Co., 1974).

5. **Harold W. Demone, Jr., and Herbert C. Schulberg**, "Human Service Trends in the Mid 1970's," *Social Casework*, 56 (May 1975), pp. 268–279.

6. "The Future for Social Services in the United States." Paper presented at the National Conference on Social Welfare, 1977.

7. **Sydney E. Bernard**, "Why Service Delivery Programs Fail," *Social Work*, 20 (May 1975), pp. 206–211.

8. **Alfred J. Kahn**, *Social Policy and Social Services* (New York: Random House, 1973).

9. Op. cit.

10. **Sol Levine and Paul E. White**, "Exchange as a Conceptual Framework for the Study of Interorganizational Relationship," *Administrative Science Quarterly*, 5 (March 1961), pp. 584–601.

11. Ibid.

12. **William R. Dill**, "Desegregation: Comments About Contemporary Research on Organization," in **W. W. Cooper, Harold J. Leavitt, and Margaret Shelly II**, eds., *New Perspectives in Organization Research* (New York: John Wiley & Sons, 1964), pp. 43–52.

13. Op. cit.

14. **James D. Thompson**, *Organizations in Action* (New York: McGraw-Hill Book Co., 1967).

15. **Carol H. Weiss**, *Evaluation Research* (Englewood Cliffs, N.J.: Prentice-Hall, 1972).

16. **Herbert Hyman, Charles R. Wright, and Terence K. Hopkins**, *Application of Methods of Evaluation* (Berkeley: University of California Press, 1962).

Coordinating Program Goals and Research Goals

GENEVIEVE BURCH
AND HOBART A. BURCH

Traditionally, there has been tension between the people who run human service programs and the researchers who evaluate these programs. This tension occurs because of conflict in several areas.

Program people often fail to spell out the values of the organization for which they work, relying on such generalities as "helping people." Evaluators, rather than insisting on a more explicit statement of values, often perform the evaluation on the basis of their own values, which may be in conflict with the values of the organization.

Program people often fail to delineate clearly the goals of the program or to describe how the program is supposed to achieve the goals (the relationship between program intervention and program goals). Evaluators sometimes evaluate the desirability of the program goals in a critical way rather than evaluating how successful the program is in achieving the stated goals.

Evaluators tend to develop research designs according to their specific discipline without reference to the discipline of the program people or the agency and with no attempt to understand the program. Program people may consider the evaluator's discipline esoteric and unrelated to the real world.

Evaluators sometimes make excessive demands on the time of program people at the expense of the program. Program people may not see the value of evaluation and as a consequence may fail to institute management procedures that would facilitate evaluation at little extra cost to them.

After making a study, evaluators may consider themselves program experts. Program people may consider that their own evaluative impressions are truer than the outcomes of "outside" evaluations.

Finally, evaluators tend to take the positive aspects of a program for granted and to focus on the negatives. Program people react predictably to such criticism by being defensive.

Of all evaluations, that most likely to cause problems between evaluators and program people is an evaluation focusing on the program process or procedures. Some of the additional tension results from increased contact between evaluators and program people, when the professional practice of program people themselves comprises much of the data of the evaluation.

Other tensions result from the nature of the program procedures. For instance, while the researcher needs specific values against which to evaluate, the agency's values may be deliberately vague or general in order to embrace as many different types of clients as possible. Or the values of the staff may not be identical to the values of the board. Or the values of professional and clerical staff members may differ.

Another problem is the clarification of goals. In order for the researcher to develop criteria of evaluation and valid measuring instruments, the goals must be explicit. However, after goals have been clarified for research purposes, a working program group may, during the study, go through the process of developing its own goals, may change goals, may change activities, or the like. Moreover, social work practice gives especially strong emphasis to allowing clients to decide their own goals and processes both in individual, family, and group therapeutic settings and in community organization and planning settings. The subject does not sit still long enough for the researcher to focus a camera.

This paper examines some of the tensions and conflicts that occur during the evaluation of human service process and suggests how they can be handled. The authors—one a program manager, the other an evaluator—have discussed, problem-solved, and argued many of these issues for 20 years. They conclude that some of the conflicts can be resolved by rational operation, some can be eased, and some must be lived with.

Many of the ideas expressed have been clarified in the last year while the evaluator author was the principal evaluator of the National Juvenile Justice Collaboration, a program funded by the Law Enforcement Assistance Administration of the U.S. Department of Justice through the National Assembly of National Health and Social Welfare Organizations. A major goal of the program was the development, in five local sites, of collaborations of affiliates of National Assembly agencies and other youth-serving local organizations, to work toward the deinstitutionalization of status offenders.[1]

WHAT IS EVALUATION?

Evaluation is currently a popular concept. Like all widely used terms, evaluation means quite different things to different people. The authors' purpose is not so much to define it for the reader as to clarify what the authors mean by evaluation.

There are many kinds of evaluation, both subjective and objective. Often the subjective assessment of a program leader or a quick survey of program participants of how successful they thought the program was is all the evaluation available for the planning of future programs. Often even large-scale evaluation research contractors do not report to program managers in time for future planning. Both subjective evaluation and objective evaluation and research are important to the program manager.

Evaluation, as the term is used here, is the application of social science methods to organizational programs or activities in order to obtain valid and objective assessment of what they are accomplishing. Its purpose is to enable program managers to plan and deliver programs or activities so as to increase the probability of achieving desired goals. This definition assumes the following:

1. There are values that an organization seeks to maximize.

2. These values are related to program goals and objectives.

3. The programs are planned and carried out so as to achieve the goals and objectives.

4. There is a way to determine the success of the organization in presenting programs and of the programs in achieving goals.

5. Evaluation is a program tool, not the primary program activity itself.

WHAT SHOULD BE EVALUATED?

Three aspects of human service programs can be evaluated: program inputs, program operations, and program outcomes. Van de Vall, using a systems model of organizational activity, explains that evaluation is the continual feedback from output and throughput at one stage, to input and throughput at a later stage in time.[2] Figure 1 shows his conception in simplified form.

Program Inputs

In human service programs, the inputs include assessment of the target population's needs, the theory behind the intervention or professional practice of the agency, and the theory behind the actual program intervention —how the proposed program practices are supposed to effect the program goal. This is the planning element. Program inputs can be evaluated in terms of soundness, for example: Are the goals clearly defined? Are the program interventions or methods logically designed to achieve program goals? Is the program material sound?

Unit of Evaluation and Different Aspects of Program Delivery Systems

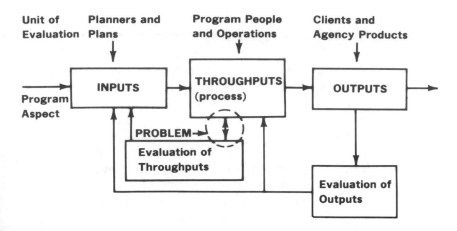

Program input can also be evaluated in organizational or community context: Is the program meeting the needs of the community? Is it duplicating other services? Is it consistent with the organization's values?

Program Operations

The second aspect of programs that can be evaluated is the nature of the program process or operations. This evaluation seeks to determine whether the program has been put into operation using processes developed during the planning stage and in a way to meet its goals and objectives most successfully. Is the program serving the client group that it is supposed to be serving? Is it serving the number of clients that were proposed? Do people complete the program? If not, why not? What are the characteristics of those who drop out? Is the staff able to present the program adequately? Is the budget adequate?

Program Outcomes

The third aspect of programs that can be evaluated is program outcomes. Did the program actually do what it said it would do? Did it change self-image, reading ability, or assertiveness patterns? Van de Vall says that human service program evaluation tends to be concentrated in this area.[3]

While outcome evaluation is what most researchers would rather do, the throughput or process evaluation will be emphasized in this paper because more tension exists between evaluators and program people in that

area. The figure indicates that only in throughput evaluation of feedback is there direct contact between those being evaluated and the evaluators.

WHAT ARE THE APPROPRIATE METHODS?

There are basically four major methods for evaluation research: the
experiment, the survey, archival/historical/cultural analysis, and systems
analysis. Reference here is to the logic by which the program is evaluated,
not to the technique or procedures by which data are gathered, measured,
analyzed, and so on.

The *experiment* or quasi-experiment is the most desirable method from
the perspective of the academic researcher. The evaluation is designed to
measure the success of the program in attaining its goals. A good design has
a before-and-after measure on both the experimental group and a control
group. Subjects must be randomly assigned to the two groups. Some form
of experimental design is sought in output evaluation although the evaluator
can seldom randomly assign clients to control groups or control process
operations well.

The logic of the *survey* method is to select subjects randomly and ex
post facto compare those who had been in the program with those not in
the program. For instance, if one wants to determine whether driver education affects driving record, one can randomly sample high school students,
determine their driving records, and compare those who had taken driver
education and those who had not done so. The assumption is that in random
selection, all extraneous variables are controlled.

A third method is the description analysis of *historical/archival/cul-
tural* data. This includes census data, historical records, running records of
organizations, vital statistics, such cultural artifacts as media presentations
and dress patterns, and many others. The logic tends to be analytical
description, either quantitative as in census analysis or qualitative as in case
study. Historical/archival/cultural records can also be a data source in any
of the other methods.

Systems analysis utilizes analysis of the operations of an agency or
organization from the planning stage through the operation of programs to
the outcomes with feedback from each process to the ongoing planning and
operation of the agency. The logic is the description of operations to maximize the achievement of both program goals and organizational stability
goals. Much process evaluation, especially in industrial organizations, is
systems analysis or operations research.

Research techniques are tools used to implement the four methodologies. Data-gathering techniques—interview, questionnaire, observation,
analysis of records, content analysis, and the like—and statistical tech-

niques (with slight differences) can be used in any of the major methods. The proper combination of methods and techniques depends on a number of factors, such as the nature of the program—and data—under study, the status of previous research on that type of data, the amount of money available, the constraints of time, the personnel available, and so on. The proper method to use for any one evaluation depends on several factors: the aspect of the program being evaluated, the nature of the program goals, and whether the program is an ongoing operation or a demonstration program.

Aspect of the Program

The aspects of the program are those from Van de Vall's model. Most *inputs* are evaluated with the survey method or historical/archival/cultural analysis. *Outputs* are most often evaluated using the experimental or quasi-experimental method. *Process or throughput* evaluation uses different methods depending on other factors:

1. Ongoing programs are successfully evaluated with systems or operations analysis with the feedback providing input for continued improvement or monitoring.

2. Model programs that are trying to establish new methods of operation are best evaluated with a carefully controlled experimental design measuring inputs and operations carefully so that comparison with former operations can be established.

3. Pilot programs that are searching for new processes to achieve new goals are best evaluated with an eclectic and innovative approach depending on case description, the history of events, and analysis of archival/historical data. Pilot programs should be able to benefit immediately from feedback from the evaluator to enable them to change immediately to improve the program.

Nature of the Program Goals

The second factor that affects choice of methods is whether the program goals are limited or broad based. Weiss and Rein suggest that a researcher who attempts to force an administrator to define a broad-based program's goals in simplistic measurable terms will merely alienate the administrator and frustrate him- or herself unnecessarily.[4] In evaluating programs with broad-based goals, they suggest a combination of methods using systems theory, a description of events that unfold and affect the program, and analysis of the political process of actors and roles in the give and take of the program process.

The authors used this approach in their analysis of the juvenile justice collaborations. The authors hope to analyze the historical events, the system subparts, and the political processes in a way that will give them a basis for generalizing from the five collaborations as to the kinds of events and processes that foster collaboration among social agencies.

Nature of the Program

The third factor in choosing proper evaluation methods is whether the program is ongoing or is a demonstration program. Suchman distinguishes the logical differences between one-shot or short-term programs and ongoing programs.[5] Short-term programs use different approaches; pilot programs should be evaluated using a variety of techniques depending on the way the programs are organized; model programs can use more rigorous experimental designs. Evaluations of ongoing operational programs usually focus on the improvement of services rather than on evaluating whether a program is worth keeping.

An administrator must beware the researcher who tends to have a favorite method and/or technique that she or he always uses. An administrator should also beware the researcher who follows completely what the administrator thinks is the proper method. The design should be developed after a preliminary review and planning phase, and the evaluator should be able to explain the logic of her or his chosen methods and techniques.

WORKING TOGETHER

Working through to the best possible evaluation of organizational process requires a great deal of trust and openness among all the people involved. While recognizing possible sources of problems will not necessarily eliminate the problems, it will make their occurrence less painful and ego-shattering. In the process of evaluating and managing several such programs, the authors have reached the conclusion that there are three areas of universal and inevitable stress between program people and evaluators: (1) areas in which differences are resolvable but the issues were never openly addressed, (2) areas in which there are reasonable conflicts because of differences in perspective, and (3) areas of inevitable, nonrational human conflict.

Resolvable Differences

Areas in which there is usually stress but for which common agreements can be reached include the goals of the program, the purpose of the evaluation, the expectations that the program administrator has of the evaluation, the nature of reports, the availability of office space, how payment will occur, deadlines for reports, and the like. These matters require rational planning between evaluators and program managers not only before the research is undertaken but before either side commits itself to the project. This may raise unexpected problems and complications, which must be resolved before the project is begun. It typically leads to some change—often substantial—in the request. It moves from what was *asked for* to what was *really wanted*. The authors like to start with the outcome, requiring a plan for the use of the findings. This clarifies what findings are essential and what data are not worth the time and expense to obtain. This in turn helps to define what methods are necessary to produce the findings and leads typically to a presentation by the evaluator of a series of choices relating cost to benefit and a sober compromise between soaring desires and hard costs, human and financial.

Finally, this tedious but essential planning must be reduced to a written plan, written specifications, and a detailed contract. A written contract is necessary even when no money changes hands, as in volunteer service or evaluation by an employee of the agency. The savings in hostility, frustration, wasted effort, and disregarded findings are well worth the effort.

Reasonable Conflicts

Those issues that cause conflicts between program people and evaluators because of differences in perspective are more difficult to deal with. One such issue is the method of putting goals into operation and measuring them. Because of the limitations of research tools and techniques, this often involves a distortion of program goals. The program people tend to have a holistic view; the evaluator must look for discrete, quantifiable fragments of hard data. Both parties are right, from their own contexts.

A second issue is the amount of staff time that the evaluation will take. The evaluator sees his or her study as having top priority. The staff members may see their services to clients as being more important. Both are right from their own perspectives.

A variation on this is the conflict between an administrator seeking to keep the cost of the evaluation down and a researcher seeking to turn out a quality product. Again, both are right.

The issue of confidentiality is another source of conflict. The evaluator must have access to confidential case records or quasiconfidential agency material such as budgets, records of meetings, and the like, which agencies are sometimes unwilling to share for legal, ethical, and self-protective reasons. Both are right.

These and similar issues can be negotiated with the following ground rules: (1) Feelings and rationales of all parties should be freely expressed. (2) Such feelings and rationales must be accepted as reasonable. (3) Conflicts between these reasonable positions will be acknowledged without resort to claims of right and wrong and without *ad hominem* overtones. (4) Compromise is accepted as a necessary evil in order to carry out the project.

(5) Parties accept, but do not have to like, the negotiated compromises. (6) These compromises must be spelled out in writing. The authors have many experiences of continued friendly relationships when conflicts are resolved by this process.

Inevitable Human Conflicts

Finally, there are some conflicts that are a result of ego needs and/or personality demands on the part of both the program people and evaluators. The personality and ego needs of participants can cause unavoidable clashes. As research draws to a conclusion, as programs end their funding, as deadlines approach, these tensions become more open. Such stresses and conflicts are impossible to avoid and not easily resolvable.

There are several sources of these problems. First, evaluation is inherently threatening. Even if it is primarily positive, it causes bad feelings.

Second, administrators need to be in control, for both ego and program reasons. Yet the evaluator cannot permit this if the evaluation is to be valid and objective. Conflict will inevitably appear at times over power and control issues.

Third, the pretense of objectivity on the part of the evaluator can cause tension. Good evaluators strive with all the techniques and tools at their disposal to be objective. However, they still have biases and blind spots in perception, in design, in the presentation of the results, and in their personal understanding of and agreement with what the agency is doing—and the program people know it. If evaluators claim total objectivity while projecting strong subjective values nonverbally, then they will antagonize and alienate the program people. The only solution is for the evaluator to strike a balance between self-confidence and honest humility.

Fourth, at times there will be feelings of mutual paranoia and mutual rejection between evaluators and program people. If the evaluators are excluded from some process or denied access to records, they may become suspicious and question what the agency may be trying to hide. Program people often perceive the activities of evaluators during process events as snooping, spying, and criticizing.

It is these human problems that make continual feedback from the evaluation into the program process unpleasant, difficult, and at times nearly impossible. While the program people want feedback to the program, paranoia, defensiveness, and attacks on the evaluator are common. While evaluators pay lip-service to wanting to be helpful to the program, their seeming disdain of program goals, critical demeanor, and suspicion cause them to present the feedback in a way guaranteed to increase paranoia and suspicion.

The foundation for resolution of these kinds of tensions should be laid in advance of the evaluation before negative feelings develop. Areas of probable future tension should be discussed, compromises negotiated and agreed on, and inevitable nonrational areas of conflict recognized. This will not eliminate the conflict, but when it occurs, it may be less upsetting.

The program-manager author has used this tension-reduction technique successfully in such areas as premarital education for engaged couples and preparation of demonstrators for hostile engagements. This was done especially well by the Southern Christian Leadership Conference in its training for passive resistance in the late fifties and early sixties.

The second ingredient is for the actors to maintain enough awareness to avoid escalating a situation when they are the targets of nonrational hostility or attack, as in a recent incident involving a threat to exclude the evaluator author from a key event. A hostile confrontation on this issue when feelings were running high was avoided by sending an alternate with whom the group was comfortable rather than attending the meeting herself. The group relaxed, yet the data were collected.

While many researchers *are* social workers, some do not have human relations skills. Social scientists are socialized for solitary work. If social scientists are going to do evaluation, they must learn human relations and planning skills. Van de Vall identified three roles for social scientists in process or throughput evaluation: They have to be social researchers, policy advisers, and planned change agents.[6]

Few program people, including social workers, can take criticism without hurt even though they are trained professionally to take criticism. Social workers will frequently encounter evaluators without planning or negotiating skills. So as persons *with* these skills, program people must take the initiative to sit down with the evaluators and negotiate the areas of inevitable tension. If the evaluators refuse to go through the process of coming to terms with conflict, they must be dismissed, because regardless of their technical competence, the evaluation will be a failure. The evaluators will not have the full cooperation of the program people, and the data will be weaker. The conclusions, however sound, will lack credibility with the program people. Since evaluation is solely a means toward improved program, it has no value if not used to improve program.

NOTES AND REFERENCES

1. Status offenders are youths who have committed actions considered illegal that would not be so considered if the youths were 18 years of age or older, such as running away, possession of alcohol, and the like.

2. **Mark Van de Vall**, "A Theoretical Framework for Applied Social Research," *International Journal of Mental Health*, 2 (Fall 1973), pp. 6–25.

3. Ibid.

4. **Robert S. Weiss and Martin Rein**, "The Evaluation of Broad-Aim Programs: Difficulties in Experimental Design," in **Carol H. Weiss**, ed., *Evaluating Action Programs* (Boston: Allyn & Bacon, Inc., 1972), pp. 236–249.

5. Op. cit.

6. **Edward A. Suchman**, "Action for What? A Critique of Evaluation Research," in **Carol H. Weiss**, ed., *Evaluating Action Programs* (Boston: Allyn & Bacon, 1972), pp. 52–85.

Skills Needed in the Use of Information and Referral Service Data

SHIRLEY L. ZIMMERMAN
AND RICHARD STERNE

Stimulated by Title XX of the Social Security Act, which mandates the use of data in social planning and encourages the provision of information and referral services (referred to hereafter as I & R services), as well as the widespread development of computer technology, the potential of I & R services' data for planning is of growing interest.[1] This interest is expected to continue into the foreseeable future, not only because of Title XX, but because data generated by I & R services could lead to decisions that would enable social service organizations to become more responsive and adaptive to existing and emerging human needs. Whether this potential is realized, however, depends largely on whether planners and administrators acquire the knowledge and skills needed to maximize the development and use of such data for planning.

An exploratory survey was designed to answer a number of questions implied in the foregoing:[2] Are I & R services' data used in social planning? If so, to what extent? What factors facilitate or impede the use of such data for planning purposes, including I & R data characteristics and their possible limitations? Derived from these findings are the kinds of planning/administrative skills needed by agency leadership to ensure the effective compilation, processing, and utilization of I & R data for social planning purposes.

FUNCTIONS OF I & R AND SOCIAL PLANNING

The reciprocal nature of I & R and social planning functions frequently is not understood or, if it is, is poorly articulated. The primary function of an I & R service is to provide information about services offered by its host organization and those of other organizations within its organization set. An I & R service also may refer people to social agencies if their needs and characteristics are consistent with the criteria established for service eligibility. In addition to these access and linkage functions, an I & R service may engage in follow-up, a function designed to obtain information about the appropriateness and effectiveness of services obtained through its referral activities. The follow-up function, in turn, provides the basis for feedback to the host organization about the efficiency and effectiveness of its performance. These interrelated functions—access, linkage, follow-up, and feedback—all suggest that information generated by I & R services has the potential for contributing significantly to social planning.

Social planning, like I & R, involves a multiplicity of functions, which, following Kahn, include (1) determination of facts and trends, (2) inventory of available knowledge, skills, and resources, (3) clarification of goals and priorities, (4) analysis of alternatives and predictable outcomes of choices among them, (5) facilitation of the expression of value preferences and the process of choice, (6) translation of policies into implications for programs at different levels, and (7) measurement of program outcome.[3] It is evident that social planning functions require the kinds of information that I & R services can provide. Such information can increase the likelihood of successful adaptation of the organization to its environment and the environment to the organization. The frequently turbulent nature of their environment presents organizations with relatively sudden, unpredictable crosscurrents of change that threaten to undermine strategies of long-range planning and innovation.[4] Social service organizations, therefore, must learn to adapt their programs to changing environmental contingencies, which can quickly be discerned through the primary information that I & R services can provide.

In short, the multifaceted functions of I & R services and social planning are strongly interrelated. The extent to which these functions are perceived as reciprocal and are performed in a reciprocal fashion can significantly enhance the capacity of social service organizations to achieve their goals. Are they so perceived in reality?

AN EXPLORATORY SURVEY

To better understand the actual and potential relationship between I & R and planning functions, an exploratory cross-sectional survey was conducted to determine how these functions are articulated in Minnesota's 85 county social service agencies; no similar studies were found in the literature.[5] While Minnesota may not be a truly representative state, it was believed that the relationship between I & R and planning functions would be reasonably reflective of local public social service agencies in similar relatively liberal and supportive environments. Further, because Title XX mandates the use of data in planning by local public social service agencies throughout the country and also encourages them to provide I & R services to everyone, regardless of income, the relationships studied may likely be characteristic of those existing in public social service agencies in other states as well.[6]

A pretested, reasonably reliable and valid questionnaire was sent to the directors of each county agency because directors were considered to be expert judges about the I & R and planning functions in their agencies. In some atypical instances, questionnaire completion was delegated to more knowledgeable persons in the agencies. Data collection extended over a two-month period, including follow-up telephone interviews with nonrespondents and those whose questionnaire responses were ambiguous. The participation rate was 83 percent of the agencies ($N=70$), indicating both a high level of participant interest and involvement as well as probable representativeness of the descriptive findings. Findings relevant to two and three variable hypotheses ($N=36$ and $N=20$, respectively) may not be representative of Minnesota agencies, however, because of case attrition resulting from "not applicable" responses relative to some of the variables used in the correlational analyses.

Findings and Discussion

I & R data were found to be used extensively in social planning by most of the agencies surveyed (67 percent). Of all the planning objectives examined, they appear to be used most frequently in relation to program and policy formulation (75 percent), while somewhat less frequently for program innovation (70 percent), priority choices (68 percent), resource allocations (67 percent), and service coordination (67 percent). The consistently high level of usage is impressive. One repetitive use of the data pertained to the identification of unmet needs that serve to stimulate program development by the agencies, such as money-management programs and programs for unwed mothers. Need identification also is used to instigate the development of programs by other community agencies, such as social work programs by the schools.

What kinds of I & R data are considered most important for planning? Of at least moderate or greater importance are data pertaining to user problems (67 percent), available services (64 percent), and service utilization (61 percent). Data pertaining to unavailable services, service quality, and inaccessible services were considered important in slightly more than half of the agencies. I & R data pertaining to user characteristics are considered of lesser importance for planning (47 percent), which is something of a paradox, considering that planning can scarcely begin without knowledge of a population's characteristics.

The kinds of information I & R services gather are relatively consistent with the planning functions outlined earlier. These include data relating to services available (83 percent), user problems (75 percent), service utilization (60 percent), and user characteristics (57 percent). Data generally *not* gathered by I & R but nevertheless considered important for planning pertain to service accessibility and service quality, suggesting a discrepancy between the kind of data gathered and the kind of data considered important for planning.

A measure of the communication of information between staff performing I & R and planning functions revealed that informal means were utilized more than twice as often as formal communications (79 percent versus 33 percent). Informal procedures implied in the use of written memoranda, consultation, and staff discussion are utilized considerably more often than such more formal procedures as assigned liaison personnel and the preparation of statistical and written interpretive reports.[7] Agency requirements for such reports apparently vary considerably, from selected monthly reports to reports produced as infrequently as annually. Regularly prepared reports tend to pertain to service utilization, services available, and user problems. Interpretive reports including other kinds of information tend to be produced on an "on request" basis, a somewhat questionable procedure in terms of the timeliness and adequacy of the ongoing kind of information I & R services provide.

The use of I & R data for social planning purposes is influenced by a number of factors. Data use is strongly related to the informal nature of the I & R and planning interface ($r = .61$), suggesting that there is recognition of the reciprocal nature of I & R and planning functions as well as a need for personal contact in the exchange of information and its subsequent use. Variables found to affect the relationship between I & R data use in planning and the I & R/planning interface to a modest degree were leadership attitudes toward I & R data $r_{xy.z} = .49$ and the stage of agency development in planning $r_{xy.z} = .52$. Contrary to theoretical expectations, variables not affecting the relationship were differences in status, professional orientation, and expertise between I & R and planning staff; the urban-rural, political, and economic environment of the surveyed agencies; female I & R/planning staff ratio; organizational size; specialization of I & R and planning functions; and stage of development of the I & R function in the agencies.[8]

In a few instances, I & R data were found *not* to be used at all in social planning. The most prevalent reasons given seem to be idiosyncratic: a few agencies prefer to use data from other sources, such as past agency experiences; in other instances, I & R data are not provided for agencies to use. Data deficiencies, such as unreliability, untimeliness, inappropriateness, and incompleteness, do not really account for much nonuse of the data. Viewing these findings somewhat differently, it can be said that when I & R data are made available, their use in social planning tends to be quite high.

Constraints on I & R Data Use

Although the potential of the use of I & R data for social planning is generally perceived as promising, a number of undercurrents were identified that could undermine its realization. Inadequate and restricted funding for programs identified through I & R data as being needed could give rise to a sense of the futility of engaging in such activity. Limited funding also has served to restrict the full development of I & R data systems in many agencies, as have agency priorities for other activities. Boards and directors do not always maintain positive attitudes toward social service programs and, in a few agencies, these attitudes actually have precluded I & R data use in planning. Further, the laissez-faire approach toward the development of I & R data systems assumed by the U. S. Department of Health, Education, and Welfare and the state agency, manifested in the lack of overt support, stimulation, and incentives they provide to local agencies, could seriously inhibit the development of I & R data systems at the local level or, at best, eventuate in the development of incompatible data systems among local agencies. Such developments could impose serious constraints on I & R data use in planning, not only at the local level but regionally and statewide as well.

Another constraint on I & R data use in planning is that follow-up information about the outcome and consequences of referrals is rarely collected. This lack of information limits the capacity to evaluate both the I & R service itself as well as the need-meeting performance of organizations providing services for which referrals are made. The lack of such information obviously also poses a constraint on effective social planning. Meaningful follow-up assessments not only would strengthen the I & R data base for planning, but would also strongly convey the notion that people-serving organizations care about what ultimately happens to people seeking help.

Given the data-based nature of both I & R and planning functions, it is surprising, in principle, to find that statistical and written interpretive reports are not common means of information-sharing, and, therefore, are rarely relied on in arriving at planning decisions. While many agencies wished for technical assistance to improve their I & R data systems— through help, for example, in developing better classification categories, more efficient and reliable methods of data processing, and better methods of data analysis—these problems probably are not the real impediments to the development and use of statistical I & R reports. In reality, the problem may be that few administrators and planners know how to draw warranted inferences from such data and then how to translate these into planning decisions. In addition, there may be lack of relevant staff involvement in the formulation of the critical questions that ought to underlie data collection so that collected statistics are viewed somewhat passively or, at best, as simply information required for reporting purposes.[9]

NEEDED SKILLS

With notable exceptions, social work education has given little attention to information development and use as a set of skills about which future social service administrators, planners, and other agency leadership need to be trained. This is not surprising, since the computerization of information is hardly more than a decade old, and its impact on social service agencies has been gaining momentum only in the past few years. Microcircuitry, however, has transformed the visionary's dream to a near reality that every key administrator or planner will have a desk top computer at his or her immediate disposal for decision-making purposes.

The effect of this rapidly approaching future is that administrators, planners, and even service delivery personnel will increasingly have to be skilled in the development of information systems and their use. To keep pace with new demands, skill training must not only take place during the course of professional education but must be complemented by continuing education programs and in-service training of agency leadership. Such complementary forms of education would give perceptive recognition to the fact that professional education cannot deliver and provide total competence, that some skills are newly emergent, and that there often is a considerable time lag between initial professional training and the acquisition of leadership positions that demand the use of never acquired or perhaps dormant and forgotten skills.

Training curricula should include didactic material about I & R services, their functions, and potential for gathering information needed for planning. Moreover, practice opportunities should be provided for designing an I & R data system that is relevant for planning, one that offers clues to emerging human problems and provides indicators that can be used for estimating existing human needs. The importance of information for the achievement of organizational goals and mission should be stressed in contrast to the more conventional reporting perspective on information use. Also, considerably more attention should be paid to the factors affecting information use in social service organizations. Although the unavailability of information clearly precludes its use, its availability does not assure its use—the vast accumulation of unread reports offers ample testimony to the contrary. Stress in principle and practice needs to be placed on using information to increase the effectiveness of social planning for meeting human needs.

The set of skills needed by planners and administrators that were identified through this research generally fall into four categories: (1) interpersonal and group skills, (2) planning skills, (3) administrative/management skills, and (4) scientific problem-solving skills. None of the skills that were identified is what could be called new, since most professional training programs expose students to skill training in these areas. The differences seem to lie in the degree of mastery required and the special contextual application of such skill training. The skills described here are intended to be illustrative of the range of skills needed for the development and use of I & R data systems for planning; by no means is this list exhaustive. Although the emphasis is on skills needed for planning, many are applicable to I & R as well.

Interpersonal and Group Skills

These skills are needed in any situation involving dynamic human interactions in complex organizations, such as social service agencies.[10] Written and verbal communication skills provide the basis for the effective performance of organization functions. Implicit in the interrelationship of planning and I & R functions is a reciprocal educational function through which informational requirements and I & R data available for planning are explained and made known.

Sensitivity to the feelings of others, self-awareness, and understanding of human behavior underlie the interpersonal skills typically needed. Since group mechanisms, such as staff meetings and staff discussions, frequently provide the means for the exchange of information between I & R and planning staff, group skills, such as those involved in oral presentations, initiative-taking in staff meetings and discussions, active listening, and group decision-making and its facilitation, are all essential.

Planning Skills

The planning functions of policy and program determination involve a range of fact-finding and analytic skills in addition to those interpersonal and group skills just mentioned.[11] These analytic skills—the ability to obtain and analyze data about services and potential and actual service users, to analyze alternative courses of action and their probable consequences, to translate policies into their implications for programming, to clarify program and agency goals and priorities, and to evaluate program outcomes

—all are critical for facilitating the adaptation of the organization to its environment and the environment to the organization.

How the bridging of I & R and planning functions is to take place is only now beginning to be articulated. Early clues from the present study indicate that the integration of I & R and planning functions depends on an intellectual awareness of their reciprocal nature and the ability to analyze and interpret I & R data in terms of their relevance for planning and programming—and to apply such data accordingly.

Administrative Skills

Attitudes are a precondition for information use in organizations because they establish the emotional and intellectual climate in which information is generated and used. Requisite positive attitudes toward data rest on the belief that data are essential to the administrative and planning processes. Such commitment, in turn, will facilitate the development of data that are relevant to planning decisions. In addition, skills in budgeting and resource acquisition are necessary for identifying and obtaining special resources to make an information system operational on a relatively long-term basis; information systems can be complex and costly and should be demonstrably cost effective to the organization. Technically oriented personnel skills also are needed to help ensure that competent people are placed in key positions both to develop and utilize the information produced. Other important administrative skills include the ability to develop the unifying mechanisms necessary to ensure the appropriate integration of I & R and planning functions and the suitable integration of I & R data at all levels of organization functioning.

Scientific Problem-Solving Skills

To develop and use information systems, it is necessary to have some knowledge of the capabilities of the hardware and software needed to process and analyze the data generated. Skills in question formulation as well as the delimitation of information needs are necessary requisites to effective data systems development. Since question formulation must be translated into some data-collection form, knowledge and skill in the construction of data-collection instruments are essential. In addition, perceptive choice-making among alternative data-collection procedures is required. Some ability in the differential selection of research designs, such as experimental, survey, or trend-analysis studies, may likely be required at various times in the gathering of I & R data. Knowledge of sampling plans and their consequences for parameter estimation is critical for decision-making based on random sampling procedures.

CONCLUDING NOTE

The findings of the study highlighted the fact that the effective use of I & R data for planning purposes requires both generalized and specialized skills that range from interpersonal and group skills to analytic and technical research skills. In addition to presenting these skill components, complementary training approaches to educating professionals are suggested to facilitate the appropriate use of I & R data in social planning. The strategic boundary position of I & R services relative to their organization suggests that the data they generate can contribute significantly to the humanizing of service delivery at the local level, but only if staff have the requisite skills to translate this promise into a reality.

NOTES AND REFERENCES

1. U.S. House of Representatives, "Social Service Amendments of 1974," *Conference Report,* December 19, 1974, p. 10; U.S. Department of Health, Education, and Welfare, Social Rehabilitation Service, "Social Service Programs for Individuals and Families; Rules and Regulations," *Federal Register,* June 27, 1975, Sections 228.31 and 228.32.

2. **Shirley L. Zimmerman**, "The Use of Information and Referral Services' Data in Social Planning." Unpublished Ph.D. dissertation, University of Minnesota, Minneapolis, 1977.

3. **Alfred J. Kahn**, *Theory and Practice of Social Planning* (New York: Russell Sage Foundation, 1969), pp. 16–17.

4. **Shirley Terreberry**, "The Evolution of Organization Environments," in **John G. Maurer**, ed., *Readings in Organization Theory: Open System Approaches* (New York: Random House, 1971), p. 60.

5. The design, methodology, and findings of this study are presented only in the broadest terms below. Interested persons may write to Dr. Shirley Zimmerman, Assistant Director of Continuing Education in Social Work, University of Minnesota, Minneapolis, Minn. 55455, for additional information.

6. Considering the early stage of planning and development among local public social service agencies and the high degree of variability and flux of programs within and between states, it is unlikely that a meaningful representative national sample could be established.

7. Similar preferences for informal communication arrangements and limited use of written reports and statistical information were also found in LaMendola's study of social service executives' use of information. *See* **Walter LaMendola**, "A Study of Preliminary Considerations in Management Information System Development

for the General Social Service Agency." Unpublished Ph.D. dissertation, University of Minnesota, Minneapolis, 1976.

8. These variables may not have been meaningful because of the small sample that was used in testing these hypotheses. Another more interesting possibility is that these variables—derived largely from relationships found in profit-making organizations—do not hold in the nonprofit, social service sector.

9. In different contexts, both authors have made these same observations about the use of statistical data and reports by decision-makers. Similar findings are reported in LaMendola, op. cit.

10. For a more extensive identification of interpersonal skills used in practice, *see* **John Crane**, "Interpersonal Competence and Performance in Social Work" (Vancouver, B.C.: University of British Columbia School of Social Work, 1974). (Mimeographed.)

11. Planning, administrative, and management skills are dealt with more comprehensively in "Educating for Management in Social Welfare" (Seattle, Wash.: University of Washington School of Social Work and Graduate School of Business Administration, 1976). (Mimeographed.)

Problems with Information Systems

WILLIAM THEISEN
AND LOIS BRAVERMAN

When one thinks of social work skills, the natural tendency is to think about skills in the traditional areas of clinical practice, supervision, administration, and research. Few social workers would think about skills in the context of computers and information systems.[1]

Carroll states that social agencies, in common with other types of formal organizations, regularly collect certain types of data about their activities.[2] Increasing demands for evaluation and accountability since the late 1960s have led a growing number of public and private agencies to turn to computers for help in tracking client-worker activities as well as in accounting for agency finances.

Since most social workers have limited skill in working with computers, specialists from other disciplines have had great influence on the design and implementation of computerized information systems. Social service information systems are usually designed by accountants and computer programmers to trace financial transactions, document client eligibility, and establish agency eligibility for reimbursement from external funding sources. Social workers have increasingly surrendered decision-making responsibility, as well as program control, to accountants, economists, and business administrators who speak the language of numbers and computer programmers.[3] But these systems are not designed to answer policy or practice questions, and an information system in and of itself does not guarantee quality services.

Current social service information systems have minimal capacity to tell administrators what practitioners are doing, how they are doing it, or for whom they are doing it. Practitioners' data-collection efforts have little relation to their ability to deliver service. Data collection may be seen as an arduous burden, with the practitioner feeling no need to be complete, thorough, or accurate in submitting reports. Thus, there may be considerable question about the validity and reliability of agencies' data.[4]

Social workers live and work in a social and political milieu that believes that forms and computers will produce efficient and effective services.[5] The current emphasis on monitoring and evaluation makes it likely that computers, with their speed and storage capacity, are here to stay. Social workers must learn how to maximize the computer's positive effects and minimize its negative effects. How, then, may computers and information systems be used to humanize services?

This paper systematically examines and discusses the types of problems social workers commonly encounter with information systems. Also discussed are some methods social workers can use to control data errors as well as to facilitate useful data analysis, thereby making the system work *for* social workers rather than *against* them.

CONTROLLING DATA ERRORS

Most information systems contain several types of data. Registry data include clients' names, addresses, and social security numbers and other types of data that identify specific clients.[6] Information systems also contain demographic variables, such as age, sex, and income, that provide data about the total client population. Information systems may also contain data about the presenting problem; service needs; and units, length, and cost of service.

The ability to do useful analysis is severely hampered by data errors.[7] Data errors create numerous problems for practitioners, administrators, and data-processing staff. Anderson notes that social workers need to know more about information systems, how they are developed, and how they work.[8] Form design, the nature of the data base, accurate labeling of variables, and missing data are factors that lead to data errors.

Form Design

What is being measured? Every social work student who takes a research course must try to answer that question. But while a student's design error has limited consequences, a design error in an agency's information system can have serious consequences for administrators, staff, and clients. One problem social workers encounter in designing measuring instruments is the need to break program goals into operational variables and for variable categories to measure specific and discrete attributes and activities. The designed product is usually some type of reporting form the purpose of which is to record certain predetermined details about an event when it occurs.

What we want to measure and what we want to learn from the data collected are integral parts of form (or instrument) design. Form design affects how data are collected, organized, and, ultimately, analyzed. Form design affects how thoroughly and accurately workers complete the form. Once variable codes and categories are established, it can be difficult and expensive, especially with large data systems, to reorder or recode variables and categories. Forms that generate large numbers of data errors are exceedingly expensive, since the resultant output is useless. Most important, data errors result in misleading interpretations when used as a basis for policy or practice decisions.

Nature of the Data Base

A second problem social workers encounter with information systems is the nature of the data, that is, whether the data are narrative (as in a case record) or coded; if coded, whether alphabetical or numerical; if numerical, whether the data are nominal, ordinal, or interval in scale.[9] These considerations affect whether data in the system are useful only for examining individual attributes and characteristics or if the data can be aggregated to provide information about characteristics of the population as a whole. If data can be aggregated, the level or scale of the data affects the statistics that can be used.[10]

A surprising number of tests can be done, even with simple frequency distributions. Table 1 is a frequency distribution of a sample of injuries reported for child abuse victims. The variable *injury* is nominal; that is, as we read through the list, there is no indication that injuries are ranked as more or less severe. Interpretation is limited to how many children were reported with burns, fractures, inappropriate punishment, or whatever, and the relative frequency of any one injury to other reported injuries.

This simple listing is typical of the unanalyzed output that most information systems generate and does not necessarily lead to better practice or policy decisions. Table 2 recodes the injury categories and arbitrarily ranks the level of severity. At the very least, some ordinal ranking of injuries is needed if one wants to talk about child abuse beyond the individual case. The procedure used to create Table 2, while admittedly risky, is one method.

The recategorization of data in Table 2 suggests interesting practice and policy questions. Why in so many abuse cases is neglect specified as the principal injury? What services should be offered when 60 percent of the reported children have no injury and only 4 percent have injuries serious enough to be classified as internal injuries, fractures, or hematomas? How seriously injured are the 36 percent reported with bruises, welts, cuts, and burns?[11]

TABLE 1. REPORTED CHILD ABUSE INJURIES[a]

Type of Injury	Frequency (number)	Frequency (percentage)	Cumulative Frequency
None	4	.2	.2
Bruises	383	22.2	22.4
Abrasions	29	1.7	24.1
Wounds	17	1.0	25.1
Sprains	1	.1	25.2
Internal	3	.2	25.4
Single fractures	9	.5	25.9
Multiple fractures	4	.2	26.1
Dismemberment	0	.0	26.1
Exposure	0	.0	26.1
Burns	50	2.9	29.0
Skull fractures	11	.6	29.6
Subdural	4	.2	29.8
Brain damage	3	.2	30.0
Poison	0	.0	30.0
Ingestion	2	.1	30.1
Prior injuries	11	.6	30.7
Malnutrition	5	.3	31.0
Failure to thrive	5	.3	31.3
Inappropriate punishment	349	20.2	51.6
Sexual abuse	133	7.7	59.3
Congenital drug addiction	4	.2	39.5
Abandonment	6	.3	59.8
Physical neglect	207	12.0	71.9
Emotional neglect	219	12.7	84.6
Medical neglect	19	1.1	85.7
Educational neglect	39	2.3	88.0
Lack of supervision	79	4.6	92.6
Lock in/out	8	.5	93.1
Unknown	21	1.2	94.3
Other	99	5.2	100.0
Total	1724	100.0	

[a]These data were collected for a midwestern state by the Region VII CA/N Center using the Nation Clearinghouse for Mental Health form.

Interval level data are necessary to measure how severely reported children are injured. Data are needed on each reported injury, the extent of each injury, the relationship to other injuries, and some additive method of arriving at the severity of injury for a given child. With interval data, the powerful statistical tools of analysis of variance and correlation analysis can

TABLE 2. RECODED CHILD ABUSE INJURIES

Type of Injury	Frequency (number)	Frequency (percentage)	Cumulative Frequency
None	26	1.5	1.5
Neglect	1040	60.3	61.8
Sexual abuse	133	7.7	69.5
External	462	26.8	96.3
Wounds	17	1.0	97.3
Malnutrition	10	.6	97.9
Internal	6	.3	98.2
Fractures	13	.8	99.0
Head	18	1.0	100.0
Total	1725	100.0	

be used to examine the population and to examine and compare subgroups within the population.

Accurate Labeling of Variables

Variable labeling is an important consideration in using information systems. A variable label needs to be clear and accurate, since it suggests the kind of data stored under the heading. In this context, concern is not only with what is being measured but also with the history of the data collection. Changes in rules and regulations regarding eligibility, program content, and service activities occur regularly in social service programs. But program changes create problems for the users of information systems. Program changes can result in new forms, and new forms can lead to changes in variable categories—or the renaming of variables.

Table 3 indicates how labeling problems affected the quarterly child abuse statistics for one state. The original form used alphabetical codes from A through Z to list the variable categories. The keypuncher was instructed to change all letters to numbers, starting with $A = 1$, $B = 2$, and so forth. One variable coded the individual making the report. However, the agency developed a supplementary report that rearranged reporters and added new categories to account for mandatory reporters listed in the child abuse law. The supplementary form also used numerical codes for the new categories. Depending on the reporter, a letter or number would be coded. The keypuncher, following instructions, entered either the number or, if a letter was entered, converted the letter to a number. But when quarterly statistics were compiled, code 22 for "Christian Science Practitioner" was a high-frequency category, even though the staff knew that only a couple of reports had been received from that category of reporter. A recheck of the labeling

TABLE 3. CHILD ABUSE FORM

First Form	Second Form
A = 1 Spouse	1 – Physician
B = 2 Paramour	2 – Medical Examiner
C = 3 Divorced/Separated	3 – Coroner
D = 4 Deceased Spouse	4 – Dentist
E = 5 Spouse Temporarily Absent	
	5 – Chiropractor
F = 6 SpousePermanentlyAbsent	6 – OPT
G = 7 Natural Child	7 – Podiatrist
H = 8 Adopted Child	8 – Resident
I = 9 Stepchild	9 – Intern
J = 10 Foster Child	10 – Nurse
K = 11 Grandchild	11 – Other Hospital/Clinic
L = 12 Self	12 – Other Health Practitioner
M = 13 Parent/Adoptive Parent/-	
Stepparent	13 – Psychologist
N = 14 Grandparent	14 – Mental Health Professional
O = 15 Sibling	15 – Social Worker
P = 16 Other Relative	16 – Day Care or Child Care Worker
Q = 17 Child Care Provider	17 – Juvenile Officer
R = 18 Institution Staff	18 – Probation or Parole Officer
S = 19 Teacher	19 – Teacher
T = 20 None	20 – Principal or Other School Official
U = 21 Unknown	21 – Minister
V = 22 Other	22 – Christian Science Practitioner
	23 – Peace Officer or Law Enforcer
	24 – Other person with responsibility for care of children

process revealed the error. The error could easily have gone undetected for a considerable length of time if the data had not been so obviously at variance with what the staff knew to be true.

Moreover, variable categories need to be discrete and defined in such a way that they are used consistently over time and across locations. For example, states using the National Clearinghouse for Mental Health form to report child abuse and neglect use the term *substantiated* differently. Some states use the concept of a substantiated report as an indicator of genuine versus malicious reports. In these states a case is substantiated if the child welfare worker determines that the report was made in good faith even if no injury actually occurred.

A second group of states uses the concept of substantiated to indicate that a worker determined an injury had occurred. In these states, the worker may determine that a report is genuine in terms of suspicion, but if no injury can be documented, the report is considered unsubstantiated. A third group of states uses the concept of substantiated to indicate that child abuse was determined in a court hearing. In these states, only reports that have been screened by a worker, referred to court, and had a court hearing with a finding of abuse adjudicated are reported as substantiated.

The problem of states having different definitions makes it difficult to aggregate data among the states or to compare data between states. Thus it is difficult to say what is happening in child abuse investigations or service delivery on a regional or national basis. Similar problems can occur within a single agency system unless everyone—administrators, practitioners, and data-processing staff—agrees on labels and definitions.

Missing Data

Missing data is another form of data error that influences the usefulness of an information system. Data may be missing from an information system for many reasons. This section discusses three prevalent origins of missing data and the problem of making inferences from missing data.

1. Missing data can originate when record-keeping systems are converted from manual to more formal and rigid processes of computerized systems. For example, one agency received funds for service to children; the agency also received funds for service to families. Accurate accounts for each type of service and for the number of service units were important. Each month a clerk simply went through the manual file and counted the number of people in a family receiving service, excluding those members not receiving service. When this method of record-keeping was converted to a computerized information system, a code to count total families versus a code to count total clients was not included. The data were not "missing" until the needed information was identified as no longer available. Missing data caused enormous problems for this agency.

2. Missing data can also result when a person responsible for recording data does not have information available at the time the form is completed. For example, some agencies log cases into the information system at intake. An initial form is completed, with supplementary follow-up later. Supplementary data may never be collected, thus resulting in missing data.

3. Poor form design may affect a worker's ability to complete the instrument under field conditions. Workers who find a form difficult or confusing to complete in the field, or who find a form irrelevant to service activities, may pay little attention to certain data categories.

The problem of making inferences from missing data is not only frustrating but also risky. Policy and practice decisions may be made from biased samples for which 50–75 percent of the data about individuals may be missing. For example, almost 40 states are using the National Clearinghouse form as the one (and perhaps only) method of registering child abuse cases and maintaining a statistical data base. It was noted earlier that different states use different criteria to determine whether an abuse report is substantiated. The form instructs workers not to complete information about injuries, family characteristics, and service activity if the report is unsubstantiated. While any given variable might be questioned, certainly service information can be useful to an agency. How do services vary between substantiated and unsubstantiated cases? What services are offered to unsubstantiated cases? What is the cost of service to these cases? If an agency reports 25–35 percent of its cases as substantiated, it is losing service information on 65–75 percent of the total caseload—and unsubstantiated cases may be consuming as much manpower, time, and energy as substantiated cases! Missing data will prevent the agency administrator from giving a fair and accurate accounting of agency service activities.

SUMMARY

Until recently, data in most social service information systems have been accessible only to data-processing staff. Administrators and practitioners did not have the skills to process data and obtain their own output. When computers were new, it was generally assumed only specialists could learn to run the machine. But recent innovations make it possible for laypersons to learn enough about the computer to use interactive systems and canned packages with relative ease.[12] Social workers need to acquire the skills to use these new developments and enable them to become designers and users of information systems.

While the field worker is concerned with the individual client, the administrator is concerned with the client population as a whole. Services cannot be humanized without resources, and resources cannot be obtained until the needs of the client population are documented. By becoming involved in the design of information systems, social workers can affect how data are collected, organized, and analyzed. No longer will social workers need to rely completely on computer specialists to obtain the desired information from the computer.

In addition, by systematically controlling for data errors, worker frustration with data collection can be reduced and the quality of data analysis can be improved. In this way, effective treatment and program decisions can be facilitated, thus ensuring clients the quality of service they need.

NOTES AND REFERENCES

1. Generally the term *information system* refers to everything from specific information (such as client and personnel files) to population variables (such as age

and sex). For purposes of this paper, *information system* refers primarily to a computerized data system capable of aggregating individual attributes to describe and make inferences about a population.

2. **Nancy K. Carroll**, "An Exploratory Study of Social Agency Effectiveness: The Open System Model Applied to a Comparative Time-Series Analysis of Selected Social Agency Performance Data" (unpublished doctoral dissertation, Washington University, 1970). These data presumably (1) provide an important source of feedback about organizational activities, (2) are useful for making future decisions, and (3) give evidence of accountability to the organization's various publics as justification for their continued support.

3. Several authors have touched on the enormous storage capacity of data-processing systems and the resultant explosion of data-collection forms to collect data for these systems. The consequence is that employees of many organizations —from private companies to social agencies—feel overwhelmed by the problems they encounter with data-processing systems. *See,* for example, **Edith Fein**, "A Data System for an Agency," *Social Work,* 20 (January 1975), pp. 21–24; **George Hoshino and Thomas P. McDonald**, "Agencies in the Computer Age," *Social Work,* 20 (January 1975), pp. 10–14; **Norman H. Nie, C. H. Hull, J. G. Jenkins, K. Steinbrenner, and D. H. Bent**, *Statistical Package for the Social Services* (2d ed.; New York: McGraw-Hill Book Co., 1974); **S. Wooldridge and Keith London**, *The Computer Survival Handbook* (Boston: Gambit, 1973).

4. Discussion of validity and reliability is largely confined to the research literature. Garbarino and Crouter and Lorch have raised questions about the validity and reliability of data in specific systems, but the issue has not been generally addressed in the literature, despite the fact that organizational intelligence, feedback, and planning have received considerable attention in organizational literature. **James Garbarino and Ann Crouter**, "The Problem of Construct Validity in Assessing the Ecological Correlates of Child Abuse and Neglect" (Omaha: Boys Town Center for the Study of Youth Development, 1977); **Steve Lorch**, "The New English Resource Center for Protective Services: A New Approach to Public-Private Collaboration," paper presented at the meeting of the American Orthopsychiatric Association, April 1977. For further discussion, *see* **James Davis and Kenneth Dolbeare**, *Little Group of Neighbors* (Chicago: Markham Publishing Co., 1968); **Daniel Katz and Robert L. Kahn**, *The Social Psychology of Organizations* (New York: John Wiley & Sons, Inc., 1966); **Melvin R. Levin**, *Community and Regional Planning: Issues in Public Policy* (New York: Praeger Publishers, 1969); **K. Rosenthal and K. Weiss**, "Feedback and Its Effects on Policy," in **Raymond Bauer**, ed., *Social Indicators* (Cambridge: MIT Press, 1966); and **Harold L. Wilensky**, *Organizational Intelligence* (New York: Basic Books, 1967).

5. **Robert Boguslaw** suggests that too often computerized systems are designed with the idea that their primary function is to deal with and get rid of human imperfection. *See The New Utopians: A Study of System Design and Social Change* (Englewood Cliffs, N.J.: Prentice Hall, 1965).

6. Emphasis on accountability has led to a push for better information systems, but various writers argue that the need for record-keeping has limitations. Collection, storage, and retrieval of client data on computer systems, while still relatively recent, generates controversy in the area of privacy and civil liberties. *See* **Edgar S.**

Dunn, Jr., *Social Information Processing and Statistical Systems: Change and Reform* (New York: John Wiley & Sons, Inc., 1974); **Verne R. Kelley and Hannah B. Weston**, "Computers, Cost, and Civil Liberties," *Social Work,* 20 (January 1975), pp. 15–19; **John H. Noble**, "Protecting the Public's Privacy in Computerized Health and Information Systems," *Social Work,* 16 (January 1971), pp. 35–41; and **Leila Whiting**, "The Central Registry for Child Abuse Cases: Rethinking Basic Assumptions," *Child Welfare,* 56 (January 1977), pp. 761–768.

7. Among others, the following discuss the monitoring, planning, and evaluation uses of data contained in information systems: **Charles W. Cobb**, "A Management Information System for Mental Health Planning and Program Evaluation: A Developing Model," *Community Mental Health Journal,* 7 (April 1971), pp. 280–287; **Theron Fuller**, "Computer Utility in Social Work," *Social Casework,* 51 (December 1970), pp. 606–611; **William J. Reid**, "Developments in the Use of Organized Data," *Social Work,* 19 (September 1974), pp. 585–595; and **Ivan Vasey**, "Developing a Data Storage and Retrieval System," *Social Casework,* 49 (July 1968), pp. 414–417.

8. **Claire Anderson**, "Information Systems for Social Welfare: Educational Imperatives," *Journal of Education for Social Work,* 11 (Fall 1975), pp. 16–21.

9. *See* **Fred W. Vondracek, Hugh G. Urban, and William H. Parsonage**, "Feasibility of an Automated Intake Procedure for Human Services Workers," *Social Service Review,* 18 (June 1974), pp. 271–278, for a discussion of one use of narrative data.

10. Most books on statistics discuss levels of data and appropriate statistics. The discussions in Nie et al., op. cit., or **John L. Phillips**, *Statistical Thinking* (San Francisco: W. H. Freeman & Co., 1973), provide especially lucid examples for laypersons.

11. A child reported with fracture(s) would generally be expected to be more seriously injured than a child with bruises or cuts. But some children suffer severe external injuries, while others sustain simple fractures. Sexual abuse is a problem because no injuries are reported, but the abuse may range from simple fondling to intercourse to mutilation.

12. Essentially, these packages allow the user to input, reorder, recode, and sort the data and obtain appropriate summary statistics in an intelligible way. Most university computer systems as well as many state agencies have these packages in their systems.

How To Testify Before a Legislative Committee

GEORGE R. SHARWELL

The need for social workers to address legislative issues has never been greater. This is true, in part, because legislation is reaching into the lives of more people and institutions every day. In part this is true because issues have arisen in recent years that are of concern both to social workers and legislators; child abuse and neglect and licensure of social workers are perhaps the best examples of such issues. In addition, legislative concern over the best use of the taxpayer's dollar and the recent legislative disenchantment with social welfare programs generally have forced social workers to defend many existing programs and to advocate more creative programs to take the place of those that have been ineffective. Finally, social workers have increasingly recognized their responsibility to speak out on a variety of issues in regard to which they have special information and insight.

It is obvious that if social workers are to be effective advocates in the Congress and in the statehouses throughout the nation, they must possess a knowledge of legislative behavior and principles of advocacy, be aware of the relevant values that guide social workers' actions, and attain skill in the application of that knowledge in a manner consistent with social work values. Unfortunately, few social workers have been exposed to the knowledge-value-skill triology during the course of their professional education. Moreover, the literature has largely ignored close examination of legislative advocacy. Maryann Mahaffey, an experienced legislative advocate and past president of the National Association of Social Workers (NASW), is one of a number of social workers who have noticed this gap in the literature. As she writes:

> How does a social worker influence the legislative and administrative process to achieve the profession's social policy objectives? The litera-

87

ture on social work—and other human service professions as well—is virtually devoid of materials delineating the discrete sequence of actions necessary.[1]

The purpose of this article is to address part of this literature gap by delineating the discrete actions necessary for competent testimony before legislative committees and subcommittees. The principles and mechanics discussed in this paper apply equally well to administrative bodies and to local legislative bodies, such as county or city councils. One assumption is that the advocate speaks in a representative capacity for a professional association, such as an NASW chapter, or for a human service organization, such as United Way or a family service agency. This assumption is made for two reasons: (1) it is probably more commonplace for a social worker to speak in a representative capacity than it is for a social worker to express individual views as a constituent-citizen or as one with expert knowledge on a specific topic of legislation and (2) the process involved in speaking in a representative capacity is much more complex than the process involved when one speaks only for oneself—but the skills involved in speaking only for oneself are identical in all important respects to the skills involved in testifying in a representative capacity.

PRELIMINARY POINTS

Before the mechanics of testimony before legislative committees are addressed, two important preliminary points must be made: (1) ineffective advocacy does not merely fail; it undermines the very cause it seeks to advance and (2) it can damage future efforts of both the advocate and the organization the advocate represents. It is better to stay out of the legislative arena entirely than to enter it and display incompetence or lack of professional responsibility to deal with facts fully, fairly, and skillfully. One must recognize a distinction between ordinary citizen groups and professional associations, a distinction that legislators make. The citizen group's justification for speaking out is purely political—that is, the group communicates to legislators the wishes of a group of persons who are constituents; their strength is tied to their right to cast votes, not to their claimed ability to give sound advice on matters of public policy. In contrast, the professional association both claims special expertise and is expected by legislators to make a sound contribution to the development of public policy. Although there is a political dimension to the clout that professional organizations can develop, the political side is secondary to the claim of expertise. Thus, while a citizen group is often free to be intemperate in its actions, inaccurate in its facts, and unreasonable in its demands—and to do so with impunity—the professional association is not. Every advocate must be aware of this legislative double standard. The trite admonition that anything worth doing is worth doing well is nowhere more true than with respect to legislative advocacy.

Inept advocacy depletes resources of time, energy, and money without a positive return, and it tends to demoralize the advocate, the organization the advocate represents, and their partners in a given legislative matter. Moreover, because timing and circumstances often are important in legislative matters, failure to advance a legislative objective in a specific legislative session often means that another effort to achieve that objective cannot be mounted for a long time; a missed opportunity may be lost forever. In addition, legislative memories can be excellent. An advocate's ineptness or lapse in judgment can tarnish the image of the advocate and of the organization that person represents for many years to come, and thus can affect the outcome of issues not yet even imagined. Fortunately, the reverse is also true. Competent advocacy not only advances a current legislative objective but enhances the ability of the advocate and of the organization represented to further future legislative objectives. Thus, the advocate has a responsibility to prepare sufficiently and approach legislative tasks in no less a professional manner than that person approaches clinical practice or other social work responsibilities.

Demonstrating Competence

In addition to the specific legislative objectives that an advocate will attempt to accomplish, the advocate needs to further one global goal. This goal is to demonstrate by words and actions that the advocate and the organization represented are competent and characterized by integrity. The full scope and nuances of competence and integrity cannot be captured in the abstract. Generally, though, competence is demonstrated through awareness of the issues involved in a proposed piece of legislation, ability to express the issues clearly and succinctly, awareness of alternate routes that legislation might take to resolve the issues, advocating a *specific* route that legislation should take, and cataloging the defects in each of the alternative proposals.[2] Throughout all of this, the advocate must demonstrate awareness of relevant facts and political realities and express ideas in a convincing manner.[3] The key to all of this is obviously that the advocate must check factual matters and the prevailing political winds as well as agonize over the choice of words, so that the advocate's statements are both factually accurate and convincingly expressed.

Conveying Integrity

Integrity is conveyed by accurately and fully disclosing all information that is relevant to the legislative issues and never misleading or being untruthful. To do otherwise courts disaster. Legislative advocacy takes place in a largely adversary arena—a setting in which opponents will seize on any improper or incorrect statement and expose it. Diligence and honesty may not always be rewarded in the legislative arena or anywhere else, but inaccuracy or dishonesty in a legislative forum is almost certain to have adverse consequences.

NEED FOR A WRITTEN STATEMENT

Legislative committees generally prefer to be furnished with a written statement of an advocate's positions on proposed legislation either at the time that oral testimony is given or, preferably, prior to that time. The oral presentation at a hearing can then consist of either reading the text of the written statement (if it is not too lengthy) or paraphrasing or summarizing the written statement. The advantages of providing a committee with a written statement in addition to oral testimony are numerous and important:

1. It demonstrates professionalism.

2. It shows a more than casual, impetuous interest in the legislative matter.

3. It assures that the committee record of the testimony will be accurate.

4. It can make the oral presentation to the committee more effective, because some of the committee members and the committee staff will read the written statement in addition to listening to the testimony.

5. It permits the advocate to say all he or she wants to say in the written statement while still being able to meet the time restraints often imposed on oral testimony.

6. It gives flexibility in that the advocate can cover all the issues in the written statement but can highlight points in the oral portion that are especially responsive to points raised at a hearing by the opponents.

7. It provides greater assurance of coverage in the media, because copies of the written statement can be provided to media representatives prior to the testimony.

8. It provides greater assurance that media coverage of the testimony will be fuller and more accurate, since media representatives can work from the written statement rather than from hastily penciled notes.

9. It enables the advocate to inform members of the organization represented and other persons and organizations as well of the content of the testimony.

10. It provides a better record for the advocate's own organization than will notes from memory.

11. It can be used as a model from which to draw in the future.

12. It forces thorough preparation prior to testimony, and this preparation in itself should lead to a more competent performance before a legislative committee.

13. It generally minimizes faulty communication within and outside the organization represented.

Figure 1 suggests the format and contents of a cover page for the prepared statement. While it may seem that some of the information contained on the cover sheet is not necessary (telephone number or descriptive information regarding the organization, for example), experience suggests that it is helpful, since the statement should be circulated and read widely —by representatives of the media, committee staff members, and various other persons and organizations.

Fig. 1. Illustrative Cover Page

Testimony Regarding

H. 2069—CHILD PROTECTION ACT OF 1977

Before the

JUDICIARY COMMITTEE
X STATE SENATE
March 27, 1977

Presented by

Jane Roe
Executive Director, Y

On Behalf of

Z Association*
0000 Nth Avenue
City, State 00000
Telephone (000) 000-0000

*If desired, include a brief description of the organization, including membership size.

Fig. 2. Structure of the Prepared Statement

A. Introductory Remarks

(This should be a brief introductory paragraph—usually requiring fewer than 75 words —in which the advocate identifies the organization represented, describes the organization briefly—including the number of the organization's members—and thanks the committee for the opportunity to be heard.)

B. Body

1. a. Most important point
   b. Rationale
   c. Flaws in opponents' arguments

2. a. Least important point
   b. Rationale
   c. Flaws in opponents' arguments

3. a. Second most important point
   b. Rationale
   c. Flaws in opponents' arguments

(The body consists principally of a series of specific recommendations, each supported by one or more reasons, and includes arguments to counter recommendations made by opponents of the advocate's position. The body is organized with the most important points coming at either the beginning or the end, while the less important points are placed in the middle portion.)

C. Closing Remarks

(This should be a brief paragraph—usually requiring fewer than 50 words—in which the advocate thanks the committee for the opportunity to testify, stating that she or he will be available at any time to provide additional information for the committee and is willing to answer questions of the committee at this time.)

Figure 2 suggests the structure of the prepared statement. The body of the statement—which is bookended by brief introductory remarks and brief closing remarks—consists of a series of points, recommendations, or arguments.[4] Each point is supported by a rationale—factual, logical, or ideological. And each affirmative point that is made and justified should also be followed with arguments to refute the arguments advanced by those who oppose the advocate's point. This final nicety—the refutation of opposing positions—is a powerful weapon that is seldom used by neophyte advocates. By refuting opposing positions, one's own arguments are strengthened in comparison. Moreover, attacks on opposing positions can put opponents on the defensive, with the result that they cannot advance their own arguments because it is difficult to attack and defend simultaneously. Any advocate who develops arguments along the tripartite dimensions of affirmative argument, justification, and refutation—the three dimensions used by lawyers in developing their arguments—is certain to have a strong case to present to a committee.

It should be noted that Figure 2 suggests that the body of the prepared statement be organized so that the most important points are presented either early in the presentation or near its end, while the least important points are placed toward the middle of the statement. Experience proves that a strong start combined with a strong finish produces a favorable overall impression. Beyond this, lawyers have learned in the courtroom, and psychologists have learned during the course of the investigation of human memory, that people tend to remember best that which comes either first or last in a presentation and that they tend to retain least well information that comes in the middle portion.[5] This tendency of the human mind to remember best the first and final portions of a presentation is sometimes called the primacy-recency rule. This rule explains not only the placement of arguments within the body of the presentation, but it also explains why introductory remarks and closing remarks should be brief.[6]

The primacy-recency rule also gives counsel as to the length of a presentation—it should be no more lengthy than necessary. As a general rule, a prepared statement should not be longer than 2500 words—and preferably not more than about 1500 words. Quality, of course, should not be sacrificed to brevity, but most presentations can be shortened considerably without sacrificing substantive content or persuasiveness. If a presentation is lengthy, this sometimes is because it contains much technical information. In such a case, it is often desirable to append one or more documents to the presentation so that the presentation itself is largely devoid of technical matters, but the technical material will be available for those who may wish to consult it.[7]

Anticipating Issues and Attacks

It has been said that it is not possible to know beforehand what specific issues and arguments will be advanced with regard to a specific legislative proposal, but this is seldom true. Investigations made prior to preparation of a written statement of positions on a bill can forewarn one of many of the issues involved, enable one to anticipate many of the arguments that will be used to attack one's positions, and may even uncover arguments that can be used both to further one's affirmative points and to counter arguments that are hurled against one.

In order to identify issues, an advocate should obtain each bill introduced in the legislature that deals with the subject matter of present concern, go back several years, and then trace changes in the bills. Each change usually signals some issue. The available committee reports and the recorded debate on the bills on the floor of the legislature should be checked. These committee reports and records of legislative debate will identify not only issues but arguments as well, pro and con. If there is federal legislation related to the subject matter, the advocate should try to uncover similar information on bills, committee reports, and debate.

Congressional committee reports tend to be especially full and to illuminate issues and arguments.

It is often helpful to follow the bills, committee reports, and legislative debate in a state other than one's own. California and New York tend to address most legislative issues before other states and to have such large and diverse populations as to assure rather thorough discussion of issues on any important legislative topic.

It is helpful to consult the professional literature—and the advocate should not neglect legal publications. Law review articles tend to identify issues thoroughly and to argue them exhaustively; they can lay the intellectual groundwork for one's testimony thoroughly.[8] Moreover, since many legislators and legislative advocates are either lawyers or frequently consult such literature, law reviews can be invaluable aids not only in avoiding embarrassment but in identifying arguments and counterarguments. Other sources of information also can be helpful: local newspapers, contacts with persons and organizations that are concerned with the specific piece of proposed legislation, experts in the subject matter of the bill, and friendly legislators.

Preparing the Written Statement

The advocate should begin to draft the written statement as soon as research has been completed. Then the advocate should circulate the draft among key members of the organization represented, those persons and organizations that are allied with the organization represented in regard to the bill at hand, and among persons who are experts on the subject matter of the bill. The advocate should begin to write the statement early so that there will be time both to get feedback and clearances from the organization represented and to modify the draft prior to testifying. It can be helpful to examine the testimony given by a variety of advocates. Copies of testimony on behalf of the National Association of Social Workers are routinely provided to state chapter offices, and the *Congressional Record* contains many fine examples of testimony given by experienced advocates.[9]

The following guidelines may be helpful in preparing a written statement:

1. Write the statement so that it stands on its own and can be understood by any reasonably literate adult.

2. Do not use jargon, except in appended materials.

3. Prefer the specific to the general.

4. Do not preach—argue on the basis of facts and logic.

5. Beware of humor; it can detract from serious argument and often appears tasteless or ghoulish. (There is little that is humorous in rape, malnutrition, child abuse, or most other topics on which social workers testify.)

6. Avoid hostility in any form.

7. Focus testimony directly on the proposed legislation at hand; do not use the opportunity to be heard to state views on a wide variety of problems. Problems are solved, if at all, one at a time, not in bunches.

BEING HEARD BY THE COMMITTEE

As soon as a bill is referred to a legislative committee, the chair and the committee staff person should be contacted. Normally it is desirable to telephone committee staff members to advise them of the advocate's name, the name of the organization represented, a brief description of the organization, and the advocate's general position on the bill. Staff members should be advised that the advocate wishes to testify on behalf of the organization and that the advocate wants to be notified of the time, date, and place of any hearings that will be held on the bill. This discussion should be followed up with a letter on the organization's letterhead addressed to the chair.[10]

The advocate should try to get a commitment that he or she will be heard and will be placed on an agenda if there is one. It is desirable to be placed on an agenda, if possible, not only because it gives some status and recognition to the organization, but also because the media may give more attention to those organizations that are scheduled to testify. A representative of an organization on the agenda also is likely to testify prior to organizations that are not on the agenda, and additional time restraints or pressures often are placed on those who testify later. Moreover, media representatives sometimes attend only part of a hearing; testifying early may permit an advocate to testify before some reporters leave.

ATTRACTING THE ATTENTION OF THE MEDIA

Other things being equal, the fact that an advocate can provide the media with a statement of testimony gives greater assurance of coverage in the media than if there is no prepared statement. Representatives of the media do read prepared statements, and if an advocate gets to a hearing room early so that copies of the testimony can be given out early, many representatives may read it while waiting for the hearing to begin. This reading reinforces the impact of later testimony.

Moreover, a prepared statement makes the media representatives' jobs safer and easier. A typewritten statement is easier and more trustworthy than a reporter's own hastily written summary of remarks. And a media representative need fear no accusation of mistatement if she or he quotes directly from a prepared statement. It is also easier for a harried reporter to bracket portions of a written statement on which to report than it is to write out excerpts from oral testimony. A copy of an advocate's testimony should be put into the hands of the media representatives before the testimony is given.

PRESENTING TESTIMONY

If the advocate has prepared thoroughly in advance and has a written statement, he or she should have little difficulty presenting the testimony. Preparation is the key. The advocate can, of course, read a prepared statement to the committee. However, this is not generally advisable. Normally it is better to summarize the major points of a prepared statement and then stand ready to answer any questions that the members of the committee may want to put. If the advocate cannot answer a question fully, it is advisable to indicate to the committee that an answer will be provided at a later time or to suggest that someone else who is present in the hearing room can answer the question capably.

The style of the advocate's presentation should be natural. It is the quality of the material and the argument that is important, not the advocate's delivery. Role-playing beforehand may help give an advocate assurance, however, and it may also help to talk with the chairperson or committee staff prior to the hearing to learn the format of the hearing.

POST-TESTIMONY ACTIVITIES

Immediately following the presentation of the testimony, the advocate should do three things: (1) start planning the next steps, which would include lining up legislative support on the bill once it is reported from the committee, (2) communicate his or her activity on the bill to the membership of the organization represented (it is recommended that the entire text of the testimony be communicated to the membership in a newsletter or otherwise[11]), and (3) place one or more copies of the statement in the files of the organization represented for use not only for historical purposes but, more important, to build a file that will be of use in the future. Professionalism depends to a large extent on the preservation of materials for future use. Files are no less important for the legislative advocate than they are for the clinical practitioner or administrator. It is largely through the preservation of the experience of an advocate that an organization can become increasingly influential.

At some point, too, the advocate should prepare lettersof appreciation to be mailed to legislators and others who have allied with or helped the advocate and the organization in relation to the bill. The end of the legislative session is one time to write these letters; clear victory or loss is another time to do so. Such letters are important, and they distinguish the professional from the inept advocate—because legislators know that most of the letters they receive are letters of complaint, not letters of appreciation.

CONCLUSION

The real key to effective legislative advocacy is preparation. Unfortunately, thorough preparation takes time and work, but there is no adequate substitute. Fortunately, however, the time and energy expended in preparing for legislative testimony lead to success. The successes are never total, and they are sometimes temporary, but they make the time and energy well spent. And beyond this, today's success makes tomorrow's victories more certain.

NOTES AND REFERENCES

1. **Maryann Mahaffey**, "Lobbying and Social Work," *Social Work,* 17 (January 1972), p. 3. Mahaffey discussed the entire range of actions in which a legislative advocate might engage. The present article focuses directly on a narrower range of actions—those related to testimony before a legislative committee.

2. Inexperienced advocates often fail to attack the positions of their opponents. This is unfortunate because it is sometimes easier to win a point by demonstrating the weaknesses of opposing positions than it is to advance a specific affirmative point.

3. Social workers often look with disdain on political dimensions of issues and focus on substantive issues only. On many issues, however, legislators cannot act counter to the wishes of their constituents—no matter how ill-informed their constituents may be—if they are to remain legislators past the next election. The object is therefore to help legislators find some alternative that will not displease their constituents and that does not represent poor public policy.

4. Some illustrations of opening remarks are as follows:
"Mr. Chairman and distinguished members of this committee: My name is Robert Cohen. I am Senior Staff Associate for the National Association of Social Workers, the largest organization of professional social workers in the world. I am here on behalf of the association, although I would note that I have resided in Montgomery County, Maryland, since 1963. NASW represents over 70,000 members, located in chapters throughout the 50 states, the District of Columbia, Puerto Rico, the Virgin Islands, and Europe. In Maryland over 2500 social workers are currently active in the national association." Testimony of Robert H. Cohen before the Economic Affairs Committee of the Maryland State Senate on January 25, 1977. Note that Mr. Cohen identified himself as a Maryland resident as well as a representative of NASW.
"Mr. Chairman, members of the committee, ladies and gentlemen. My name is George Sharwell. I represent the South Carolina State Chapter of the National Associ-

ation of Social Workers, the only body of professionally educated social workers in South Carolina. There are more than 450 members in this chapter." Testimony by George R. Sharwell before the Medical, Military, Public and Municipal Affairs Committee of the South Carolina House of Representatives, March 9, 1977.

The following are illustrations of concluding remarks:

"We appreciate the opportunity to testify before this committee and will be pleased to answer any questions the members may have." Testimony of Robert H. Cohen on behalf of NASW before the Economic Affairs Committee of the Maryland State Senate on January 25, 1977.

"In conclusion, may I thank you for permitting me to testify and urge you to support the passage of H.B. 5984, an act concerning the licensure of social work." Testimony of Sondra K. Match on behalf of NASW before the Public Health and Safety Committee of the Connecticut State Legislature on March 25, 1977.

5. **Bernard Berelson and Gary A. Steiner**, *Human Behavior: An Inventory of Scientific Findings* (New York: Harcourt, Brace & World, 1964), pp. 164–165.

6. The rule also is sometimes termed the "serial-position effect." *See* ibid.

7. Committee staff members or those drafting bills may be interested in technical information, while committee members may be less interested in such information.

8. Law review articles can be located by consulting *The Index to Legal Periodicals.*

9. One of the most instructive examples of testimony before a legislative committee is the testimony of Senator Hubert H. Humphrey reported in the *Congressional Record* of June 27, 1974, p. S11697 (daily edition). His testimony is especially noteworthy because although Senator Humphrey had a reputation for being verbose, his testimony was given in fewer than 700 words!

10. The body of such a letter might read somewhat as follows:

"I am writing to inform you that X wants to present its view on H. 2069 before the House Judiciary Committee.

"I have been informed by Y, Secretary to the Judiciary Committee, that hearings on H. 2069 have not yet been scheduled. I request that the Judiciary Committee provide X with an opportunity to be heard on this bill when a hearing is scheduled, and that I be notified of the time, date, and place of the hearing when it is scheduled.

"For purposes of planning, it may be helpful for your committee to know that our association will provide the committee with a written statement containing the views of our association's nearly —— members and that oral presentation will be limited to a summary of the written statement. It is anticipated that our position will be essentially supportive of H. 2069."

11. The full text is the best communication to provide to the membership. A summary is never adequate and, in any event, members deserve to be informed. A summarized statement is sometimes defended on the ground that members will not read a full statement. This is not necessarily true. But beyond this, members deserve to have the fullest possible information made available to them.

PART 3
SERVICES TO INDIVIDUALS AND GROUPS

EDITOR'S COMMENT

Whereas the articles in Parts 1 and 2 provided a broad, more abstract, issue-focused context for current practice, the following group of articles primarily describe direct services provided by social workers. These articles encompass descriptions of programs and social work skills, with the mix of these two elements varying from article to article. Since most of the articles emphasize particular aspects of programs or treatment modalities, they do not include evaluations of effectiveness or other relevant aspects that might be susceptible to research. This gap is hardly surprising, given what is know about the existing staffing patterns of agencies and the predisposition of social work practitioners to do and serve rather than evaluate.

If evaluation were to be emphasized in assessing these articles, one might ask such questions as these: What is the precise nature of the phenomena being dealt with? Given an initial baseline, is it possible to demonstrate systematically and objectively that the described intervention program or modality was responsible for the desired changes as set forth in the goals stated before the intervention? Is it possible to show by evaluative research that the particular intervention program or modality is superior to others involving the same variables—such as type of problem or size and type of target population described in the article? Further, while recognizing the limitations of cost-benefit analyses, how would the interventions described in the article compare to cost-benefits for other types of programs for different social problems or target populations? Could such a comparison in a given community help determine more objectively priorities in allocating scarce resources among competitive social services?

In addition to assessing the articles in terms of evaluation, other perspectives come from viewing the articles with respect to how they relate to particular target groups, settings, or modalities. For example, to what extent do the articles express a concern with specific ethnic or cultural groups? None of the articles emphasizes any one group, although the social work-related literature has historically given considerable attention to blacks and increasing attention to Chicanos in the 1970s.[1] Is this lack of representation indicative of the current diminution of public, and perhaps professional, concern with such target groups as contrasted with the civil rights emphasis in the 1960s and early 1970s?

By contrast, a professional focus on sexuality as an emerging interest is reflected in three articles, and two articles deal with aging. Subjects related to women's problems, in keeping with current social developments in the woman's movement, are manifested in three of the fifteen articles in this group. Health (interpreted broadly as covering both physical and mental health), including the health of the elderly, receive attention in four articles, which may indicate the continuing and growing importance of this social problem. The schools and industry are represented by one article each; these two settings have been receiving increasing emphasis in the profession and special program leadership from NASW. Only one article, that by Shulman, discusses a specific treatment modality throughout the article. Neither behavior modification nor ego psychology, as current treatment models, are incorporated in any of the articles. Similarly, drug addiction—a subject of marked concern in the social work-related literature of 1965–76—is not addressed in any article.

Any content analysis of the articles along dimensions of target groups and problems, modalities, or settings, at best, only suggests the range of emphases in social work practice. The selection of articles stressed quality alone; no consideration was given to representativeness within those three dimensions. Furthermore, the number of articles is so small that the absence or range of numbers of articles along a particular dimension is not substantially significant.

Turning now to the individual articles: Shulman's "The Skills of the Helping Process" deserves particular attention because it is foremost in discussing skills and in having model-building and empirical testing as a goal. Utilizing the mediating theory of William Schwartz, Shulman gives an abbreviated account of his research, which is part of a larger study. Readers whose interest is stimulated by this article may wish to follow additional reports of Shulman's work, one of which appeared in the July 1978 issue of *Social Work*.[2]

Kane and Glicken's "Compliance and Consumerism: Social Work

[1]Sidney E. Zimbalist, "Social Work Abstracts: A Clue to Trends," *Social Work Research and Abstracts*, 14 (Spring 1978), pp. 41–46.
[2]Lawrence Shulman, "A Study of Practice Skills," *Social Work*, 23 (July 1978), pp. 274–279.

Goals in the Health Field" is the first of four articles in the collection that stress practice in a health setting. The authors recognize that the use of the term *compliance* has ambiguous and negative connotations with respect to what might otherwise have been called the patient's acceptance of, or cooperation with, physicians' recommendations for medical treatment. Given the reported excessive use of medications and surgery by physicians, in some instances the patients may be wise not to comply. The authors' discussion of the right of the patient, as a consumer, to accept or reject treatment balances their informative delineation of the problems of compliance by the patient. The authors describe factors associated with and efforts to improve compliance, as well as those to enhance consumerism. Both aspects are construed as mutually supportive rather than contradictory or antagonistic. Sharing the medical record and contracting are discussed as specific tactics, along with a discussion of the general implications of consumerism and compliance for the social work practitioner.

Gamble's "Dignity and Success: The Experience of Welfare Rights Members" is the most specific reminder in this collection about the profession's continuing concern for low-income clients, who happen also to be black. It is also unique in that it deals with practice in a rural setting, although differences in methods and skills needed in rural practice are not considered. With the diminished thrust of the welfare rights' movement nationally, the article has elements of nostalgia for a movement that was both promising and complex just a few years ago. The article purports to show success by what appears to have been a "generalist" practitioner working with individuals, groups, and the community. The success of individual welfare rights members, as well as the group's attainments, are reported subjectively and unsystematically, although they appear to have been substantial. The interventions by the practitioner are eclectic, with no single modality being described or systematically applied or tested.

Warmsun, Ullmann, and Nyland's "Client Record-Sharing: A Solution to Problems of Confidentiality, Clients' Rights, and Accountability" describes the innovation of having a client of a mental health center cooperate with the therapist in writing his or her records. The authors refer to the costs and benefits of dealing with problems of confidentiality, clients' rights, and accountability. Although mentioned in the subtitle as a "solution," the recording procedure is more appropriately assessed as a limited approach to those three problems. The client's participation in writing the client's record is closely related to the current mode of contracting with clients. The article suggests, but does not purport to confirm, that shared recording facilitates the treatment process as well as approaches the three problems more specifically addressed. Although researchers may question aspects of the research methods used, the article has a special value in that it attempts to subject an innovative method to empirical testing.

Bryce and Ryan's "Intensive In-Home Treatment: An Alternative to Out-of-Home Placement" is relevant to the recurrently sharp policy issue: to treat in an institution or in the community? The article is also significant in highlighting the role of the voluntary agency in providing program innovations. However, the voluntary aspect is qualified, typically as it is in these times of mixed funding, by the fact that the agency is subsidized contractually by tax moneys from a public agency. The program involves family therapy delivered in the home, rather than in an office setting, and its goal is to strengthen parental functioning to avoid placing a child in an institution or in foster care. Team approaches and the management of crises with round-the-clock services are stressed. The subjective description of the program appears to be promising, but this article exemplifies the need for cost-benefit analyses and other comparisons, systematically and scientifically implemented, to support the value of this program per se and in comparison with other approaches, particularly institutional and foster home care.

Bridgeman and Willis's "Families in Transition: A Divorce Workshop for Parents and Children" is especially pertinent for the growing social concern with divorce and its effects on children. Using a workshop that includes both parents and children, the program uses a grief model (adapted to the specific situation), communication and step-parenting skills, and adaptations from transactional analysis procedures. No evaluation or subjective report on effectiveness is provided regarding this project which received a regional award for its program design.

Shoham's "Psychiatric Social Work with the Aged: A New Look" challenges "the currently conventional attempt to reorient the patient to reality" and focuses on the treatment of anxiety or depression as symptoms among the elderly. The author's use of the term *insight therapy* will be challenged by practitioners from the psychoanalytic school. The term *psychiatric social work* as used by the author may be challenged by those who have abandoned that terminology in favor of the generic term *social work.* However, readers can find value in the author's geriatric center experience wherein he attempted to modify a relationship therapy model for use with the elderly. The article also has value in that it is concerned with the aged—a growing target population.

Fishman's "Human Sexuality and the Institutionalized Elderly" shares Shoham's concern for the elderly and highlights the need to recognize the sexuality of patients in nursing homes. The author contends that the sexuality of such patients has been neglected compared to sexuality among the noninstitutionalized majority of the elderly. After giving an overview of the particular needs and problems of nursing home patients, the author discusses a range of social work interventions. No evaluative material is included, but this article evokes certain research questions such as the following: Assuming social work intervention, what behavioral changes might be associated with the acceptance of sexuality in nursing home patients by the patients themselves, the staff, and the administrator? Similarly, would a nursing home population that received social work intervention be different from one that did not receive it?

Continuing the theme of sexuality, but with a different target population, Mantell and Green's "Enhancing Sexuality: A Humanistic Approach to the Mastectomee" targets a group of patients subjected to radical surgery that involves emotional trauma. After providing informative background information, the authors are helpful in the specificity with which they address the skills needed by social work practitioners to assist this group of patients. The positive consequences of skilled social work intervention for such patients —should that outcome be demonstrable—would be a significant contribution from research related to the skills delineated in this article. Similarly, were such skills to be shown to be either ineffective or detrimental, that research result would be important, even though it did not support the value of social work intervention in this instance.

The consequences of sexuality for both the victim and the perpetrator are addressed in Ensminger and Ferguson's "Sexual Abuse of Children: Child and Offender as Victims." The article benefits from a Philadelphia agency's twenty years' experience with rape victims. It describes the treatment given to the offender (primarily group therapy) as well as to the child and family. The authors also suggest how a follow-up study can be useful to assess the outcomes of an innovative program, although they provide only subjective descriptions which intimate that there are positive results from the interventions.

Star's "Treating the Battered Woman" exemplifies another of the multiple concerns of the women's movement. Drawing from the literature and interviews with and personal investigations of fifty battered women, the author examines the psychosocial dynamics of abused women, their marriages, and the problems in wife-beating some social workers might encounter. Considerations for treatment are then suggested. The author reports stereotypes, largely stemming from psychoanalytic nomenclature, used to describe battered women. These comments are useful reminders that research undertaken simply to describe a phenomenon is shaped by the conceptual framework which guides, or as often narrows or constricts, the perspective of the researcher. Although the author refers to her research about battered women, no data or conclusions from a specific research design are reported in the article. Furthermore, none of the treatment suggestions in the article were validated by the author's research, as alluded to in the article.

Miller, Johnson, and La Celle's "Hidden Victims: The Effects of Disaster on Caregivers" moves on to a new emphasis on the helper's own behaviors under the stress of a natural disaster. Natural disasters are unique in their suddenness and widespread, usually tragic, effects on a total population in a limited geographic area. The authors describe the experience of five mental health teams sent to provide crisis intervention to victims of a major flood. Based on three questionnaires administered immediately after and within an eleven-month period after the flood experience, the article assesses staff reactions to the flood and discusses disaster skills training in three categories: (1) experiential, (2) crisis theory, and (3) self-awareness. The article is supported by descriptive research from which the authors draw their conclusions about caregivers as victims. The reliance on crisis intervention theory in assessing staff reactions, as well as its use as a basis for future training of practitioners for disaster work, brings up the same question raised about Star's article. Nevertheless, many readers will find that this article adds to their awareness of practitioners' reactions to and the training needed to enhance practitioners' skills in disaster work.

In contrast to the previous article's concern with a sharply limited disaster, Wetzel's "The Work Environment and Depression: Implications for Intervention" addresses a more pervasive social phenomenon: work. The article has a stronger research component, primarily from a social psychology view, than most of the articles in this collection. Personality traits, variables in the environment, and the symptomatology of depression are examined. The research background is then utilized to suggest the macro- and micro skills needed to deal with work-related depression. This is an outstanding article in that it is an example of the potential application of social research to practice. One implication of the article for future research would be how the interventions suggested by the author might modify the work-environment variables identified in this article.

Whereas most of the articles in this section deal with direct intervention, Munson's "Consultation in Group Homes for Adolescents" pinpoints the indirect role of the consultant as a helper. Although this article was not based on research, it has the special merit of taking a particular role theory, whatever its limitations, and applying it as a consistent conceptual framework. Consultative skills are then viewed within that perspective. Readers may wish to compare this approach with other theoretical approaches in a similar setting or to determine the degree to which role theory for consultation is transferable to settings other than a group home for adolescents.

The emphasis on child welfare is continued in Lapham and De Christopher's "Education Laws: The Silent Revolution." This article substantiates the profound impact on school social work of recent education laws. It is of special topical interest because of the growth in school social work and the current emphasis by NASW on this specialized setting. The immediate program skills occasioned by the new laws that are needed by social workers in working with children, parents, and educators are delineated by the authors with respect to what they characterize as "the silent revolution" in the schools. Special attention is given to handicapped students and to children's and parents' rights.

Skills of the Helping Process

LAWRENCE SHULMAN

This paper focuses on the skills of the helping process—what it is the worker does while interacting with clients. There is an increased awareness in the helping professions of the need to translate theoretical frameworks into specific behaviors so that middle-range theories can be developed for use by practitioners, teachers, and researchers. This marks an important revolution in professions that have long been plagued by a lack of clarity about method.

The first part of this paper presents a model describing the mechanisms of the helping process. Specific worker skills are identified and organized into categories. While the model and the skills are related to a specific practice frame of reference, this author believes they also describe a central process relevant to other frameworks. The second part of the paper briefly reports the related findings of a four-year research project in which the impact of these skills on the development of working relationships with clients and the provision of help is examined.

A MODEL OF THE HELPING PROCESS

The frame of reference providing direction to the model-building and empirical testing described in this paper is the mediating theory developed by William Schwartz.[1] While the behaviors described in this paper were generated by this theoretical framework, they can all fit comfortably within other theories of the helping process.

One widely accepted concept of helping involves the worker's using his or her skills in early encounters with the client to develop a positive relationship, which is a precondition for helpfulness. Questions that can be raised in connection with the concept include the following: Specifically which behaviors on the part of the worker will lead to this construct called relationship? What are the elements that make up a good relationship? Exactly how does a positive working relationship set the conditions for effective work? Are there skills that should only be used after an effective relationship has been developed? The attempt to answer questions of this order can be called interactional research. The model described in the following sections is a step in a continuing process in which theory provides direction for empirical examination. The results of the research are then used to modify the theory. These constructs and research findings are not presented as completed products but rather as steps in an ongoing process.

Five of the nine skill categories in the model are presented in this paper: contracting, empathy, elaboration, the demand for work, and offering feelings.[2] The underlying assumptions related to each skill grouping are described and the specific skills identified. Many of the skills are illustrated with excerpts from a process recording of a first interview with a father in a child welfare setting. It is the author's belief that the skills and dynamics described are relevant to other clients and settings.

Contracting

There are two types of contracting behavior. The first are those worker behaviors utilized in the beginning phase of work with clients that are designed to negotiate a mutual understanding about the overall nature of the work. The second sense of contracting relates to the beginning phase of each session when the worker attempts to determine the client's agenda for that day.

An emphasis on contracting in the beginning phase of work relates to the assumption that all clients approach their first sessions with varying degrees of ambivalence. New situations—especially encounters with people in authority—will tend to heighten the client's feelings of inadequacy and concerns about the demands to be placed on her or him. If a client has had previous experiences with helping professionals, the client may bring in a preconceived notion of the process that may serve to keep her or him on guard.

The other side of the client's feelings may consist of hope that the engagement will be helpful. There is a part of every client that is always reaching out toward life and growth, even though for some this strength may be glimpsed only faintly. Differences in degree of ambivalence can relate to the given client, the setting, whether or not the engagement is voluntary, and so on. These factors will contribute some of the variant elements that need to be dealt with.

Because of this ambivalence, effective work with clients will be hampered unless clarity about the working relationship is established early. The three skills designed to encourage this are *clarifying purpose, clarifying role,* and *encouraging client feedback on purpose.*

To illustrate these skills, an excerpt follows from an interview with the 25-year-old father mentioned earlier. His wife had signed the agreement forms to place their three children voluntarily, and the worker asked the father to come in so that she could inform him of his legal rights, ask him to sign the forms, and see whether she could offer some assistance. The father was described in the agency records by past workers as "difficult, hostile, and uncooperative."

> WORKER: You know that your wife has signed forms to place your children under the care of the agency. I wanted to meet with you to have you sign agreements, but before that, to discuss what this means for you and your children. I know it can be an upsetting time, and I thought you might also have things on your mind you want to discuss.
>
> CLIENT: For how long are my kids going to be in care?
>
> WORKER: Your wife has signed forms for six months, but with 24 hours' notice, you or your wife can have your children home.
>
> CLIENT: It's a long time for the kids.
>
> WORKER: Yes, it is, and for you also.

In this example, although the worker made a direct offer to the client, the client politely refused to accept it and continued to discuss his children. He was guarded, possibly wondering what the worker was up to and whether she would be like the others he had experienced. The worker was not thrown by the first subtle refusal, however, and returned to her offer in the comment "Yes, it is, and for you also."

Sessional contracting got under way in this excerpt as the worker began the session tentatively, attempting to read as quickly as possible what issues might be immediately relevant to this client. She had prepared herself through the process of "tuning in," in which she attempted to gain a preliminary empathy for potential themes of concern. As the session unfolded, she tried to pick up indirect cues that would help her stay with the client. During the middle phase of work, sessional contracting is seen at the start of each session when the worker uses the skill of *reaching for between-session data*. It is simply the process of checking at each session for the emergence of any new issues.

Empathic Skills

A critical factor in determining whether the client will begin to open up and accept the worker's offer will be his sense of her ability to respond empathically. His internal question will be "Can this young woman really understand, or will she be like all the rest, harsh and judgmental?" The empathic skills are reviewed and illustrated next.

As the client tells his story, the worker uses a number of skills designed to keep the discussion real by having the client invest his talk with feeling. Clients often withhold their affect, for a number of reasons; however, the affect is there and can exert a powerful force on the client unless it is acknowledged and dealt with. The worker's acceptance and understanding of the client's emotions frees the client to drop some of his defenses and to allow the worker and himself more access to the real person.

It is important to underline that the empathic skills must be genuine. Workers who ritualistically express understanding without really feeling the emotions themselves are perceived as phony. Willingness to feel the real emotions of the client is a gift the worker provides that contributes greatly to the development of the construct called working relationship. The specific skills of *understanding client's feelings* and *putting the client's feelings into words* are illustrated in the next excerpt from the interview (note the sentences that are in italics). When the client said, "It's a long time for the kids," the worker began to demonstrate her capacity to feel his emotions with her response.

> WORKER: Yes, it is, and for you also.
> CLIENT: Yeah, I haven't seen them yet, but I hear they're doing fine.
> WORKER: Would you like to see them?
> CLIENT: I thought I wasn't allowed to.
> WORKER: Sure you are. You have the right to see your children whenever you wish.
> CLIENT: I was told it would upset the kids, especially Andy, to see me, so it would be better not to.
> WORKER: Sure it will upset him; it will upset you too. *It's hard to see someone you love and can't be with.*
> CLIENT: Yeah, Andy has been in care before, and he's confused and sad.
> WORKER: *That must make it hard on you to see him.*

As the relationship begins to develop in response to the worker's use of her skills, the client begins to move into the work. In the next excerpt, the skill of *putting the client's feelings into words* just before he has articulated them is illustrated. In a sense, the worker was slightly ahead of the client and helped the client move into what might be perceived as a hard subject to discuss—his sense of guilt.

> CLIENT: Yeah. Like what do I say to him?
> WORKER: Like when he asks, "When do I come home?"
> CLIENT: Well, yeah.
> WORKER: What do you say?
> CLIENT: Oh, I change the subject and cheer him up.
> WORKER: Does it work?
> CLIENT: Not really.
> WORKER: What do you want to say?

CLIENT: Well, I don't know when he's coming home.
WORKER: I guess that hurts you.
CLIENT: Well, kids don't understand.
WORKER: Have you tried telling him?
CLIENT: No, not really.
WORKER: I think it's hard to tell your child you don't know when he's coming home, but clearing that up might make it easier for you both.
CLIENT: Yeah, I won't feel like I'm holding out. Can I see him at my wife's house this weekend?
WORKER: Whatever visiting arrangement you want can be worked out if I know in advance. You can see him at your wife's if it's OK with her.
CLIENT: I want to know, are you going to be my social worker? You see my wife, and you help her, so how does it work? Are you on her side or mine, or do I get another social worker?

As the client was pulled into the work, he suddenly caught himself and stopped. He needed to sort out some important issues with this worker. The suddenness and directness of his comment caught the worker off guard and she responded, not with her real feelings, but with a long and involved speech.

WORKER: I'm on no one's side. I try to help your wife with what's on her mind. I'm here to help you with whatever you want. I do this so you can both come to the point of finally making a decision about your children. Whatever we discuss is confidential, and the same for your wife and me. When the two of you will make decisions that will affect each other, we'll do it together. Then I won't take sides. [Quiet. . . .]

The worker provided an answer to the client's question without fully understanding the implications of the question. It is at this moment that elaboration skills would help. Fortunately it is not necessary for interviews to be perfect. Real skill involves the ability to catch mistakes as quickly as possible. These elaboration skills are discussed next, and the process of catching a mistake in action is illustrated.

Elaboration

The elaboration skills are designed to help a client tell his or her story. First offerings by clients are often vague and indirect. This represents, in part, the client's ambivalence about dealing directly with difficult subjects. Skills in this area would include the following: *moving from the general to the specific* (asking for details of a general concern), *reaching inside of silences* (exploring the communication hidden in each silence), *supporting the client in taboo areas,* and *dealing with the authority theme.* Supporting the client in taboo areas recognizes that clients will have difficulty discussing concerns that carry societal taboos (for example, sex and dependency). The authority theme, the relationship between the client and the worker, is one of the most difficult areas for clients to discuss openly. Returning to the point of silence in the interview, we see the worker catching her mistake and using a number of skills in helping the client elaborate.

> WORKER: Why did you ask? It sounds like you have had trouble with social workers before.
> CLIENT: I did. All the other social workers seemed to be with my wife and against me. I was always the bad one.
> WORKER: And you're worried that I might do the same thing?
> CLIENT: Yeah, well, you might.
> WORKER: I try to help the two of you decide to do what's best for you and your children. If you feel I'm siding, or if you don't like how things are going with me, I want you to tell me, because I want to help you both.
> CLIENT: Don't worry, you'll know. Are you new at this job?
> WORKER: No, I've been here for a while. Why do you ask?
> CLIENT: Well, the last worker I had was really green—she knew nothing. She took me to court, didn't get anywhere, but what a mess.

The elaboration skills of the worker opened up an important conversation that will go a long way toward deepening the beginning working relationship. Mutual expectations and the terms of the relationship are discussed with remarkable directness partly because of the skill of the worker and partly owing to the strength of the client that emerges from his anger. It is this anger that may have frightened previous workers.

The Demand for Work

Central to an understanding of the helping process is the issue of ambivalence. Clients will be of two minds about proceeding with the work. Their strength will move them toward the work and the understanding and growth that follow. Their resistance will pull them back from what is perceived as a painful and difficult process. This ambivalence is normal and represents a signal that the work is going well. It is because of this natural process that the worker must present a consistent demand for work. It is precisely this demand, when expressed in conjunction with empathic understanding, that helps the client to mobilize his or her energies for further work. Without empathy, the demand will be experienced as harsh. Understanding without demand may lead to a warm relationship, but it can also allow an illusion of work that blocks the client's progress.

Some of the skills involved can include *partializing client's concerns* (breaking global problems into manageable parts), *holding to focus* (helping the client to discuss specific themes one at a time), and *pointing out the illusion of work* (letting the client know when it appears the work is super ficial). The demand for work is also evident through a number of skills already mentioned. For example, when the worker in the interview excerpts responded to the client's comment "It's a long time for kids" with "Yes, it is, and for you also," she was making a gentle demand for work. As the interview excerpts continue, we see her making another demand in the area of the authority theme.

> CLIENT: . . . She [the other worker] took me to court, didn't get any-where, but what a mess.
>
> WORKER: Are you wondering if I'll take you to court?
>
> CLIENT: Oh, no. And if you did, I'd go ahead and fight.
>
> WORKER: I think it's important for me to let you know under what condi-tions I'd go to court. You have a voluntary placement. Unless I see your kids harmed when they are with your wife or when you are visiting, or not fed or supervised, then I wouldn't go to court. I'd go if they were beaten or neglected.
>
> CLIENT: What if I want to take my kids home—can you go to court and stop me?
>
> WORKER: No, you can take your children whenever you want.
>
> CLIENT: What if I'm not working, can't care for them? You won't let them come.
>
> WORKER: I can't stop them. If, however, once they're home, they don't get fed, clothed, taken care of, then I can go to court and bring them back.
>
> CLIENT: [Smiles.] I really knew the answers to this, but I was misin-formed by other people in the past. I used to sort of test my last worker to see if she'd tell me the truth.
>
> WORKER: Did I pass?
>
> CLIENT: Not you—her. [Quiet.] Yeah, you passed. [Smiles.] I had to do it to see where we stand. The first meeting's really important, you know.
>
> WORKER: Yes, it is. And it's scary since you don't know what's happen-ing.
>
> CLIENT: Yeah. But it looks OK. [We talked a bit more about procedures, rules, etc., then summed up and arranged a next meeting.]

In a short period of time, the worker's clarity of purpose and role, her empathic responses, directness, and gentle demand for work made a start on a working relationship. Her work turned this stereotyped "hostile" client toward the agency service and, in turn, toward his children. He had to deal with a worker who refused to act like a stereotype, and he decided that, so far, "it looks OK."

Offering Feelings

A critical factor in this model and in the interview just described is the worker's ability to present him- or herself as a real human being. Direct expressions of worker feeling, anger, fear, and ambivalence have often been presented as "unprofessional." Workers have been faced with the dilemma of having to choose between their personal or their professional selves. This model suggests that workers can only be effective when they are able to synthesize their personal feelings and professional function. The client needs to experience the worker as a real human being who demonstrates the same degree of spontaneity of expression that the worker expects from the client.

Workers often express concern about spontaneity and the expression of related feelings. They are worried that they will act out, make mistakes, and perhaps hurt a client. What they fail to recognize is that clients can forgive a mistake more easily than an image of perfection. When a worker's reactions are direct, a client may find it easier to be trusting. Two skills that reflect this behavior are the *worker displaying feelings openly* and *sharing personal thoughts and feelings.* It should be clarified that the feelings expressed must relate to the work of the client. It would be a mistake to turn the interview over to the concerns of the worker.

It has been possible to share only a portion of the model in this paper. In the next section, a research project designed to test some of these theoretical constructs is described briefly and some of the major findings are shared.

A STUDY OF THE HELPING PROCESS

A four-year research project, funded by the Welfare Grants Directorate of Health and Welfare, Canada, was undertaken to explore the relationship between the use of the identified behaviors and the development of working relationships and helpfulness. The portion of the study briefly described here involved the development and testing of client perception instruments that allowed the research team to measure worker skills (independent variable) and the worker's relationship with clients and helpfulness (dependent variables).[3]

All of the 118 workers in two child welfare agencies (the Children's Aid Society of Ottawa and the Children's Service Centre of Montreal) were included in the study. Questionnaires were mailed to over 4000 of their clients and foster parents, with a return rate of better than 53 percent. This was a good response, considering that many of those on the case load were relatively inactive clients and the mailing was interrupted by a postal strike. However, an element of self-selection may have biased the returns, resulting in a more positively inclined sample. Half of the clients (randomly selected from each case load) reported on their workers' behaviors, and the other half, on the state of the worker-client relationship and the worker's helpfulness. This procedure was followed to maintain independence between the two questionnaires by preventing any influence on the results of one by clients who had completed the other. Each client had an equal chance of receiving either questionnaire. Table 1 lists the 15 skills mentioned in this paper (out of a total of 27 in the study). Each skill is followed by the phrasing of the questionnaire item attempting to describe the behavior in nonjargon terms. Respondents would read the item, followed by an example (not included in the table), and then indicate the frequency of use by their worker (for example, often, fairly often, rarely, never). The average score of all respondents for a given skill became a worker's score for that behavior.

Key items on the questionnaire relating to the worker-client relationship and the worker's helpfulness included such questions as "How satisfied are you with how you and your worker get along?" and "In general, how helpful has your worker been?"[4] The findings reported next are the correlations between the clients' perceptions of their workers' behaviors and their perceptions of the state of the worker-client relationship and how helpful their workers had been.

There are a number of obvious limitations to a study of this type. The analysis is limited to workers in two agencies, both in the child welfare field. Would these results generalize to other workers in other types of agencies? Although all workers and all clients/foster parents were included in the study, a mail questionnaire means returns were self-selected. Was there a bias in the sample, and would it affect the results? Although instruments were tested, they are still in a developmental stage, and there is always some degree of error; in effect, this is a study of client perception. These limitations and others are examined in detail in the full report.

The composition of the worker and respondent samples are also limitations. Of the 118 workers in the study, 83 percent were female. Sixty-one percent reported some form of social work education (junior college, 12 percent; BSW, 15 percent; MSW, 34 percent). With respect to total social service work experience, 37 percent had three or fewer years' experience, 41 percent had from three to nine years' experience, and 22 percent had more than ten years' experience. Of the respondent sample of 1,783, 23 percent were natural parents, 33 percent were foster parents, 19 percent were adolescents over 14, 8 percent were unmarried mothers, and 17 percent were adoptive parents. Seventy percent of the respondents had not gone beyond grade 13 in school. In terms of duration of contact with the worker, 13 percent reported contact of two months or less, 45 percent three to 11 months' contact, 20 percent had known their workers one to two years, and

TABLE 1. WORKER BEHAVIOR QUESTIONNAIRE ITEMS

Item	Behavior	Corresponding Questionnaire Item
1	Clarifying Purpose	In our first meetings, my worker explained the kinds of concerns we might be discussing.
2	Clarifying Role	My worker explained how we would work together, describing the kind of help a social worker could give.
3	Encouraging Client Feedback on Purpose	During our first meeting, my worker asked me for my ideas on specific subjects we would discuss together.
4	Holding to Focus	When we began to discuss a particular concern, the worker kept me on the topic.
5	Moving from the General to the Specific	When I raised a general concern, the worker asked me for examples.
6	Reaching for Between-Session Data	The worker began our visit by asking if anything had happened between visits that I wanted to talk about.
7	Pointing out the Illusion of Work	When the worker thought I was not working hard in our discussions, she let me know.
8	Reaching Inside of Silences	When I was unusually silent during our visits, the worker tried to find out why.
9	Supporting the Client in Taboo Areas	The worker helped me to talk about subjects that were not easy to talk about.
10	Sharing Personal Thoughts and Feelings	The worker shared her personal thoughts and feelings, which helped me to get to know her better as a person.
11	Understanding Client's Feelings	When I told my worker how I felt, she understood.
12	Dealing with the Authority Theme	When I was upset about what my worker did or said, she encouraged me to talk about it.
13	Putting the Client's Feelings into Words	The worker seemed to understand how I felt without my having to put it into words.
14	Partializing Client's Concerns	The worker helped me look at my concerns one at a time.
15	Worker Displaying Feelings Openly	The worker let me know her feelings about the situations we discussed.

17 percent reported contact of more than two years. There were no data on this variable for 5 percent of the sample. More complete descriptions of the worker and client samples, as well as an analysis of the impact of these variables on the results, are contained in the complete report.

It should be noted that this is essentially an exercise in theory-building, and any results must be viewed as tentative. It is less an effort to prove a hypothesis than it is an effort to understand more deeply the complex processes involved when one person attempts to help another. The findings need to be supported by replications in other settings with different populations before a value can be placed on them as proven theoretical generalizations.

Summary of Findings

It is possible to highlight some of the tentative findings that relate to the skills described in this paper. One of these indicated that the skill of *sharing personal thoughts and feelings* was most positively associated with good working relationships and helpfulness (see Table 2 for correlation levels). This finding conforms with those of other studies that have indicated

TABLE 2. CORRELATIONS BETWEEN WORKER BEHAVIORS AND RELATIONSHIP/HELPFULNESS

Relationship		Helpfulness	
Item	r	Item	r
Sharing personal thoughts and feelings	.45	Sharing personal thoughts and feelings	.47
Understanding client's feelings	.41	Understanding client's feelings	.46
Clarifying role	.34	Supporting the client in taboo areas	.33
Worker displaying feelings openly	.33	Putting the client's feelings into words	.32
Putting the client's feelings into words	.31	Encouraging client feedback on purpose	.31
Partializing client's concerns	.29	Partializing client's concerns	.27
Dealing with the authority theme	.26	Clarifying role	.23
Supporting the client in taboo areas	.24	Reaching for between-session data	.21
Reaching for between-session data	.23	Worker displaying feelings openly	.21
Encouraging client feedback on purpose	.20	Dealing with the authority theme	.18

NOTE: All correlations are significant at $p \leq .05$. The number of workers included in this analysis totaled 88 after workers with fewer than four returns on either the S.W.B.Q. or the S.S.O. form were dropped. Deletion of cases with no data on certain variables (the normal option with a partial correlation program) also reduced the number. The higher the correlation *(r)*, the stronger the association between variables. Correlations lower than .30, although statistically significant, are not high enough for theoretical interpretations. In addition, *partializing client's concerns* and *dealing with the authority theme* indicated low individual item reliability in the test-retest procedure.

that self-disclosure may make an important contribution to helping.[5] In the written comments portion of the questionnaire, one respondent summarized the feelings of many on this issue with the following statement: "I got along well with my worker because she wasn't like a social worker; she was like a real person."

The skill of *understanding client's feelings* was next in importance for its contribution to both helpfulness and relationship. At this point it is helpful to return to the general model described earlier in which relationship was a precondition for helpfulness. In this study, scores on relationship were positively associated with helping ($r = .76$). It would be quite legitimate for the reader to wonder whether these skills appeared to be associated with helpfulness only because of their association with relationship. One could argue that sharing feelings and empathic responses helped to build relationships and that correlation with helpfulness was a result of the association between relationship and helpfulness.

Exploring this question could yield findings that would help determine which skills were most important to relationship-building, which to helpfulness, and which to both. An additional analysis was undertaken (third-variable analysis using partial correlation), and the results suggested that *sharing personal thoughts and feelings* and *understanding client's feelings* contributed to both. At one and the same time, empathic responses could help the client work on specific concerns while also serving to cement the bond between worker and client. The same was true for *sharing personal thoughts and feelings.* Our understanding of the process increases as we see that a single skill can have more than one impact.

It is interesting to note in Table 2 that under relationship skills, the next behavior on the list is *clarifying role,* while under helpfulness, the third skill listed is *supporting the client in taboo areas.* The stronger association between supporting the client in taboo areas and helpfulness (as compared to relationship) tentatively supports the theoretical notion that a positive relationship can be built with worker openness, empathy, and clear role, but for the worker also to be helpful, she or he needs to develop skills to help clients move into the discussion of difficult subjects. This finding also tends to support the argument in this paper that, contrary to some thinking, one helps to build a relationship by defining role rather than first building a relationship and then defining role. Clients simply cannot open up to a worker until they know clearly what the worker is all about.

The skill of putting the client's feelings into words appeared to be related equally to relationship-building and helpfulness; however, when the second analysis was performed, it indicated that the main contribution of this skill was to relationship-building. This was a most interesting finding. Workers have long been concerned about getting too far ahead of the client and "putting feelings into their mouths." One interpretation of this finding is that the greater risk may be in failure to share empathic hunches soon enough. Perhaps, early in the relationship, the client cannot risk some of the more difficult feelings. By articulating these for the client, the worker may demonstrate an understanding that helps to build the bond, even if the client is not ready to deal with the issue. The important thing is that the client knows that the worker understands. This question, as with all the interpretations in the study, needs further study.

One skill that appeared to be associated positively with helpfulness was *encouraging client feedback on purpose*. It makes sense that clients will perceive workers as more helpful if the workers are dealing with issues and concerns that the client feels are urgent.

Table 2 lists additional skills with correlations high enough to be statistically significant; however, those with an *r* score of less than .30 are too weak to carry much weight.[6] They present interesting possibilities for future study, but the behaviors account for so little of the change in helpfulness or relationship that it is not possible to make inferences about their importance based on these findings alone.

What is interesting, however, is the lack of significant correlations between some of the demand for work skills and the outcome measures. A pattern in the study seemed to indicate that more gentle demand for work skills (for example, *supporting the client in taboo areas*) appeared to be better received than those that may have implied harshness or criticism of the client (for example, *pointing out the illusion of work*). While the demand for work appears to play an important part in the helping process, questions are raised about the specific nature and timing of demands. Lower individual reliability for some of these items is an alternate explanation for these findings. It is these unexpected or unusual findings that help to focus our attention back onto the theoretical assumptions so that the cycle is continued from theory to research work, back to modification of the theory and the development of an agenda for more empirical work.

SUMMARY

A model for describing several aspects of the helping process has been presented and illustrated. A brief description of a research project exploring the model and a sample of the findings have been discussed. It is important that the limitations of the study be kept in mind when reviewing these findings. This work has been presented not as a conclusion but as an illustration of a process in action. The specific findings are not as important, in this author's view, as the demonstration that it is possible to develop theoretical models and associated middle-range theories, to put them into operation, and then to test them empirically in an effort to strengthen the theory-building process. The many models in the literature today provide frameworks for research efforts that can make contributions to our general understanding. It is through such a process that we can develop the scientific structure that will free the individual artistry of each practitioner so that she or he can operate more effectively.

NOTES AND REFERENCES

1. This approach suggests a worker function of mediating the engagement between the client and the specific system involved at the moment (for example, peer group, family, agency), attempting to have an impact on both client and system. The function is defined broadly and can include client advocacy. For a fuller description of Schwartz's model and this author's elaborative efforts, *see* **Lawrence Shulman**, *The Skills of Helping Individuals and Groups* (Itasca, Ill.: Peacock Press, to be published in 1979); **William Schwartz**, "Social Work with Groups: An Interactionist Approach," *Encyclopedia of Social Work*, Vol. II (New York: National Association of Social Workers, 1977), pp. 1252–1263; **William Schwartz**, "The Social Worker in the Group," *New Perspectives on Services to Groups: Theory, Organization, Practice* (New York: National Association of Social Workers, 1961), pp. 7–34; and **Lawrence Shulman**, "Social Work Skill: The Anatomy of a Helping Act," *Social Work Practice* (New York: Columbia University Press, 1969), pp. 29–48.

2. A total of 27 skills were identified and grouped into nine categories. Limitations on the size of this article prevent the full description of the model.

3. This research was supported by a grant from Health and Welfare, Canada. Findings are the author's sole responsibility. For a description focusing on methodology, *see* **Lawrence Shulman**, "A Study of the Helping Process, *Social Work*, 23 (July 1978). A full report of the study written by this author is titled *A Study of the Helping Process* (Vancouver, B.C.: School of Social Work, University of British Columbia, 1977). A series of six videotape programs titled *The Helping Process in Social Work: Theory, Practice and Research* also describes the underlying model, the research design, and study results (Instructional Communications Centre, McGill University, Montreal, Quebec, Canada). All instruments used underwent testing for reliability and validity during the first two years of the project. Full descriptions are included in the study; however, the results for the questionnaire designed to measure worker behaviors are reported here briefly. A test-retest design to measure stability indicated a correlation for the overall test score of .75 (standard deviation = 0.29). Internal consistency, using a split-half method, yielded a correlation of .79. Face validity was explored and supported. Approaches to criterion validity were attempted. In the first, a comparison of selected questionnaires of clients whose interviews had been videotaped and rated by trained observers using a second instrument, developed by the researcher, did not support validity. A number of design-related reasons may have accounted for this. In a second effort,

clients' perceptions were compared to workers' self-judgments on their use of skills, yielding positive results. Workers and their clients agreed or were one scale apart 81 percent of the time. However, this finding is limited because of the low variance in responses to many items. A comparison of 15 workers with positive skill scores and 15 with negative skill scores indicated significant differences in relationship ($p \leq .05$) and helpfulness ($p \leq .02$) scores, favoring the workers with positive skill scores (analysis of variance: relationship—$F = 5.56$, d.f. $= 29$; helpfulness—$F = 7.42$; d.f. $= 29$). Individual item analysis was also undertaken. In the test-retest design, seven items had correlations of less than .30; nine, correlations between .30 and .50; and 13, correlations between .51 and .86. The author considers this instrument to be in the embryonic stage.

4. This questionnaire was also tested for reliability and validity with similar subdesigns and results as described earlier. Additional data on the content of the work were also gained and reported in the full report.

5. For an example of such a study from the field of psychotherapy, *see* **C. B. Truax**, "Therapist Empathy, Warmth, and Genuineness, and Patient Personality Change in Group Psychotherapy: A Comparison Between Interaction Unit Measures, Time Sample Measures, and Patient Perception Measures," *Journal of Clinical Psychology,* 71 (April 1966), pp. 1–9.

6. While the scores listed were significant at the .05 level, the amount of variance the skills account for in the dependent variables (r^2) are fairly low.

Compliance and Consumerism: Social Work Goals in the Health Field

ROSALIE A. KANE AND
MORLEY D. GLICKEN

From its inception, social work practice in the health field has eluded specification of goals and processes for goal achievement. In 1919, a founder of social work in the hospital wrote:

> Even now I think that the value of the social worker and his proper recognition are considerably limited by the fact that he cannot recognize himself or tell you what the value of his profession is. He is an expert. *But in what is he an expert?* What is his special field of knowledge or skill?[1]

These words sound distressingly modern as the struggle to articulate social work functions in the health field continues.

Despite lack of precision in definitions and a paucity of outcome studies, it is generally acknowledged that the social worker contributes to direct patient care through a variety of purposes, including (1) helping the patient and the patient's family adjust to illness, disability, and sometimes death, (2) helping the patient accept and adjust to treatment itself, (3) helping alleviate the fear and anxiety associated with medical procedures, and (4) assisting with concrete arrangements for health-related services. Those who have studied the social work role in the hospital have developed task lists that break social work activities down more finely, but most direct service tasks may be associated with the four purposes listed.[2]

Historically, the social worker's contribution to the health team has been anchored in insights derived from psychoanalysis and developmental psychology. In addition to knowledge of community resources, the worker has contributed skill in psychosocial assessment and an ability to view the patient as "a whole person." Over the decades, Cabot's question, "But in what is he an expert?" has been answered with the statement "The social worker is an expert in bringing forward a point of view about the patient as a person." Although such a viewpoint is sorely needed, it is hardly a *raison d'être* for the presence of the social worker on the health team, especially since other professions have been developing psychological sophistication and a humanistic stance.

Professional survival in the health field requires that the social worker translate general objectives into specific outcomes of social work practice and begin to test the ability of the profession to achieve predetermined goals. It also requires that social workers be cognizant of research that has emanated from behavioral scientists in the health field (including psychologists, sociologists, and educators) regarding patient behavior and its determinants. With such a perspective, the social worker may then be the member of the direct care team most able to interpret such concepts to other team members and to introduce them into ongoing practice.

This paper will briefly explore two concepts that have become increasingly prominent in the health care literature—compliance and consumerism. Both ideas are compatible with social work values and purposes; moreover, they offer a route to greater specificity in goal-setting and measurement for social workers in the health field.

COMPLIANCE

The word *compliance* may have an odd ring to social workers. It seems to smack of manipulation by the professional and a passive role for the patient. In fact, however, compliance with therapeutic regimens requires the opposite of a submissive patient; except for extremely ill inpatients, compliance with medical instructions is ultimately the prerogative of the patient and the patient's family.

Compliance has been defined as "the extent to which the patient's behavior (in terms of taking medications, following diets, or executing other life-style changes) coincides with the clinical prescription."[3] Social workers have long recognized that patients do not automatically understand or follow medical advice. The role of the social workers has always included facilitation of compliance, although that term may not have been used.

Patient compliance is no longer taken for granted. In the area of medication alone, it is accepted that between 25 and 60 percent of patients do not take their prescribed medicines; whether one accepts the more conservative or the larger figure depends on the studies one prefers to endorse. Similarly, compliance rates are poor in the areas of preventive

TABLE 1. FACTORS ASSOCIATED WITH NONCOMPLIANCE

Category	Factor
Disease	Psychiatric diagnosis Alcoholism
Regimen	Complexity Duration Degree of behavioral change required
Therapeutic source	Inconvenient, inefficient clinics
Patient-therapist interaction	Inadequate supervision Patient dissatisfaction with therapist
Patient	Inappropriate health beliefs Previous noncompliance Family instability

measures, return appointments, maintenance of diet, or such habit changes as modification of smoking or drinking patterns, weight loss, or, for that matter, use of a seat belt in an automobile. Sackett and Haynes have reviewed 185 compliance studies, selected on the basis of methodological rigor; from their and other works, generalizations may be drawn about those at high risk of noncompliance and about promising strategies for improving compliance.[4]

Factors Associated with Compliance

Sociodemographic characteristics are not especially linked to compliance with therapeutic regimens, except as social class is associated with ease of access to medical care. Even intelligence and general health knowledge are not positively correlated with compliance, with the obvious exception of patients with limited mental capacity. One cannot assume that the well-educated, sophisticated patient will follow medical instructions.

Table 1 lists factors associated with poor compliance. More than one of these factors is likely to occur in a single situation. As an example, a psychiatric diagnosis or a diagnosis of alcoholism increases the likelihood of family instability and of high patient dissatisfaction with the patient-therapist interaction; the latter is true, in part, because of the stereotyped negative responses such patients encounter from health personnel.

Most of the items in the table are self-explanatory and predictable on a commonsense basis. Compliance decreases with the complexity and duration of the regimen and the degree of life-style or behavioral change required of the patient. Compliance is also negatively correlated with inaccessibility of clinic and long waiting periods but is positively associated with supervision of the regimen through frequent appointments or other means.

Of special interest to the social worker are the factors related to the patient and the patient-therapist interaction. If the satisfied patient tends to follow the regimen, patient satisfaction can no longer be dismissed as merely a desirable by-product of care; instead it becomes a goal for which the health team must strive and to which the social worker can systematically contribute. A follow-up study of 800 pediatric outpatient visits dramatically underscores this point.[5] Mothers who perceived physicians as lacking warmth, being disinterested, or giving inadequate explanations tended not to follow instructions; other than the mothers' subjective impressions of the seriousness of the problem, no other variables were associated with compliance.

Inappropriate health beliefs, an item associated with noncompliance, requires some explanation. Becker has developed a model for examining health-related behavior that is predictive of those who seek out preventive care and early treatment and that has recently been applied to curative care.[6] In summary, this theory asserts that the patient's subjective views about health, the patient's own susceptibility to illness in general and particular illnesses, the bodily harmfulness of the illness, the interference of the illness with social roles, the presence of symptoms, the proposed regimen's safety, and the proposed regimen's efficacy in contributing to recovery are all linked to compliance. Stated another way, the compliant patient believes in the existence of disease, his or her own vulnerability, and the effectiveness of medical care. Interestingly, belief in the harmfulness of the illness is positively associated with compliance until anxiety over the disease reaches inhibiting levels—a strong fear is negatively associated with compliance. Social workers will find this point reminiscent of Ripple's findings on motivation for casework treatment in which the motivated client presented a balance between the "push of discomfort" and the "pull of hope."[7] Duff and Hollingshead dramatically demonstrated that many noncancer patients leave the hospital with the firm conviction that they are really suffering from a malignancy, and the consequent fear becomes immobilizing; health team members using the health belief model must ensure that patients do not harbor such unexpressed fears while also correcting the belief that nothing can be done about cancer among those patients who really do have the disease.[8]

Strategies Associated with Improving Compliance

Both educational and behavioral strategies may be used to improve compliance rates. Educational approaches include fixed content health messages, programmed instruction, lectures, demonstrations, counseling, and even emotional role-playing around the consequences of noncompliance. Behavioral strategies include simplification of regimens, behavior modification (such as rewards for compliance administered by family members or a contract approach with forfeiture of deposit for noncompliance), mechanical devices (such as warning bells on medicine bottles), telephone reminders of appointments, and home visit follow-ups. Educational and behavioral strategies may, of course, be combined; while both kinds of intervention have been shown to improve compliance, behavioral strategies have proved to be more effective.

Neither educational nor behavioral strategies are unfamiliar to social workers. The overlap between education and therapy is increasingly apparent; both pursuits have as their goal behavioral change. The behavioral strategies are not limited to classic behavior modification but include variations on the traditional social work theme of environmental manipulation. In the context of this article, environmental manipulation involves an assessment of the patient and the patient's environment and, based on this, the implementation of structural changes directed toward the specific and measurable goal of improved compliance with medical recommendations.

A recent annotated review of 230 reported efforts to influence health consumer attitudes through health education describes the state of that art.[9] Many of the efforts described lacked evaluation data, yet some general conclusions may be drawn from the accumulated literature:

1. Educational efforts directed toward increasing the understanding of a procedure to be administered in the near future or accurate expectations of an imminent hospitalization are effective, not only in reducing anxiety, but also in increasing cooperation and minimizing pain.[10]

2. Efforts to change health behavior in low-income and ghetto areas seem most effective when indigenous health workers are utilized to engage the consumers in an education-counseling model.[11]

3. The anxious individual is more likely to seek out health information, and a message with some appeal to fear attracts more attention than a reassuring message.

4. There is enormous variation in the way in which individuals understand the same health messages, including the instructions on a medicine bottle.[12]

While a role exists for social workers in the area of compliance, only fragmentary efforts in that direction have been reported in the literature. As one example, social workers in a burn unit provided an educational brochure for the patients' relatives, describing procedures and offering a glossary of terms. In addition, a support group for relatives was conducted. Although no formal data are provided, the authors believe that, in addition to reduction of the relatives' anxiety, the interventions permitted family members to become important adjuncts and reinforcers of the regimen.[13] In other instances, a group approach has been utilized to help parents bring about desired behavioral changes in their children.[14] For the most part, however, social workers have not been involved in systematic efforts to in fluence patient compliance and measure the results.

CONSUMERISM

At the same time that behavioral scientists are considering ways of helping patients to change health-related behavior and to comply with medical regimens, health personnel are increasingly aware that the patient is a consumer of health services, with both a right to treatment and a right to refuse treatment. Mandatory consumer representation on health planning and community health center boards has somewhat altered the power structure in the health field. The many issues related to consumer representation have been discussed in detail elsewhere.[15] These include questions about who the consumer is, whom the consumer represents, how the consumer remains representative, and how responsibility should be divided between the consumer and the technical experts, or providers.

Many factors are driving a wedge into the traditional trusting relationship between physician and consumer. The high costs of medical care have led to public exploration of alternative delivery systems and funding mechanisms. The burgeoning malpractice suits have shown that a physician's judgment is not sacrosanct. For example, at this writing, consumers are demanding the right to use Laetrile despite professional opposition. Certainly the feminist movement has caused many women to question the practices of a male-dominated profession with regard to such female concerns as pregnancy and delivery, birth control, menstrual disorders, and breast cancer.[16]

A distinction can be made, however, between the consumer-as-citizen and the consumer-as-patient. McNerney points out that the consumer in need of medical care is less likely to be concerned with cost-saving measures.[17] In addition, she or he may prefer reassurance to an assertion of the right to make decisions. Yet evidence exists that an active, inquiring patient is more likely to derive maximum benefit from medical care. Helping the patient become a better informed, more active decision-maker should lead to better compliance and better health for the patient.

Since both patient and health team members tend to be mobile, the more informed patient is better able to maintain continuity of care. Again, social workers in the health field have helped patients articulate their questions to physicians and gain a sounder understanding of medical recommendations. Unfortunately, little systematic work has been done to study such interventions and their outcomes.

Two current ideas related to treating the patient as an informed consumer are worth discussion—the open medical record and the contract for care.

Open Medical Record

The seemingly radical suggestion has been made that all patients should, by legal requirement, receive a copy of their medical records.[18] The rationale is that access to records would render the patient more informed, more capable of seeking information, less subject to costly duplication of tests, freer to change physicians or get a second opinion without costly new work-ups, and better able to communicate with physicians. At the same time, advocates believe this plan would offer physicians satisfaction in improved patient communication.

Field trials of record-sharing with the patient show promising results. In an inpatient rehabilitation unit, patients were given copies of their initial admission work-up and, later, their discharge summary. This practice was evaluated positively by 125 patients. Moreover, physicians had not expurgated their records except in the choice of language.[19] Similarly, an Australian study compared 25 patients who had continuous access to their hospital records with a control group; no differences were found between the two groups in either anxiety levels or medical knowledge following the record-sharing. Since the experimental group members were given their records during rounds and participated in the discussion, better communication was facilitated; in addition, patients were able to correct the occasional factual error in the records. Interestingly, patients did not tend to consult their records often, and those denying that their illnesses were terminal seemed able to protect themselves from unwanted knowledge.[20]

Another project in an outpatient setting offered 48 patients a cassette recording of the final doctor-patient interview during which findings were discussed. A three-month follow-up showed enormous enthusiasm for this innovation. Many patients had played the tape several times; almost all felt it helped them understand their illness better, and 75 percent had found it useful to play the recording for family members.[21]

Contract for Care

Fink uses the term *tailoring the consensual regimen* to describe all strategies that "attempt a negotiated regimen or management plan by health provider and consumer."[22] More than 25 years ago, Szasz and Hollander discussed the doctor-patient relationship as a continuum ranging from the comatose patient who is the passive recipient of care, through the hospital patient who is expected to be cooperative, to the patient who is necessarily a full partner in the health care plan.[23] Most outpatients or chronically ill individuals fall in the last category. Since a contract establishes the mutual expectations of both partners in the effort, health contracts have been advocated as useful for all patients with chronic illnesses.[24] In addition, contracts may be established to give inpatients increased responsibility for such matters as the timing of medication, dosages of certain painkillers, and schedules for therapy.

Social Work and the Informed Consumer

Social workers in the health field convey information to patients both about their specific diagnoses and the patient role. In an unusual experiment, a social worker in a pediatric cardiology unit tested various kinds of social work intervention during the period immediately after parents were told about their child's heart problem. According to a random procedure, the social worker focused interviews with some parents on helping them conceptualize the meaning of the child's illness for the family and to anticipate with them future problems and questions. In other cases, the social worker merely reiterated the diagnosis in lay language. A follow-up questionnaire showed that the former group raised more questions about their children's illnesses; these were referred to the cardiologist for reply. Interestingly, this difference occurred despite the fact that during the interviews the worker had met with little response from parents.[25]

Other interventions might be structured by the worker to develop a more active health consumer as patient or parent-of-patient. The authors' position is, however, that such strategies are insufficient without built-in measurement techniques and preferably a control group. In working toward the goal of a participatory patient, the social worker may encounter initial resistance from other team members. When connections are drawn between the active consumer and compliance, such objections should diminish.

GENERAL IMPLICATIONS FOR SOCIAL WORK

This paper has presented concepts and data from the health care literature on the related subjects of patient compliance and the patient-as-consumer. It is argued that the social worker is well equipped to make deliberate efforts to facilitate compliance and active patient participation, as well as to interpret these factors to the health team. Attempts to influence compliance have usually been introduced as studies superimposed on practice by social scientists. The authors believe that it is now time to incorporate this goal into routine service; if social workers lead in the task, such efforts will lend greater specificity to social work practice in the health field.

It is expected that the two goals of compliance and consumer participation will most often be consistent with each other, but occasionally an informed consumer will make a decision not to comply with treatment. If so, team members may have to cope with their own anger and frustration and, hopefully, the social worker can be an effective intermediary.

Some specific implications of the theme for social work practice are suggested:

1. As social workers become more concerned with compliance, the present models of service, which place heaviest emphasis on social service for inpatient populations, will require reexamination. It is outpatients who need help in achieving a measure of compliance with medical advice.

2. Social workers may need to forsake consideration of social work goals in global terms that encompass improvements in all dimensions of life for the patient and the patient's family. Rather, practice should be considered in the more narrow terms of achieving specific, measurable goals.

3. In order to advance practice knowledge in health, the social worker will need to implement clinical trials of specific interventions with control groups that do not receive the service. Since social work is a scarce resource in the health field and there are seldom enough workers to meet all social needs, such trials pose ethical questions.

4. Social workers in hospitals will need to consider new technology to facilitate compliance and achieve the related goals of providing information and relieving anxiety. Tape-recorded messages describing painful procedures in detail have been shown to reduce anxiety, leading to a lesser response to pain and improved cooperation. Similarly, it is impossible to reach all presurgery patients with the one-to-one casework method, so that new methods will need to be devised.

5. The social worker can make an impact on compliance through the linkage between compliance and patient satisfaction. Social workers are in a good position to document the correlates of patient satisfaction as well as to work toward structural changes that will reduce dissatisfaction with the delivery system.

6. To facilitate compliance, social workers in hospitals will need to develop resources and allies in the patients' families and communities to help apply an individualized plan for the given patient.

7. Close interdisciplinary cooperation is necessary for an effective program in facilitating compliance and patient participation in health care.

In conclusion, a knowledge of the compliance phenomenon offers the social worker a route to achieving some of the goals that have already been incorporated into the all-encompassing objectives of social work practice in the health field. Compliance concerns are not, of course, the exclusive domain of the social worker, but the issue is a natural one for social work involvement and leadership. The technological advances of medical science are rendered less valuable if the patient does not or cannot follow through with recommendations. In the case of chronic illness, few miraculous cures are available. In the absence of curing, a demonstration of caring is crucial. The attentions required to ensure that the patient is informed, consulted, reminded, and, as much as possible, satisfied seem to have rewards in improved compliance.

NOTES AND REFERENCES

1. **Richard Cabot**, *Social Work: Essays on the Meeting-Ground of Doctor and Social Worker* (Boston: Houghton Mifflin Co., 1919), p. 38.

2. *See* **Jules Schrager**, *Social Work Departments in University Hospitals* (Syracuse, N.Y.: University of Syracuse School of Social Work, 1974); and **Shirley Wattenberg, Michael Orr, and Thomas O'Rourke**, "Comparison of Opinions of Social Work Administrators and Hospital Administrators Toward Leadership Tasks," *Social Work in Health Care, 2* (Spring 1977), pp. 285–294.

3. **David Sackett and R. Brian Haynes**, eds., *Compliance with Therapeutic Regimens* (Baltimore: Johns Hopkins University Press, 1976), p. 1.

4. **Sackett and Haynes**, op. cit. *See also* **Robert Kane**, ed., *The Behavioral Sciences and Preventive Medicine* (Washington, D.C.: U.S. Government Printing Office, 1977).

5. **Francis Vida, Barbara Korsch, and Marie Morris**, "Gaps in Doctor-Patient Communication: Patients' Response to Medical Advice," *New England Journal of Medicine,* 280 (March 6, 1969), pp. 535–540.

6. **Marshall Becker**, "Sociobehavioral Research on Determinants of Compliance," in Sackett and Haynes, op. cit., pp. 40–50.

7. **Lilian Ripple**, *Motivation, Capacity and Opportunity: Studies in Casework Theory and Practice* (Chicago: University of Chicago, School of Social Service Administration, 1964).

8. **Raymond Duff and August Hollingshead**, *Sickness and Society* (New York: Harper & Row, 1968).

9. "Annotated Bibliography and Selective Literature Review on Patient/Consumer Health Education" (Cambridge, Mass.: Arthur D. Little Co., 1975).

10. **J. E. Sauer**, "Preadmission Orientation: Effect on Patient Manageability," *Hospital Topics,* 46 (March 1968), pp. 79–83; **Jean E. Johnson and Howard Leventhal**, "Effects of Accurate Expectations and Behavioral Instructions on Reactions During a Noxious Medical Examination," *Journal of Personality and Social Psychology,* 29 (May 1974), pp. 710–718; **K. M. Healy**, "Does Preoperative Instruction Make a Difference?" *American Journal of Nursing,* 68 (January 1968), pp. 62–67.

11. *See,* for example, **Norman Epstein and Anne Shainline**, "Paraprofessional

Parent-Aides and Disadvantaged Families," *Social Casework,* 55 (April 1974), pp. 230–236.

12. **J. M. Mazzullo, Louis Lasagna, and P. F. Griner,** "Variations in Interpretations of Prescription Instructions," *Journal of the American Medical Association,* 227 (February 1974), pp. 156–162.

13. **G. A. Brodland and J. J. Andreason,** "Adjustment Problems of the Family of the Burn Patient," *Social Casework,* 55 (January 1964), pp. 13–18.

14. *See* **John Hicks and Daniel Wieder,** "The Effects of Intergenerational Group Counseling on Parents and Children in a Vocational Rehabilitation Agency," *Rehabilitation Literature,* 34 (December 1975), pp. 358–364; and **Sheldon Rose,** "Group Training of Parents as Behavior Modifiers," *Social Work,* 19 (March 1974), pp. 156–162.

15. *See,* for example, **Rosalie Kane and Robert Kane,** "Galloping Consumption," in **Robert Kane,** ed., *The Challenge of Community Medicine* (New York: Springer Publishing Co., 1974), and **Harry Rosen, Jonathan Metsch, and Samuel Levey,** eds., *The Consumer and the Health Care System* (New York: Spectrum Publications, 1977).

16. **Gena Corea,** *The Hidden Malpractice: How American Medicine Treats Women as Patients and Professionals* (New York: William Morrow & Co., 1977).

17. **Walter McNerney,** "Medicine Faces the Consumer Movement," in **Rosen, Metsch, and Levey,** eds., op. cit.

18. **Budd Shenkin and David Warner,** "Giving the Patient His Medical Record: A Proposal to Improve the System," *New England Journal of Medicine,* 289 (September 27, 1975), pp. 638–691.

19. **Arnold Golodetz, Johanna Ruess, and Raymond Milhous,** "The Right to Know: Giving the Patient His Medical Record," *Archives of Physical Medicine and Rehabilitation,* 57 (February 1976), pp. 78–81.

20. **David Stevens, Rhonda Stagg, and Ian MacKay,** "What Happens When Hospitalized Patients See Their Own Records," *Annals of Internal Medicine,* 86 (April 1977), pp. 474–477.

21. **Hugh Butt,** "A Method for Better Physician-Patient Communication," *Annals of Internal Medicine,* 86 (April 1977), pp. 178–180.

22. **D. L. Fink,** "Tailoring the Consensual Regimen," in **Sackett and Haynes,** op. cit., pp. 110–118.

23. **Thomas Szasz and Mark Hollander,** "Contribution to the Philosophy of Medicine," *Archives of Internal Medicine,* 97 (1956), pp. 585–592.

24. **Donnell Etzweiler,** "The Contract for Health Care," *Journal of the American Medical Society,* 224 (May 14, 1973), p. 1034.

25. **Sandra Blatterhauer, Mary Jo Kupst, and Jerome Schulman,** "Enhancing the Relationship Between Physician and Patient," *Health and Social Work,* 1 (February 1976), pp. 46–57.

Dignity and Success: The Experience of Welfare Rights Members

DOROTHY N. GAMBLE

The relationship between work and welfare has been the subject of many books, articles, senate hearings, presidential speeches, newspaper articles, and Social Security amendments, especially in the recent past. Although much of this material has been marked by heated, ideological discussion, there have been some more enlightened analyses that help to explain the complexity of the systems involved.

Piven and Cloward, for example, have offered the historical view that welfare programs are expanded in response to mass disorders that are the result of dislocations in the work systems.[1] When such disorders diminish, welfare programs are restricted to enforcing work. Much of the work that is available to welfare recipients is described by Doeringer and Piore as the labor market's "secondary sector" jobs—jobs that have little security, no fringe benefits, low pay, and capricious supervisory practices.[2] Goodwin has shown that welfare recipients are as committed to the work ethic as other Americans; however, both he and Liebow have also shown how repeated frustration with secondary sector work experience leads people to be more accepting of their status as welfare recipients.[3]

In addition to these aspects of the work/welfare issues, we now know that welfare recipients, even recipients of Aid to Families with Dependent Children (AFDC), are not as homogeneous a group as was once assumed. Recent studies show that there are considerable individual variations in age, length of time receiving welfare, and geographic mobility.[4] In addition, these studies show cyclical movements in and out of welfare and work, indicating that most welfare recipients have previous work experience.

133

The Work Incentive (WIN) program was, from the beginning, an extremely questionable effort to decrease the welfare rolls by channeling recipients into work or training situations. For the first three years of the program, $250 million were spent, and only 36,000 people completed the program.[5] Even the government employment agencies established to serve the poor have been found to have really best served the labor needs of low-wage industries.[6]

Another problem with the WIN program was that it presumed that any employment and the income earned from it would be sufficient to solve the problems of the poor. However, as Miller and Robey—as well as many others—have pointed out, defining the poor or welfare recipients solely as income deficient is grossly inadequate because economic inequality usually has significant ramifications as well for the physical, social, and psychological well-being of the individual.[7]

Those who have worked at a grass-roots level with these various work and welfare issues had an early education into their complexity. The author's own work with members of a Welfare Rights Organization in Orange County, N.C., from 1969 to 1974 was such an experience. The purpose of this article is to describe how members of that organization dealt with the issues, challenged the welfare system head-on, made it work for them in spite of itself, and finally escaped from the system with pleasure.

THE SETTING

The Welfare Rights Organization was begun in 1968 when three mothers, clients of a private social service agency, began discussing mutual problems engendered by their poverty status. In the beginning and throughout the life of the organization, additional members were recruited in two ways. One source was the clientele of the agency. The second, and by far the most effective, recruitment source was friends and acquaintances of current members of the WRO. Although there were about 300 welfare families in the county during the years the organization was active, only 20 could be considered active members (that is, involved in welfare rights activities at least three times a month).[8]

The group established linkages with the National Welfare Rights Organization early, and in order to be able to send delegates to the national convention each year (which they did from 1969 until 1975), they always maintained a membership of 50 dues-paying members. The majority of the 50 dues-paying members changed from year to year, but the 20 active members, including the leadership, remained relatively constant. As a county-wide organization, the group included former sharecroppers from a small town and rural tobacco lands, as well as urban recipients from a university community of 40,000.

The 20 active members of the organization were all black women. The women in the organization often emphasized their blackness in responding to welfare slurs that carried racist implications. This perhaps inadvertently discouraged whites from becoming active members, although white recipients attended meetings from time to time, and active black members helped them with specific problems. To join an organization that was clearly led by black women would have even further diminished a white welfare recipient's status in a southern community.

The organization with which the author was employed is a small, private, church-sponsored agency that concerns itself with individuals who fall in the cracks between other social service programs and with groups that would like to make changes in social policies that affect their lives. Unlike many private agencies, it has not turned its back on the poorest in our society. It often provided emergency services (for example, a grant to prevent electricity from being shut off, a ride to the hospital, a used mattress to provide additional sleeping space, and so on) to members and potential members of the WRO. While some of the WRO activities and strategies were not acceptable to all of the 23 member churches that sponsored the agency, the agency board never tried to impede the development or autonomy of the WRO.

To complete the picture, it is important to describe the county welfare department and welfare programs available to recipients in the late sixties and early seventies. Welfare employees are as heterogeneous a group as are recipients. The employees have varying degrees of training and wide differences in their value orientations. But, because of the education systems from which they came and the highly bureaucratic systems within which they work, their differences are often diminished and their behavior generally criticized by their clients as cool or callous. There is some evidence that professionally trained social workers in public welfare agencies would prefer to provide treatment as opposed to concrete environmental services, which they see as second-class activity.[9] In addition, the bureaucracy within which they work rarely, if ever, rewards public welfare employees for treating clients with dignity or developing concrete individual plans around client strengths. In spite of the system, some workers do not succumb to the metamorphosis from caring to cool to callous. Others, however, come already hardened.

The county welfare board was dominated by people who had a traditional view of welfare recipients.[10] Most were from rural environments and believed that their Depression years' view of poverty was adequate for understanding the issues of poverty in the early seventies. Having suffered from poverty themselves during the Depression, and having now reached levels of considerable economic security, which they attributed to their own hard work, they believed welfare recipients could do the same. They did not or could not see how the mechanization of southern agriculture and their ethnic advantage had enhanced their own post-Depression economic success while at the same time devastating the lives of many black sharecroppers who were forced off the land.[11]

The first and most comprehensive training program for welfare recipients in Orange County was Title V of the 1964 Economic Opportunity Act (Work Experience and Training Program). Several members of the WRO were able to take advantage of this program, a program that actually recognized the need to provide a woman with a watch and good shoes if she were in training to be a licensed practical nurse. A more restrictive WIN program, signed into law in 1967, was implemented in the county in early 1969.

By the time the Talmadge amendments to the Society Security Act were passed in 1971, it was well understood that the emphasis was on *work,* and training and education took a back seat. These programs offered opportunities to recipients *only* if they were well enough informed of the program's inherent complexities and contradictions. This will be explained in more detail later.

ACHIEVING GOALS

Welfare recipients knew, without reading Miller and Robey or Doeringer and Piore, that the only way to get the welfare monkey off their backs was to get jobs that were not in the secondary sector and that, in addition to more income, success meant the income had to be steady, the job had to offer some self-respect and opportunity for advancement, and it was necessary to become involved in decisions that affected their lives. The majority of the active members found their way to many of these goals, in spite of the welfare system. This article tells how they did it.

Building Camaraderie

Although welfare recipients have had to share their life secrets too many times with their caseworker, health nurse, housing authority social worker, and loan company, it was not something they did naturally with friends and neighbors. In fact, it was often important for a welfare recipient to keep her personal activities (fortunes and misfortunes both) to herself lest another neighbor, eager to look upright in the eyes of the welfare department, inform on her. Sharing their lives, their misfortunes, and their methods of survival with each other came gradually to the members of the organization. It came with practice and increasing trust.

It seemed that to join the group, members had to acknowledge that the public had no respect for them, without denying their own self-respect. This was an easier position for the more urban members to accept, having been exposed to a heavier media barrage than the rural members asserting the negative characteristics of welfare recipients. The more urban members assumed that the public would not allow them any dignity, so the only place to go from there was up. The actual distance (15 miles separated the two county meeting places, one to accommodate the rural members, the other to accommodate the urban members) and the awareness distance tended to separate the group until the main leadership and the group itself were made up primarily of urban recipients.

The nucleus of women around which the group developed felt it was right to be angry when you were treated disrespectfully or capriciously, but it was also right to be able to laugh at yourself and the incredible situations in which you found yourself. Women who could not allow themselves to get angry felt uncomfortable in the group. Women who were so angry that they stayed hostile to the world were also hostile to the group.

The official leadership of the WRO rotated among the 20 active women. The leadership style of the women was not authoritarian, and a strong consensus was necessary for any planned activity to be successful. The women participated in activities because they believed in the general goals of the organization and because they genuinely enjoyed each other. They were not motivated by the dictates of strong leadership or fear of ridicule.

Their concern for each other and their sharing grew steadily as the group evolved. When one member was dying of cancer, other group members made the 15-mile trip to visit her and her family with sincere compassion. If one received some produce from a country relative's garden, she often shared this with others. Most important, they shared with each other their various experiences with the welfare department and began to see that there were differences in the payments they received, differences in the ways they were treated, and differences in the services they received. They shared equally disagreeable experiences about how their children had been treated badly or not been treated at all by the local hospital. They compared the ways in which their children were regularly thwarted by the public schools simply because they carried with them tell-tale signs of poverty: free lunches, no money for special school projects, and inadequate clothing.

It was basically this information that they gathered in a supportive social organization that became most important to them as they pursued their goal. The goal was never something they voted on or even explicitly discussed; it was something implicitly shared among all members. Perhaps it was also implied in much of the literature received from the National Welfare Rights Organization. The main goal was clearly some form of economic survival with personal dignity.

Learning New Skills

Trying to keep up with the complexities and constant changes of welfare regulations is a formidable task, even for welfare bureaucrats. It was made even more difficult for the WRO because information was sometimes not available. It was not until 1968 that the state department of welfare allowed the regulations to be made public. However, once the regulations were made public and members of the organization became increasingly familiar with them and the ways in which they might be interpreted, they became expert at the interpretation and the calculations. These skills were especially important in 1970, when the state decided to pay only a certain percentage of a recipient's normal payment in an effort to trim welfare costs.

WRO members became so proficient that they acted as consultants to new welfare applicants, helping them to prepare appropriate budgets before they ever saw an eligibility specialist. With these new skills—understanding of the regulations and ability to apply them—members were able to detect errors in their own budgets and the budgets of friends and neighbors. Often these were errors that had left recipients with less money than they should have been receiving.

Learning to do the calculations and explain the regulations was an important step for many of the recipients. It was a skill that put them on an equal level with the eligibility specialists. In fact, they knew that often they had a better understanding of the regulations than the eligibility specialist, the very person who held control over the meager allotment on which they and their families tried to survive. It was an important threshold.

Applying Knowledge and Confidence

Gradually, the new knowledge, confidence, and ability began to affect nearly all aspects of the members' lives. Initially they began to encourage other recipients to appeal various decisions about their welfare budgets. Members of the WRO joined recipients in appeal hearings, regardless of whether the recipient was a member of the organization. Some cases were won and some were lost, but the department of welfare knew it was dealing with well-informed, confident recipients, something it surely had not seen before.

It is unlikely that anyone other than the board members themselves ever attended county welfare board meetings before the organization of the WRO. The very presence of WRO members at these meetings meant that issues had to be discussed in a more calculated way. Although the WRO had limited substantive impact on the board, members were able to institute or change some policies. For example, they urged and achieved the acceptance of a policy to allow a small clothing grant for school-age children each year in September and a small Christmas grant to each family. These are policies currently still in effect. Although the WRO suggested names to fill vacancies on the board, it was not until more profound political changes occurred in the county that a former recipient was appointed to the board.

Public school issues began to be challenged by the organization. Teacher conferences took on new meaning for the individual members. A list was circulated to the superintendent and all the principals in the school system indicating the specific ways children who received free lunches were singled out by some teachers and principals. The most common problem was the practice of giving a different color lunch ticket to students receiving free lunches so they could be counted more easily. After a meeting with the superintendent, some practices were changed, including the one just cited.

Members of the organization began to be active on the Title I (ESEA) advisory board in an effort to see that school funds earmarked for poor children were spent on the children rather than on the system. Title I funds originally planned to be spent on a mobile classroom were redirected toward such things as eyeglasses and shoes for poor children.

Problems with the local housing authority began to be challenged, as well as problems relating to private rental housing that was in poor repair or unheated. The group joined others in the community to urge the mayor to appoint a tenant to fill a vacancy on the housing authority board. In 1973 a tenant was appointed to the board for the first time.

A hospital policy that refused treatment to anyone with an unpaid bill was challenged and changed. Local doctors began to feel the ripples of WRO members' new knowledge and confidence as demands were made for adequate care through the Medicare and Medicaid programs.

When the company that owned both the telephone and electric services in the town decided to cut off the *electricity* of people who failed to pay their *telephone* bills, the WRO challenged the practice in a meeting with the director of the company. Although no commitment was made at the meeting, the practice was quietly stopped. Hardly a public or private agency in the area has not at some time or other been challenged by members of the organization to provide more adequate services.

In addition to these activities on a local level, the WRO members also participated in activities on a state level, sometimes by themselves, sometimes in conjunction with other county organizations. When the state welfare board cut welfare payments in 1970, the organization joined a large demonstration and discussion with the state welfare administration. The payments were restored to their former levels a few months later. When H.R. 1, the Nixon-Mills welfare measure, was proposed, members of the WRO planned a hearing with the WRO in a neighboring county to describe how the bill would actually affect poor people.[12] While the hearing was expressly planned for elected and appointed officials in the two counties, hundreds of people attended in order to learn about the potential impact of the proposed welfare reform.

On other occasions the group met with state welfare officials to persuade them to make two changes in state welfare policies. The first was to reduce the welfare recipients' out-of-pocket cost for prescription medicines from $1.00 to 50 cents. The second was related to the practice of cutting off the welfare payment completely if a recipient had earned income through temporary, part-time work. The policy was changed to reduce the recipient's AFDC check by only 2 percent until the "fraudulent income" was recouped by the welfare department.

One of the most important areas in which the members showed their assertiveness and support of each other was in their WIN training programs and classes. As the work emphasis of the WIN program evolved, members of the organization were faced with new obstacles. Some of them had been in training for three years or more. They had periodically been forced to drop out of their classes when family matters consumed all their time and energy, but they usually came back with a new determination to finish. They were trying to complete high school, typing courses, or licensed practical nursing school. They knew that unless they could get enough training to get a decent-paying, steady job, they would just be back on welfare again. It was a vicious cycle between jobs and welfare. The cycle always left gaps of several months without an income while a woman was trying to get another job or to get back on welfare. Those agonizing months were simply not worth the physical and psychological trauma. That is why a bad work experience often becomes an incentive to accept welfare status. Consequently, when the employment security job counselor came to encourage the WIN participants to accept various low-level job offers, she was confronted by a new breed of knowledgeable welfare recipients. Even when they were threatened with being cut off welfare if they did not accept the jobs they were offered, WRO members refused, holding out for additional training, more education, or a job that was not a dead end.

Strategies Used

On only two occasions from 1969 to 1974 did the group participate in street demonstrations in order to dramatize issues related to welfare problems. By the end of the sixties, towns and cities had so regulated street demonstrations that if carried out according to the letter of the law, demonstrations had little or no impact. While the mothers were passionate and embittered about some of the issues they challenged, they often expressed in meetings that, for the sake of their children, they would not be willing to risk spending a night in jail. More important, perhaps, was that in the street the welfare mothers could talk to each other and possibly a few reporters. In meetings and offices, however, they could talk face to face with the official who made and influenced policy. As their experience in discussion increased, they knew that was what they did best.

If one were to compare their strategies to Roland Warren's three models of collaboration, campaign, and contest, their most common strategy would have been campaign, with some use of contest.[13] As campaigners they were relentless. As soon as they could put together the "who" and the "what" of an issue that affected their lives, they were present and informed. If they were thwarted in one meeting, they went back again or brought the issue up at an unexpected moment. Their sheer presence at many meetings made some officials behave in a more calculated and sometimes uncomfortable way. Corresponding again with Warren's description, when they spoke with students, groups from the League of Women Voters, and church groups, the WRO members tried to turn apathy into interest. When they spoke to county commissioners and welfare board members, they tried to turn opposition into agreement.

Specht suggests specific tactics that might be related to campaign and contest strategies.[14] Some of these were clearly a part of the WRO's efforts. As part of their campaign strategy, the members bargained and negotiated with policy-makers in order to influence change. Their bargaining power lay in their relentless spirit. If unsuccessful they would return, and in the meantime they would whenever possible expose the issue in the community. When the issue related to the county welfare department's decision, they would appeal to the state welfare department.

The most notable and effective tactic they used in contest strategy was their refusal to interrupt their training and take jobs they knew would only lead them back to welfare. The courage required to say "no" at this important time was surely the result of their individual struggles with poverty and their many hours and days of mutual struggle with a system they now understood and challenged.

THE OUTCOME

In the end, four, five, and even six years after these women entered initial training to get themselves off welfare, they did so. Most have jobs that pay a decent wage and have some degree of security with regular, built-in pay increments and fair disciplinary policies. Three are bus drivers, one is a social worker, one is a clinical assistant in a health center, five are licensed practical nurses in the same hospital that once refused to treat them, and four are secretaries. Although some of these women still receive benefits in the form of decreased child care payments or supplemental rent, they no longer have the welfare monkey on their backs.

The organization continued to hold meetings until the summer of 1976 but has been dormant since that time. Many circumstances have contributed to the organization's current dormant status, including the demise of the national organization and the fact that an organizer is no longer available to the group. In spite of the lack of an organization, one of the officers continues to encourage welfare mothers to question and challenge certain policies. She recently assisted a recipient in appealing a charge of fraud by the county welfare office—and won.

The former active members who are now employed do not feel the same personal need for the organization, but they feel strongly that welfare recipients should continue to be organized. These former members have not turned their backs on recipients, and many spend many hours of volunteer time helping others to understand and negotiate the intricacies of the welfare system.

ORGANIZER'S ROLE

There were five important things the writer did with this group in order to help them build their organization. There is nothing earthshaking, new, or even clever about these things. They are simply a series of human responses to human problems.

First, it was important to *listen* to how various programs and problems affected the women's lives in order to comprehend them. Often a piece of one person's problem helped to clarify a piece of the problem described by another, resulting in useful information for the whole group. It was also important to respond to the women's stories by *reinforcing the latent anger* they felt. If a member or potential member said that she had been threatened with being cut off welfare unless she accepted a specific job offer, for example, the writer, instead of asking, "How do you feel about that?" would say, "Now that would make me mad!" or "How can those idiots do that to you when they know you only have another year to go to finish your course!" People who have been hurt so many times sometimes forget that it is quite natural to react to something that hurts.

Second, it was important to *identify the main goals* of the group. In this case their goals were perceived to be success—meaning to get a job that would be in the primary sector—and dignity—meaning maintaining self-respect and having some control over decisions that affected their lives. While some organizers have argued for the importance of goal specification, the writer feels it is unimportant to have such goals formalized by some sort of group process. Suggestions were often made about group strategies and activities, but the group never responded to them unless they fit the strong purpose they themselves felt. To identify the group's goals and assist them in the realization of these goals seemed to be the most supportive thing that could be done.

Third, it was important to *collect and share information* about the issues so that the group could sort out important things and analyze implications of policies. The linkages the group had with the national organization alerted them to proposed federal legislation and provided information about various programs that could be activated or improved on a local level. Everyone shared in collecting state and local laws and regulations, but because of available time, the writer could do more of this.

Fourth, it was important to encourage activities that would *acquaint members with their own latent strengths* and abilities. Whether it was the organization of a fund-raising party or a discussion of welfare in front of a university sociology class, members of the organization learned new things about themselves, how well they could express themselves, how much money they could raise, or how well they could sort out the essence of complicated regulations.

Finally, it was important to *manage internal conflict to the degree possible.* Personal problems, ideological problems, and organizational problems crop up in any organization and sometimes effectively drain energy away from group goals. The writer tried to minimize those problems in order to allow the group to move forward. When conflict could not be managed, the group dealt with it, usually by cutting themselves off from it or moving away from it. One example was an effort to keep the urban and rural recipients together in order to have a larger, stronger organization. The rural members felt the urban members were too aggressive in some of their strategies. Urban members felt that the rural members should be more aggressive. Resolution of these divergent approaches at each meeting was beginning to consume large amounts of time. The two subgroups began planning fewer activities together, and eventually the urban group made a cordial but definite move away from the rural members.

Various aspects of the role the writer played in being supportive to this group have been described in part in similar case studies, community organization texts, and organizing handbooks.[15] It does not seem important or useful to advocate one community organization approach over another. What does seem important is the need to initiate and stimulate these kinds of informal social organizations, especially among the poor.

CONCLUSION

In conclusion, the writer believes that these women were able to reach the level of economic success and personal dignity they achieved because of the support and encouragement they provided to each other. Without the group, they would not have reached these levels as effectively, and probably not at all. When one is all by oneself, it is difficult to ignore the threat of being cut off welfare. The knowledge and skills these women gained as a result of keeping the group viable served them in many different ways, principally as they became more assertive with the health, welfare, social, and economic systems that touched their lives.

While these women's achievements have had an enormous impact on their personal lives, what they have done has not changed the way the local welfare department operates substantively, nor can it be considered the solution to national welfare problems. This mini-process cannot take the place of the massive social and economic reforms needed to prevent the situations in which some of these women found themselves at the outset. Indeed, had they been white and gone through the same process, their level of success would have been still higher.[16] The changes needed to prevent some of the basic social and economic injustices in this country would require a commitment to a major redistribution of goods and resources, thus far not likely to be accepted by the public. In the meantime, a human response to the problems of the poor is the least we can ask of the social work profession.

NOTES AND REFERENCES

1. **Frances Fox Piven and Richard A. Cloward**, *Regulating the Poor: The Functions of Public Welfare* (New York: Pantheon Books, 1971).

2. **Peter B. Doeringer and Michael J. Piore**, "Unemployment and the 'Dual Labor Market,' " *The Public Interest*, 38 (Winter 1975), pp. 67–79.

3. **Leonard Goodwin**, *Do the Poor Want to Work: A Social-Psychological Study of Work Orientations* (Washington, D.C.: Brookings Institutions, 1972), pp. 51, 112; **Elliot Liebow**, *Tally's Corner: A Study of Negro Streetcorner Men* (Boston: Little, Brown, 1967), pp. 29–71.

4. **Judith Mayo**, *Work and Welfare: Employment and Employability of Women in the AFDC Program* (Chicago: University of Chicago Community and Family Study Center, 1975); **Miriam Ostow and Anna B. Dutke**, *Work and Welfare in New York City* (Baltimore: Johns Hopkins University Press, 1975).

5. **Sar A. Levitan, Martin Rein, and David Marwick**, *Work and Welfare Go Together* (Baltimore: Johns Hopkins University Press, 1972), p. 100.

6. **Yeheskel Hasenfeld**, "The Role of Employment Placement Services in Maintaining Poverty," *Social Service Review*, 49 (December 1975), pp. 569–587.

7. **S. M. Miller and Pamela A. Roby**, *The Future of Inequality* (New York: Basic Books, 1970), p. 12.

8. In February 1969, there were 929 AFDC recipients in Orange County, all of whom were women and children. The number increased to 1,342 in 1971 and then

began decreasing again to 953 in 1976. About 400 individuals in the county received Aid to the Aged and Aid to the Disabled in the early seventies. The average monthly payment to AFDC recipients in 1970 was $31.51. *North Carolina State Government Statistical Abstract* (Raleigh: Division of State Budget and Management, 1976), p. 47. *Profile: North Carolina Counties* (Raleigh: Division of State Budget and Management, March 1975), p. 139.

9. **Richard M. Grinnell, Jr., and Nancy S. Kyte**, "Delivering Concrete Environmental Services in a Public Welfare Agency," *Journal of Social Welfare,* 2 (1975), pp. 69–82.

10. For further discussion of rural views of welfare, *see* **Mary H. Osgood**, "Rural and Urban Attitudes Toward Welfare," *Social Work,* 22 (January 1977), pp. 41–47.

11. **Piven and Cloward**, op. cit., pp. 200–221.

12. **U.S. Congress**, *Social Security Amendments of 1971,* H.R. 1, 92nd Cong., 1st Sess., June 1971.

13. **Roland L. Warren**, "Types of Purposive Social Change at the Community Level," in **Ralph Kramer and Harry Specht**, eds., *Readings in Community Organization Practice* (2d ed.; Englewood Cliffs, N.J.: Prentice-Hall, Inc., 1975), pp. 134–149.

14. **Harry Specht**, "Disruptive Tactics," in **Kramer and Specht**, eds., op. cit., p. 341.

15. **Fred M. Cox, John L. Erlich, Jack Rothman, and John E. Tropman**, eds., *Community Action, Planning, Development: A Casebook* (Itasca, Ill.: Peacock Publishers, Inc., 1974), pp. 46–62; **Geroge Brager and Harry Specht**, *Community Organizing* (New York: Columbia University Press, 1973), pp. 67–87; **Daniel J. Schler**, "The Community Development Process," in **Lee J. Cary**, ed., *Community Development as a Process* (Columbia: University of Missouri Press, 1970), pp. 113–140; **Saul D. Alinsky**, *Rules for Radicals: A Practical Primer for Realistic Radicals* (New York: Random House, 1971); **Si Kahn**, *How People Get Power: Organizing Oppressed Communities for Action* (New York: McGraw-Hill Book Co., 1970).

16. **Sally H. Baker and Bernard Levenson**, "Earnings Prospects of Black and White Working-Class Women," *Sociology of Work and Occupations,* 3 (May 1976), pp. 123–150.

Client Record-Sharing: A Solution to Problems of Confidentiality, Clients' Rights, and Accountability

CAROLYN H. WARMSUN, LEONARD P. ULLMANN, AND JEAN NYLAND

Social workers providing clinical services face many challenging problems. Legal, professional, and humane considerations influence traditional service delivery. These pressures neither can nor should be separated from good practice, because good practice serves the client as well as the profession. The purpose of this paper is to provide empirical material on one way of improving confidentiality, protection of clients' rights, and accountability. The solution to problems in these three areas used in the authors' research involved having clients participate in creating their case records. When the record is the private domain of the therapist, clients often view it as a potential threat or symbol of power. Sharing in creation of the record demystifies it for the client.

THE STUDY

The client/therapist shared-recording study described here was done in the Alternative For Women Program, a comprehensive community mental health services program for nonpsychotic women aged 18 or over, located in Honolulu, Hawaii. The program is state funded and has one full-time and two 20-percent-time staff persons. The majority of the service delivery is done by graduate social work and psychology students interning in the program. The bulk of the client/therapist shared recording was therefore done by students and their clients.

Design

The study was suggested by Antonio J. Dy, MD, Chief of the Diamond Head Community Mental Health Services Branch where the Alternatives For Women Program operates. In working out the details, the authors decided to design and implement the study to learn the answers to the following questions: (1) What percentage of clients coming for individual therapy will opt to write the notes of their sessions with the therapist? (2) What are the characteristics of these persons compared with those who decide not to take such an option? (3) What are some of the costs or benefits in terms of time spent writing notes with clients versus time spent writing notes alone and in terms of the effects on the therapy itself?

Methodology

The subjects of this study were 101 women coming consecutively to the Alternatives For Women Program for intake that, in most cases, led to individual therapy. Women coming to the program for group therapy only, who did not have an individual face-to-face intake, were excluded. At the start of intake, the women were asked to look at a short typewritten option sheet explaining that a study was being done and their help was needed. The sheet went on to explain that they had to make a choice between writing the notes of sessions together with their therapist (who would teach the format used) and having the therapist write the notes of the sessions alone. Intake workers were careful to present the sheet in a standardized way and to avoid giving further information. They also noted comments on the bottom of the sheet after the intake session was over and the client had gone. The clients who chose to write notes with the therapist were called Novelists —because they chose the more novel approach—while the clients who chose not to do so were called Traditionalists, reflecting the fact that the notes were being written by the therapist alone in the traditional manner.

The Novelists and Traditionalists, then, assigned themselves to these respective groups by choosing a given option; they were not assigned randomly. In this way, the first question could be answered: What percentage of clients coming for individual therapy will opt to write the notes of their sessions with the therapist?

In order to assess differences between the women who chose the novel approach and those who opted for the traditional one, each woman was

Fig. 1 Problem Goal List

Therapist's Name _____

Client's Name _____

P/C #	Problem	Date Iden-tified	Goal	Date Iden-tified	Date and Problem Resolved	/or Date Goal Attained

Therapist's Signature _____ Date _____

Client's Signature _____ Date _____

given a Minnesota Multiphasic Personality Inventory (MMPI) booklet and answer sheet to take home, fill out completely, and return to the therapist at the first session. Clients were told that this was needed for the study, it was long, and they should complete it even if they could not manage to finish it for the first session with their therapist.

After the intake interview, the intake worker typed up the material, including the Problem/Goal List (see Figure 1). The Problem/Goal List is a modification of the Problem List used in the problem-oriented medical record style of making notes on clients.[1] It was modified to include as much time and attention to goals and skill-building as to problems and pathology. The Problem/Goal List is a working tool for therapist and client, to be added to as therapy progresses. It can also be used as a contract between therapist and client, which is the way in which it is used at Alternatives For Women. The Problem/Goal List becomes the base from which notes are made following sessions, since the focus of the sessions is on those problems and goals specified by the client and agreed on for work by therapist and client in the sessions.

The notes, again following the problem-oriented medical record system, are done in a form called STRAP. The letters *STRAP* stand for the separate components of each problem and/or goal covered in a session. *S* stands for "Subjective"—what the client said about this specific problem/-goal in the session. *TR* stands for "Therapist's Response"—how the therapist responded to the client's subjective material. *A* stands for "Assessment" —what is going on. *P* stands for "Plan"—what the client and the therapist are going to do about this problem/goal. A STRAP note is made on each problem/goal discussed in a session. It was decided to have Novelist clients do *S*, the therapist do *TR*, and both do *A* and *P* together. With Traditionalists, the therapist made all the STRAP notes alone. STRAP time, or charting time, was in addition to the therapy session—time added on so that it was possible to answer the question of how much time it took. The therapist also received a data sheet on which time spent making STRAP notes was to be recorded for each session and, for Novelists, comments from both the client and the therapist on the procedure or process.

Results

Of the 101 women studied, 74 chose to write notes with the therapist and 27 chose not to. The average age of the Novelists was 32.1 and of the Traditionalists, 35.6. The difference in age was not statistically significant. The average education of the Novelists was 14.3 years and of the Traditionalists, 13.4. Again, the difference was not statistically significant. Ethnically, of the entire study population, 71 women were Caucasian, 14 were Asian, and 16 were other—Hawaiian, Samoan, and so on—or mixed—for example, Hawaiian/Chinese, Caucasian/Hawaiian, and the like. There was no significant association between ethnicity and choice. This still held true when a test was run between Caucasians versus all others.

Finally, the association between marital status and choice was computed. Forty-four clients were married or living with a person as though married; 38 were divorced, separated, or widowed; and 19 were single/-never married. There was no significant statistical association between marital status and choice.

The MMPI was given to all subjects. Fifty-five of the clients completed and returned the MMPI, while 46 did not. The association between completion of the MMPI and choice was essentially random.

The next series of computations deals with the 40 Novelists who completed the MMPI and the 15 Traditionalists who completed it. Again, age and education were computed, and again there was no statistically signifi-

NUMBER OF MINUTES TAKEN TO WRITE STRAP NOTES

	Session 1	Session 2	Session 3
Traditionalists			
Mode	15	20	20
Median	18	20	20
Novelists			
Mode	15	15	10
Median	15	15	12

cant difference between the two groups. The three validation scales, the nine clinical scales, and the commonly used social introversion scale were computed. Of these 13 differences between the means, not a single one attained statistical significance or even approached the .10 level. In short, the decision to participate in writing the case record was not associated with any of the psychological measures incorporated in the wide-ranging MMPI. The validity scales are of interest since they would indicate potential differences in creating an impression, whether deviantly good or bad or relatively defensive. The clinical scales indicate that choice was not associated with intensity or type of problem. In short, the demographic and psychological material indicated no difference between Novelists and Traditionalists.

The number of minutes it took to write STRAP notes for the first three sessions for both Novelists and Traditionalists is presented in Table 1. An average number of minutes was not calculated, since the range of time taken to write STRAP notes was enormous—some therapists took as long as 35 minutes and others as little as 5 minutes doing this with the client; the time taken by a therapist working alone ranged from 5 to 45 minutes.

When the 11 therapists were interviewed, it was found that 9 felt that writing STRAP notes with their clients was much more beneficial to both client and therapist than doing this alone—that is, they preferred the Novelist approach. They felt record-sharing was therapeutic for the client and clarifying and direction-giving for both themselves and the client. Two therapists preferred writing STRAP notes alone; one felt constrained as to the content of notes written with clients and the other was in a fearful time bind. What also emerged from interviews with the therapists from the comments recorded on the data sheets was that the clients felt that writing STRAP notes with the therapist was therapeutic, enlightening, and beneficial for them, and some felt this strongly.

DISCUSSION

A first step in humanizing the social services is to find out what the client wants. Rather than forcing the client to participate in writing the case record, the first step is to provide this as a choice and find out how many people wish to take it. Essentially three-fourths of the clients in this study chose the Novel approach.

Although the researchers thought there would be differences between Novelists and Traditionalists, not a single MMPI or demographic characteristic differentiated the two groups. On the one hand, this is welcome, because it indicates a potential for generalizing to the entire population served. It leaves the question of what the reasons behind the choices were. Two observations may be helpful.

1. In maintaining ethical openness about the research, the researchers told the women that their help was needed. The intent was to indicate clearly that the Novel approach was not compulsory and that the nature of the help requested was to make a choice. The result, however, as evidenced by a large number of comments, was that many clients felt that their help was needed in getting the notes written, and making this choice afforded them an opportunity to repay the help they were receiving. Aside from the informed consent efforts, the researchers had humanized the entire process by inadvertently giving the message that the clients were a vital and needed part of the recording process. Human dignity does not seem to be significantly differentiated by demographic characteristics or even the MMPI.

2. Some of the Traditionalists were under time pressure. The time required to write case notes with the therapist, because it was added onto the therapy session, was a crucial variable in these women's choice. Some had children waiting for them, others were taking time off from work, and still others had a long commute.

The process of writing STRAP notes with the client was in itself interesting. Therapists differed in the way they approached the process with the client. Some therapists wrote the STRAP notes with the client watching and then asked the client whether the client wished to add to or delete from them. Other therapists gave a sheet of paper to the client, asking the client to write out the *S*. Then the therapist took the paper and wrote out the *TR*. The two then collaborated on the *A* and *P*. The latter process took longer than the former, so therapists with heavier case loads tended not to follow this process. Variations among therapists were also significant in terms of amount and quality of content of the notes. The two therapists who disliked writing notes with clients felt that the quality of their notes varied considerably—that they omitted a great deal of relevant material in notes written with clients. It was noteworthy that the two persons who disliked writing notes with clients were staff persons rather than students. The one other staff person involved and the eight students were highly enthusiastic about the process.

IMPLICATIONS

Sharing the client record is a solution to problems of confidentiality. Those clients who chose to participate in creating their records were not only aware of what was in their case folder but also contributed extensively to it. Therefore, decisions about releasing a folder or any part of it could be made by the client with full knowledge of what information would be sent to an inquiring agency. In short, informed consent was really informed.

In these days of rapidly changing laws governing such things as mental health records, policies are in effect in many states, or are in the making, regarding who owns the client chart—the institution, facility, or agency or the client. The traditional style of record-keeping could cost the mental health profession a great deal of rapport, professional credibility, and continued contact with many clients if their records suddenly became available to them.

Another benefit provided by this method stems from its openness to the client and the quality of the material included in the chart. Since inferences, hypotheses, and interpretations are not included in the problem/goal-based record, the therapist may decide, when called on to testify, whether it is in the interest of the client to share such material. The problem/goal-based record thus affords an optional discretion hitherto not available.

Again, in some states (Hawaii being one), therapists and clients' charts may be subpoenaed by a judge at any time. If the client knows what is in the record, she or he is better informed and can advise an attorney about whether to ask for the therapist and/or record in court. If, in turn, a prosecutor has the therapist and/or record subpoenaed, at least the client knows what information the prosecution will be getting. If therapists and clients' records are not immune to public scrutiny, then it behooves therapists to record carefully, as though talking in public before attorneys, judges, and the client.

In addition to the benefits mentioned, clients' rights are protected in many other ways by the method described. First, the client and therapist are agreed as to the problems and their related goals. Both the problems and goals are public and open and in front of the client. Therapy does not begin until a contract (Problem/Goal List) has been made by and between the therapist and the client as to what problems and goals are to be worked on together. All too often, therapists have hidden agendas and are working on problems or toward goals that have not been specified to the client or indicated by the client as areas of desired change. This is clearly in violation of clients' rights. As Reed Martin puts it, ". . . the consistently demonstrable thrust of all intervention should be focused on the problem behavior that led to a decision to become involved."[2] In short, informed consent is enhanced.

Both the sharing and the method of sharing increase accountability. The focus of therapy with clients in the Alternatives For Women Program, the Problem/Goal List, and the objectification and specificity of the problem/goal-oriented recording procedure enormously increase accountability at all levels. (1) There are problems and goals that are specified and written down. (2) The goals are objectified, concrete, and measurable. (3) The goals are visible—it is easier to ascertain whether they are being attained. (4) The goals are objectively stated so that the professional, the supervisor, the administrator, the client, the judge, the significant other, and all other persons involved can agree on the results. (5) The goals are divided into a sequence of tasks, each of which builds on the preceding ones and each of which is measurable and capable of being evaluated. (6) There is a model to teach the desired behavior to the client if the client does not have the skills to perform the task or do the behavior desired. (7) The therapist shapes the desired performance. Progress toward the goal is rewarded and encouraged, and feedback is as immediate as possible. (8) There is reliable reporting so that feedback can occur. Reporting and data-collection focus on evaluation of performance rather than opinion or judgment. (9) Decisions are based on performance. If an approach is working, it is continued. If an approach is not working—and the data will tell—the model is changed. (10) Specific results are communicated to all parties in objective, intelligible terms. With this sort of information and communication, the therapist can claim effectiveness and can back up that claim with data.

Specifically, the Problem/Goal List indicates the date of the decision about problems and goals and the date of problem resolution and/or goal attainment. This information specifies not only whether problems were resolved and/or goals attained but also how long it took.

The procedures described are methods for obtaining the objectives and resolving the problems in being accountable outlined by numerous authors in the social work literature.[3] The problem/goal-oriented recording procedure does not by itself assure high quality of either assessment or treatment. The individual therapist can still be slipshod and inadequate. A problem list and an accompanying goal list are only as good as the persons constructing them, and the treatment plans that are made are still limited by the knowledge and ability of the persons devising them.[4] Use of this method does, however, force a systematic rather than a random collection of data, enhances communication between persons, functionally defines problems and goals, provides a feedback mechanism, and documents specific therapeutic actions and their outcomes.[5] Finally, the problem/goal-oriented format has been shown to be superior in allowing students to demonstrate their ability to identify problems, help clients set goals, devise treatment plans, and help the client make changes.[6]

To summarize, the researchers found that clients were ready, willing, and able to share in creating their own session notes. The time required did not seem to be any greater than that taken by a therapist working alone. The procedure was welcomed by the majority of the therapists and warmly endorsed by the clients. In the broader professional context, the practice of record-making with the client combined with the specific problem/goal-oriented method used in the present research provides a method for solving some of the problems of confidentiality, protection of clients' rights, and accountability. Beyond all else, however, by sharing the recording, the responsibility for problem definition, goal-setting, treatment-planning, outcome, and evaluation were shared, thus communicating in deeds rather than words respect for the client as a mature and capable human being.

NOTES AND REFERENCES

1. **Rosalie Kane**, "Look to the Record," *Social Work*, 19 (July 1974), pp. 412–419; **Richard L. Grant and Barry M. Maletzky**, "Application of the Weed System to Psychiatric Records," *Psychiatry in Medicine*, 3 (April 1972), pp. 119–129.

2. **Reed Martin**, *Legal Challenges to Behavior Modification: Trends in Schools, Corrections and Mental Health* (Champaign, Ill.: Research Press, 1975), p. 63.

3. *See*, for example, **Marvin L. Rosenberg and Ralph Brody**, "The Threat or Challenge of Accountability," *Social Work*, 19 (May 1974), pp. 344–350; **Edward Newman and Jerry Turem**, "The Crisis of Accountability," *Social Work*, 19 (January 1974), pp. 5–16; **Emanuel Tropp**, "Expectation, Performance, and Accountability," *Social Work*, 19 (March 1974), pp. 139–148; **Joel Fischer**, "Is Casework Effective?" *Social Work*, 18 (January 1973), pp. 5–20.

4. **Wilma M. Martens and Elizabeth Holmstrup**, "Problem-oriented Recording," *Social Casework*, 55 (November 1974), pp. 554–561; **Roger C. Katz and F. Ross Woolley**, "Improving Patients' Records Through Problem Orientation," *Behavior Therapy*, 6 (January 1975), pp. 119–124.

5. **Katz and Woolley**, op. cit.; **George C. Burrill**, "The Problem-Oriented Log in Social Casework," *Social Work*, 21 (January 1976), pp. 67–68.

6. **Pamela H. Mitchell and Judith Atwood**, "Problem-oriented Recording as a Teaching-Learning Tool," *Nursing Research*, 24 (March-April 1975), pp. 99–103.

Intensive In-Home Treatment: An Alternative to Out-of-Home Placement

MARVIN E. BRYCE AND MICHAEL D. RYAN

There has been great reliance in the United States on institutions and other out-of-home programs as a means of managing social problems. Rothman notes that substitutes of various kinds were used as tools for social control prior to 1900, when punishment and cure were thought to be related. He observes that we still live with many of these institutions: "We tend to forget that they were the invention of one generation to serve very special needs, not the only possible reaction to social problems."[1] Institutions have contributed greatly to the special needs of the blind, deaf, retarded, delinquent, and disturbed. But Queen notes that as early as 1850, an increasing number of people began to question the wisdom of bringing large numbers of children together. Yet he points out that as late as 1910, Dr. Hastings Hart estimated there were still 100,000 children in orphanages, some of which contained as many as 2000 children.[2] Foster care has since 1910 likewise been the choice of treatment for large numbers of children. In the past two decades, use of group homes and day care has mushroomed.

These various approaches based outside the family and community are frequently used as a means of providing welfare, educational, and health services to children. Costs for out-of-home service have increased markedly over the last two decades, now ranging from over $150 a month for foster care to more than $3000 a month for residential and inpatient treatment. Unfortunately, the increased cost has not guaranteed quality services to children. Thomas points to the more recent growing disenchantment with

155

institutionalization as a way of caring for groups of dependent and/or deviant citizens.[3]

Many rationales are made for out-of-home placements. Some of the more common ones include separation of the youngster, especially the delinquent, from the peer group (however, institutions are not noted for their positive peer models) and protection from a dysfunctional family system. With respect to the latter, usually little or nothing is done to alter the family system, and the child or adolescent is either returned to the family or kept out of it permanently. Other children remaining in the family often take their turns for placement as they become older.

Some children are placed in order to take advantage of the special educational resources an institution can offer, but in several states legislation and public schools are increasingly making provision for the education of children who may be different in some way. A growing number of youngsters are placed for several weeks "for evaluation only." This action is most often taken by courts or clinicians who do not know what else to do. In many instances numerous evaluations have already been made with little or no treatment provided. In addition, observations of the behavior of an individual occurring outside that person's familiar habitat may not be valid beyond that setting. Numerous researchers have raised other, more profound, issues about the feasibility of institutional and foster care.[4]

Today perhaps as many as one million children are in placement. Nearly half of those (400,000) live in custodial institutions for the neglected, dependent, delinquent, disturbed, retarded, and physically handicapped.[5] It is variously estimated that another 300,000 are in foster care.[6]

FAMILIES' IN-HOME TREATMENT OF IOWA

Iowa is currently involved in establishing community-based services that will assist families, even with the most extraordinary circumstances, to continue in their irreplaceable role of parenting children. The program began in 1974. One of the large state institutions had been closed, and progressive legislators were calling for alternatives to institutional care. An intensive in-home, family-centered, community-based service to families was designed and proposed to the Iowa State Department of Social Services by a newly organized lay board. The state department funded the program on a contractual basis for a two-year pilot phase. The service is now in its fourth year of operation.

Families' In-Home Treatment of Iowa (FAMILIES) is a private, nonprofit, uniservice agency originally designed to offer families and communities an alternative to institutional or group home treatment. Virtually no limitation is placed on the availability, day or night, of service to a family *in its own home.* Staff persons are available on a daily basis according to need.

The original catchment area consists of six counties with a total population of 435,000 within a 4800-square-mile geographic area. The area contains two cities of 125,000 population. The rest of the population lives in small towns and on farms. The lay board consists of representatives from the counties served. After the two-year pilot phase, the program was extended to nine counties. After almost three years, a sister agency was generated, with its own staff and board, to provide service to a comparable geographic area.

Staff Deployment

The staff training center and administrative office is located near the center of the geographic area served. The 15 case managers for the original area are community based, living within the community or catchment area they serve. Case managers are thus able to be part of and conversant with the community and are promptly available to the family and community in times of crisis. Staff persons are on call around the clock for emergencies. Case managers drive to the central office one day a week for staff-development, supervisory, and administrative meetings. An attempt is made to employ persons with diverse backgrounds, training, and experience. This diversity better equips the agency to address itself to the many facets of family life—family relationships, finances, legal matters, education, and so on. Continuous staff development is an integral part of the agency.

Each case manager is responsible for two to three families at any given time, devoting as much time to the cases as is indicated. Actual time with the family, or some part of it, has ranged from 10 to 40 hours a week, depending on the phase of treatment, the nature of the problem, and the family's proclivity for crises.

At times, family needs have led case managers to work in teams. Not only is this approach an asset to treatment with some families, but sharing of talents and techniques is possible, mutual staff support has been facilitated, and staff illnesses and vacations are covered. Thus each family has a minimum of two and sometimes as many as five staff persons upon whom to rely.

The treatment coordinator, director, and some of the more experienced staff members currently also function as family workers, meeting at least weekly with the case managers and conferring by phone when necessary. In addition, the family worker and family case manager meet conjointly with each family in weekly family therapy sessions. Local community agency representatives sometimes participate in these sessions.

Referral

Referrals come from the county departments of social services and are usually made initially by phone. The referring agency makes the determination as to which families will be served by virtue of its own screening. The family is accepted for service if staff time is available and if the referred child has not been in placement outside the home, other than for evaluation purposes, during the past year. Any family with a youngster at home who is judged by the departmental worker to be in danger of out-of-home placement is eligible for in-home service. If service cannot commence immediately, a projection is made as to whether it can begin within 30 days. This information assists the referral source in making a decision about possible utilization of other resources.

Intake and Assessment

FAMILIES is introduced to the family by the referring agency. The first meeting, conducted in the home as is almost all the agency's work, is used to describe the in-home treatment program. All family members are present. The intensity of the program is stressed, and the problems this might present for the family are examined. (For instance, since the focus is on the family rather than on a single family member, at least one parent is expected to be in the home when in-home treatment staff persons are present.) Questions are encouraged, and every effort is made to clarify why the staff persons are present, what the agency has to offer, and the general manner in which the workers will proceed. The family may choose to make a commitment to accept service at the time of the introductory session, or they may wish to reflect for a time before making a decision. If both the participating agency and the family agree to in-home treatment, the participating agency then refers the family for service.

During the first week, the case manager is present in the home daily, observing the family routine, individual differences, interaction, behavior, coping patterns, and disciplinary procedures. Different times of the day are chosen to get a representative sample. Conflicts and problems are recorded. Collateral contacts in the community are made if this has not been done during the intake phase.

The first structured family therapy session usually takes place near the end of the first week. All family members are included and are expected to participate. The first two or three family sessions are designed to begin the process of structured, purposeful family interaction. Although family study is a continuous process, the initial family sessions provide useful information about the family dynamics. Provision is made for individual recognition and representation. Roles are identified, value conflicts are noted, and procedures for discussing and solving problems are demonstrated. An attempt is made to integrate all family members into family therapy.

During the first few days, program negotiation with the family is associated with the study phase. The family is engaged in daily dialogue about vital and routine family matters. In the process, information is gained by the case manager from the family sessions in the home and from community resources such as the school and other agencies. In addition, helpful written information is sometimes provided by the various family members on family information forms. Each family member is asked to record five undesirable family or individual problems needing change and five desirable family events or characteristics each wishes to keep or expand.

These data are compared for match, problem themes are identified, and primary problem behavior is noted in terms of location, severity, duration, frequency, and causality. This information becomes the basis for formulation of hypotheses and identification of priorities. Results of the assessment are shared with the family, and amenability to change is assessed.

Program Planning

Contractual program-writing is elective. The decision to prepare a written contract depends on the nature of the problems at hand, whether the problems seem to lend themselves to this approach, preferences of the staff involved, and the estimated degree of difficulty anticipated in holding a family to a focused commitment. A primary task has been to find ways of getting families to take initiative in the treatment process. Contracts are sometimes helpful in this regard. A general contract may be used that specifies, for instance, the day, time, and frequency of meetings and who will be present, as well as what the family may expect from the agency and the general expectations the agency has of the family. More specific task-accomplishment, environmental, or behavior-related problems may also be contracted. Respective expectations are discussed and clarified as written, and the family members are asked to sign the agreement. The family retains a copy of the agreement.

The team composes a program profile for each family based on the information obtained from assessment and negotiation as outlined. This profile gives the agency and the family full and honest benefit of the projected possibilities. The program profile must be reviewed often. It serves as a guide for the team and the family. No single profile or therapeutic technique is adequate for all families because each family is unique and complex, and family assessment is a continuous process. In addition, families, individuals, and circumstances change.

Program Implementation

Executing the program as outlined in the program profile often involves many people (family, agencies, employers, and the like). Family experiences, methods of coping, external-internal impact, relationships, behavior, and what may be done to alter these and other family and individual patterns become a daily focus. Problems extending into the community are given attention, and planned collateral exchange is made. Negative and positive behaviors are noted and responded to, either directly at that moment or mentally recorded for future attention. The ebb and flow of the quality and quantity of relationships in the dyads and triads in the family unit and in the community are manipulated for therapeutic purposes. A paramount factor in the in-home program is the daily contact, that is, the availability of or ready access to the family. Planned or on-the-spot judgments as to the most therapeutic use of self and the observed need are made on the basis of the worker's acquaintance with the family. The worker may assume many roles during the course of treatment, determined to a large extent by the family-life experiences.

The team strategically undergirds the individual with personal responsibility and lifts up the client's potential to effect desired change. Family and individual strengths are highlighted and supported. Team members may assume complementary roles, with one being authoritative and insistent while the other is supportive and benevolent. Family sessions focus on current interaction as it occurs and the facilitation of constructive communication with the use of structuring techniques. In the family sessions, periodic review and/or revision of the program profile is considered. What the family brings, both in feelings and content, is given serious attention.

As others have noted, work with the family in the home is a useful tool in both diagnosis and treatment.[7] Seeing a family or individual in a clinic or hospital setting exposes the treatment team to a biased concentration on pathology rather than health. Discovery and confirmation of family and individual strengths that can be utilized in problem-solving can be accomplished best in the home and can positively influence the attitude of the therapist. On-the-spot child management coaching opportunities abound.

The mystery often associated with what goes on between therapist and client behind the closed office door is quickly dispelled when working in the home with the family unit. The protection of agency structure and dependence on privacy are markedly diminished. The comparative ease of structuring one-to-one communication is decreased. Procedural organization becomes more complicated, and a balance between formal and informal interaction is made necessary.

Techniques

A concentrated effort has been made to avoid the application of a single theory or technique. One last answer, or a "stone tablet" approach—like the Ten Commandments, unquestioned and valid at all times for all people

—is appealing, perhaps because there is a sense of security in knowing in advance how one will proceed. The human need for a prescription—a formula to rely on—to be able to say, "This is what we do and how we do it," is felt no less here than in any other arena. But it is important to be flexible, to have an arsenal of alternatives rather than a single one to be applied with every family or in every situation. The following case histories are illustrative:

The K case. K was a 14-year-old boy, the fifth youngest in a family of ten children who was referred as a severe behavior problem at school. The family accepted service. The mother worked nights as a nurse in a rest home for the aged. The father was a chronically unemployed alcoholic. The two oldest daughters were married. Another had been confined to a girls' training school prior to service. The two oldest sons, both over 18, were adopting the father's life-style at home. Neither was employed, and they joined the father in his daily drinking. The family lived in the country, and the mother could not drive. She bought alcohol for the boys in exchange for transportation. She often found reasons to be away from home when she was not at work, leaving the 14-year-old and four younger children for the father to look after. The 14-year-old was refusing to go home after school and often stayed out all night without permission. The father refused to stop drinking.

The treatment staff made the following hypotheses:

1. The mother was essentially cooperating with the drinking pattern.

2. The three eldest boys (aged 16, 18, and 21) and father were mutually supportive of the drinking and nonemployment syndrome.

3. K, like his mother, was at the mercy of the chaos in the home and found ways to avoid being home.

4. K was fighting his father's declared intention to drink himself to death.

5. The four youngest children were being neglected and felt the loss of both parents.

6. K was badly in need of a relationship with his father, who seemed to be unaware of his existence, and was acting out his depression.

The treatment team found it necessary to proceed as though the father was not an asset to the family. The object was to facilitate the grieving over the loss of the father. The team assumed an aggressive role with the three oldest sons, finally managing to help them find employment (with the mother's active support, who limited her role with them as a supplier of drink and food) and establish residence outside the home. We worked daily with the school, mother, and police in regard to programming expectations, reinforcements, and penalties for K. Marriage counseling sessions were held with the parents, and the father was told in clear and direct terms that K was acting out fear and anger about his father's refusal to be a parent. The mother was utilized as the authority with K and was supported in this role. K became destructive toward staff property and blamed the treatment team for "changing" his mother (she required him to be home at night, to stay at school, follow rules, and so on). The police were used as a supplemental authority, and the father was required to be in court for a hearing after the police picked up K and he refused to go home. At the court hearing, the father was held publicly accountable together with his son. The boy wept at the hearing, and the father and son made an emotionally charged commitment to each other. With the continued help of in-home staff, the father obtained employment and ceased his drinking, took a renewed interest in the family finances, and began to socialize with and establish a structure for the family. In particular, he was able to discipline K, who responded positively.

The P case. P, age 10, was one of seven children. He had been in a mental hospital for two years, followed by a year in a residential treatment center. He had never attended public school. P had multiple diagnoses, including autism, brain damage, and schizophrenia. Work with the school led to his enrollment for one hour a day, with the condition that the worker would be with him in the classroom. He was taken to school by car. P was a severe management problem both at home and at school. After several months, the time spent in school was increased. Outings to the park, grocery store, and recreation center were useful in the socialization process (P had previously been confined at home because of his dangerous impulsiveness). School personnel and other children became more confident around P. After one year of intensive service, he was riding the bus to school, and school personnel were assuming management responsibility for the boy. He was enrolled in a newly created class for children with learning disturbances, and he attended regularly.

While the method of delivery and intensity of service are new, the techniques are, for the most part, familiar. Development of parenting skills is perhaps the most frequently used service, often in association with meeting of basic needs and use of such community resources as the police, mental health, and other traditional services. One of the key characteristics of the program is that no area needing attention is excluded. It is possible to meet family needs in many areas.

Termination

Closing may occur under any one of several circumstances: when goals have been attained; when the family feels confident it can cope in a reasonably constructive and effective manner; when there is insistence for closure by the family and/or the referring agency; or when there is agreement among the agency, family, and referring agency that the program is not sufficiently effective.

Table 1 gives the breakdown on terminations. Most families are terminated by mutual agreement. Service may be renewed on referral and by mutual agreement by the family, the referring agency, and FAMILIES.

TABLE 1. SOURCE OF TERMINATION

Source	Number
Mutual agreement	60
Client	8
FAMILIES	3
Referring agency	2
Total*	73

*This total reflects the fact that 16 of the 89 families in the study were still active-service cases.

A written summary of the program and its results in retrospect, along with recommendations for continued work when indicated, are shared with the family and the referring agency. An effort is made to leave the family with a positive feeling about the experience, in order to augment its receptivity to possible future intervention as well as to increase retention of what has been gained.

CHARACTERISTICS OF CLIENT FAMILIES

The following data are based on an analysis of 89 families containing 299 children, or approximately half of the families served during the first three years of the program. Half of the children in the families were in need of intensive service. Half of the children referred were age 13 or older. Fifty-six percent were male. Most of the families were multiproblem families.

The marital status of the parents is shown in Table 2. As can be seen, almost half were single-parent families, only two of which were headed by a male. Almost 16 percent of the families had adults living in the home who were not family members. The mean educational level of the parents was 11 years, with a range from grade five through a Ph.D.

Seventy-nine percent of the families lived in the city or in a small town. Almost half (42) were recipients of Aid to Families with Dependent Children. Table 3 shows the income level of the families.

Dysfunctional family relationships, stealing, running away, delinquent

TABLE 2. MARITAL STATUS OF PARENTS

Marital Status	Number
Single (divorced, widowed, separated)	43
Two-parent—biological	25
Blended (stepparent, adopted child)	21*
Total	89

*This figure includes seven families with common-law type relationships.

acts, noncompliance, and school problems have been the most frequently noted complaints. More than one-third of the families had nonreferred children who had previously been or were currently placed outside the home.

It would be confusing and misleading to attempt to categorize families by use of the medical diagnostic nomenclature designed for individuals. Most of the youngsters had been diagnosed at least once. Categories ranged from severe autism with retardation and various personality disorders to more positive terms, such as adjustment reaction to adolescence, childhood runaway reaction, hyperkinesis, or overanxious reaction. Some labels seem to have a negative conditioning effect on caregivers, community, and family. It appears that some communities and parents are influenced to make a decision in favor of placement based on strategic manipulation of diagnostic terms. Frequent absence of fit has been found between diagnoses applied to an individual and that person's functioning in the family system. In addition, contrasted with daily assessment of the family in the home and community, diagnosis based on an office evaluation, following which one family member is procedurally designated the sick one and treated accordingly, seems inadequate, inappropriate, and harmful to the family.

TABLE 3. INCOME RANGE*

Income Range	Number
Below $5000	40
$5000–$10,000	26
$10,000–$15,000	10
Above $15,000	13
Total	89

*Forty-eight percent of the families were AFDC recipients.

Fifty percent of the families had at least one member who had been placed prior to service. One-third of the referred youngsters had histories of prior residential, hospital, or outpatient psychiatric treatment ranging from three years to a few outpatient contacts. Almost all the youngsters referred were having significant academic and/or behavioral problems in school.

OUTCOME

The average length of service per family has been 7½ months. Seventy-three percent of the youngsters whose families have received in-home service have remained in the home. This statistic covers the first three years of the program. Ten percent of the families have been referred and accepted for renewal of service.

Review of Costs

The cost for one year of intensive in-home service has averaged $9000. The next-most-intensive home-based program in Iowa reported an expenditure of $6000 for a year of service. A national review of the home-based programs shows a wide variation in costs; the difference in the intensity of the program accounts for this variation. Ferleger and Cotter report that a family may receive a full array of supplemental and supportive services for $17,000 a year in New York City.[8] This is about $2000 less than the average cost of substitute care for a year. Home-builders of Tacoma, Washington, report a similar savings.[9] Geismar, in his research on a less intensive home-based program, found the cost of home-based care to be about 8 percent that of institutional care and 40 percent that of foster care.[10] When computed on an hourly rate, the cost is slightly more than half that of outpatient service at mental health centers in Iowa. It should be noted that for every child whose family is served, four additional individuals also receive service. When calculated on this basis, a very different cost factor is given.

PROBLEMS, IMPRESSIONS, AND PROJECTIONS

The issues of community intolerance and desire for physical control (the two major factors that seem to lead to placement) have been encountered. Chronic runaways and highly disorganized families seem especially prone to involvement in community tolerance-control problems. The communities seem more willing to extend tolerance when the family is primarily at risk (as in abuse cases) than when the community is at risk (as in juvenile delinquency cases) when intensive in-home service is present. The risks present in any treatment approach should be recognized, weighed, and taken deliberately and conscientiously. This area is one in which professionals often disagree.

Better coordination among agencies would do a great deal to meet the need for control and reduce the risk factor. Therapeutic use of immediate short-term control could help make long-term placement outside the home unnecessary. An "all-or-nothing" syndrome would then be avoided. Hospitals and courts in particular are prone to act without regard for what has come before or what may follow.

There appears to be great variation among communities in the criteria used to determine placement, which seems to be done on a random basis. This finding is in agreement with the findings of Shyne, Sherman, and Phillips in a study done for the Child Welfare League of America.[11] The researchers note that the relative use of institutions and foster homes in different communities has more to do with historical accident than with the needs of children. They found that in about half the cases examined, a group of highly experienced child welfare practitioners disagreed with each other and with the less experienced workers who were making the decision on both the reason for placement and the decision to place. It is suspected that disposition variation also reflects the personalities and philosophies of juvenile judges, county attorneys, and other personnel involved.

The discrepancy between what is done and what is needed appears to be an honest difference in interpretation of what constitutes an acceptable extent of work with family and community and its importance to a whole and effective treatment program for a family member. Many clinics and agencies continue to recommend residential treatment, institutional placement, hospitalization, boarding school, or foster care with the same frequency and for the same reasons used for the past 50 years. The number of recommendations for placement and the untold billions of dollars expended in maintaining the placement industry undergird the neglect of allocation of time, effort, finances, and professional skill at the local level for the development of alternatives to placement away from home.

Perhaps even more serious is the absence of a unified community development plan for human services with all service agencies working for all the family. This void undoubtedly reflects the absence of and need for a national family policy around which the country can deliberately and purposefully shape programs and policies. A family policy should adhere to the principle that no child should be removed from home and community until society has demonstrated as strong a willingness to invest resources in the child's own home as it does in caring for the child outside the home. As Schorr has noted, policies affecting families are adopted on the basis of the questionable assumption that "families are served."[12] Human underdevelopment in the family (the school for life and interpersonal relationships) continues almost unabated as we expend the vast share of our money, skills, and energies on nonfamily and antifamily endeavors.

NOTES AND REFERENCES

1. **David J. Rothman**, *The Discovery of the Asylums: Social Order and Disorder in the New Republic* (Boston: Little, Brown, 1971), p. 295.

2. **Stuart A. Queen**, *Social Work in the Light of History* (Philadelphia: J. B. Lippincott Co., 1922), pp. 146–147.

3. **George Thomas**, *Is Statewide Deinstitutionalization of Children's Services a Forward or Backward Social Movement?* (Athens: University of Georgia, Regional Institute of Social Welfare Research, 1976), p. 1.

4. For documentation of these issues, *see* **Ner Littner**, *Some Traumatic Eff ects of Separation and Placement* (New York: Child Welfare League of America, 1956); **Marvin E. Bryce**, "144 Foster Children," *Child Welfare,* 50 (November 1971), pp. 499–503; **David Fanshel**, "The Exit of Children from Foster Care: An Interim Research Report," *Child Welfare,* 50 (February 1971), pp. 65–81; **Henry S. Maas and Richard E. Engler**, *Children in Need of Parents* (New York: Columbia University Press, 1959); **Betty M. Ricketts**, "Child Placement and Its Effects on the Child and His Family" (unpublished master's thesis, Smith College School of Social Work, Northampton, Mass., 1959); **D. L. Rosenhan**, "On Being Sane in Insane Places," *Science,* 179 (January 1973), pp. 250–258; **John Bowlby**, *Maternal Care and Mental Health,* Monograph Series II (Geneva: World Health Organization, 1951); **Irving Goffman**, *Asylums* (New York: Doubleday, 1961); **Martin Wolins**, "Group Care: Friend or Foe?" *Social Work,* 14 (January 1969), pp. 35–53.

5. *Statement of Priorities for Research and Demonstration Activities in the Area of Children at Risk and the Child Welfare System* (Washington, D.C.: Office of Child Development, Department of Health, Education, and Welfare, 1976), pp. 1–2.

6. **Robert H. Mnookin**, "Foster Care—In Whose Best Interest," *Harvard Educational Review,* 43 (April 1973), p. 610.

7. *See,* for example, **Roy H. Schlachter**, "Home Counseling of Adolescents and Parents," *Social Work,* 20 (November 1975), pp. 480–481; and **Mary Bloom**, "Usefulness of the Home Visit for Diagnosis and Treatment," *Social Casework,* 54 (February 1973), pp. 67–75. Bloom describes the use of limited work in the home by a children's psychiatric hospital staff. Home visits are included as a part of the admissions process. *See also* **Rachel A. Levine**, "Treatment in the Home," *Social Work,* 9 (January 1964), pp. 19–28. Levine develops demonstration as a technique, combining it with recreational and concrete services.

8. **Mary J. Cotter and Beatrice Ferleger**, eds., *Children, Families, and Foster Care* (New York: Community Council of Greater New York, December 1976).

9. **Jill M. Kinney** et al., "Homebuilders: Keeping Families Together," *Journal of Consulting and Clinical Psychology,* 45 (August 1977), pp. 667–673.

10. **Ludwig Geismar**, "Home-Based Care to Children: Harmonizing the Approaches of Research and Practice." Paper presented at the National Symposium on Home-Based Services to Children, Iowa City, Iowa, April 1978.

11. **Ann W. Shyne, Edmund A. Sherman, and Michael H. Phillips**, "Filling a Gap in Child Welfare Research: Service for Children in Their Own Homes," *Child Welfare,* 51 (November 1972), pp. 562–573.

12. **Alvin Schorr**, "Family Policy in the United States," *International Social Science Journal,* 14 (Fall 1962), p. 457.

A Divorce Workshop for Families

JUDITH ANNE BRIDGEMAN AND BEVERLY ANN WILLIS

The impact of divorce on a family is significant and is often the major presenting or precipitating problem for many of the families served by social service agencies. Although this impact can range from devastating to growth producing, families often do not question whether their adjustment to the divorce and the pain they feel might be an opportunity for growth rather than dysfunctional. Divorcing families often view divorce as a "completed failure" that requires legal services only. Often they do not seek supportive services unless the conflict among the family members has become dysfunctional. Children, especially vulnerable to a disruption in their family system, receive little help in coping with their grief. Divorcing parents may need outside support to understand their child's feelings and to deal with them. Family units need some means by which they can mourn their loss and express their feelings.

Traditionally, social workers have examined the individual family member in treatment for the dysfunction that contributed to the divorce.[1] At times social service agencies have focused on the aftermath of divorce if there was a noticeable behavioral change that affected the family or the community.[2] The number of divorcing families makes more traditional services impractical, and, in the authors' opinion, these are frequently not relevant to the needs of divorcing families.[3]

There are numerous supportive and community-based programs for divorced parents and for adults in the process of divorcing.[4] But other than traditional supportive, treatment-oriented social services, the authors are not aware of any programs especially developed for children whose families are divorcing or of programs that focus on the divorcing family unit.

This lack of resources has been felt by many. In response to this need, the authors initiated a program the target of which was both the divorcing

169

parents and their children. In one year, ten workshops were held involving 176 participants. This program, titled "Families in Transition—A Divorce Workshop for Parents and Their Children," has focused on these goals:

1. To help families understand the meaning of their decision to divorce

2. To assist each family member with the struggle to cope emotionally with the divorce by helping parents to give up the husband/wife roles and by focusing on the meaning this transition has for family members in terms of their sense of identity and self-esteem

3. To facilitate open, honest, and factual communication among family members with specific emphasis on communication with children

4. To encourage development of the skills necessary to cope with the decisions and problems common to divorcing families (for example, visitation, custody, division of property, support payments, and changes in values or life-styles)

Personal responses to the divorce crisis itself have often been likened to depression or to the response to death, viewed as "ill" by outsiders (including social workers). The divorcing person perceives him- or herself as being "crazy," or dysfunctional.[5] The environmental and personal structures that formerly supported the individual within the marriage are abruptly removed, and the person feels crazy, or different. The authors, while recognizing the contributing factors of individual personalities, family system dysfunction, and environmental influences, view divorce not as an indicator of failure (although it may be) but as a significant life crisis that can be moved through productively or nonproductively. In this sense, *productive* is defined as including enhanced risk-taking and heightened self-esteem, both of which facilitate the ability to form future attachments.

In the workshops, a crisis approach was used that was based on the assumption that how family members cope with the changes divorce brings often depends on both the knowledge and the skill with which family members have coped with other life crises and the new knowledge and new skills that family members can acquire. Divorce is considered as a crisis having natural stages and creating feelings that are common to all divorcing families. These common feelings include anger, fear, insecurity, guilt, failure, and abandonment. In this framework, a crisis is not resolved productively if a family member (or a family unit) becomes stuck in a stage or is unable to overcome a feeling. If the family member does not let go, conflict will continue in some manner.

BASIC CONCEPTS

The authors have defined five basic concepts to help families cope with the major role loss of spouse (for parents) and shift in parenting (for children). These are (1) grief model, (2) separation triangle, (3) stepparent-ing skills, (4) open, direct, and honest communication, and (5) pain games.[6]

Grief Model

The authors have, for simplicity, adapted Kubler-Ross's stages of the grief process in confronting death to the grieving process families experience in divorce.[7] This facilitates family members' understanding of their own mourning, the necessary anger that results from loss and conflict, and their behavioral responses as each stage is experienced. These stages are denial, anger, bargaining (insecurity), resignation-depression, acceptance (quiet-ness), and growth. The authors have found that family members (or entire family units) are most likely to become stuck in the stages of anger, bargain-ing, or resignation-depression.

Separation Triangle

This concept clarifies the kind of communication families need to continue after the divorce. As Norris states: ". . . in marriages with children each partner plays basically two roles: spouse (husband or wife) and parent (father or mother). In divorce, the husband-wife roles are broken which means that the husband-wife no longer relate to each other as husband and wife."[8] However, because the child is mutually theirs, they continue to relate to each other as father and mother. Often in the early stages of separation, the partners also continue to relate to each other as husband and wife, primarily to resist loss or to maintain old security patterns. This continuation of former roles presents conflicting double-messages to the children (and to friends and relatives as well).

Stepparenting Skills

Many divorced parents continue to have conflicts with their former spouses after their (or their spouses') remarriage. Often the new spouse (stepparent) senses the partner's inability to let go of the former marital relationship and becomes embroiled in conflict (ostensibly over the chil-dren) with the partner's former mate. To complement the separation trian-gle and to help stepparents and natural parents understand newly defined roles, the authors have developed the concept shown in the stepparenting skills chart on the next page.[9] When this concept is used, stepparents can quickly see the role they are taking and whether this is interfering with their partner's effective parenting and coping with the previous divorce.

Open, Direct, and Honest Communication

Many divorcing parents do not offer clear information to their child about their decision to divorce. The parent's own pain and inability to share

STEPPARENTING SKILLS

+	−
Stepparent enables, supports, and facilitates the natural parent to do her or his job.	Stepparent acts as a spokesperson, decision-maker, and central parent.
Low Profile	High Profile
Strong Family	Vulnerable Family

it with his or her child may be related to a desire to protect the child from added unhappiness and may also prevent such communications. Indirectly, attorneys or social workers may support this tendency by advising parents not to give a child too much information (which might place the child in a position whereby he or she feels a choice must be made) or by excluding children from knowledge of legal proceedings that may affect them. The authors' findings are in agreement with those of Gardner, who states that children adjust more readily to divorce if given open, direct, and honest information about the divorce.[10] To convey this, the authors use Satir's communication model: open (involves choice-recognition of the importance of others), direct (meaning is clear), and honest (reality and facts are correct).[11]

Pain Games

The fifth concept is of "Pain Games," behavioral games, or expressions, that the authors have found to be basic to the feeling responses of families to divorce. Seven such games are presented in videotaped dramatizations.[12] These are "Don't Worry, It'll Be OK," "The Messenger Game," "Disneyland Daddy," "Cut Down," "I Spy," "The Friendly Divorce," and "I Wish."[13] Use of dramatizations has helped participants in the workshop to understand the meaning of letting go in divorce. The videotape clarifies the hazards of playing these games and identifies the natural feelings that are the basis of each game.

The concept of Pain Games has assisted helping professionals to understand better the change and movement that take place in a divorcing family. They are helped to recognize that, in divorce, conflict is inevitable, and thus its expression in game-playing is also inevitable. The authors identify as dysfunctional not the existence of the game called "Cut Down," for example, but its continuation beyond the grieving period.

REACHING DIVORCING FAMILIES

The original workshop began as a six-week program meeting two hours each Saturday morning. After this series, the workshop was redesigned as a weekend experience, lasting eight hours each on Saturday and Sunday. The weekend format proved most useful in maintaining high participation and as a way of working intensely with families in a relatively short period of time.

The families that participate must have made the decision to divorce, although the divorce need not yet be legal. Some families had decided to divorce just before the workshop; others had been divorced for three or four years and were still experiencing conflict. One or both parents may attend; however, parents are not included unless at least one child also attends. In recent workshops, stepparents have also been included. Adults who are struggling with alcoholism (maintaining initial sobriety) are screened out of the program. The ages of the children who participate range from 6 through 17 years. Generally on Saturdays the children's section and the parents' section meet separately except when films are viewed. On Sunday, a variety of meetings take place. For example, one meeting includes the entire group of families to view tapes and discuss common issues, while another (the final meeting of the workshop) is held with each family unit separately to discuss their goals, share feedback, recommend follow-up resources, and generally address any issues remaining.

Each workshop averages approximately six families, comprising 8–13 parents and 13–15 children. There is one workshop per month. Workshops are held in one of the offices of the agency since videotape, kitchen, and play facilities are required. Each participant (adult and child) contributes a dish for a pot luck lunch both days.

Early in the design of the workshop, four ways of reaching divorcing families were selected: (1) helping (social service) agencies, (2) volunteers who would contribute from their own divorce experiences, (3) the news media, and (4) the legal system.

Helping Agencies

The authors held in-service meetings with the staffs from the agency where the workshops were held, the local welfare agency, the public health agency, and the juvenile court. At these meetings program content, philosophy, and experiences from each workshop were discussed. Other meetings were held with ministers and community support groups. Follow-up contacts were made with local physicians in family and pediatric practice and with social workers in private practice. Social work students were addressed in two university settings; in turn, they shared the content of the workshop within their respective field settings. Training workshops have been held for other professionals desiring to offer this program.

Volunteers

The authors recruited 50 volunteers (adults and children), who contributed 4,052 hours to the workshop. Volunteers acted as coleaders in the children's or parents' sections of the workshop and assisted in the writing and production of the *Pain Games II* videotape. Most volunteers were divorced parents or children from divorced families. The requirements for volunteers were as follows:

1. Experience of at least one major loss, either through divorce or death
2. Possession of a special skill or attribute (if an adult), for example, a member of Alcoholics Anonymous, a father who has custody of his children, an attorney, a mother without custody of her children, and so on
3. Nine years of age or older
4. Agreement to participate in a four-hour training session
5. Agreement to participate in two weekend workshops and to be available during both of these weekends essentially from 7:00 A.M. Saturday morning through 5:30 P.M. Sunday evening

There is a waiting list of volunteers, which is a tribute to the community. The use of such volunteers has added a remarkable richness to the program and has ensured the relevance of the workshop experience for divorcing families.

News Media

The third means of reaching the target group was using the news media to inform the metropolitan area public about the workshop and to address some of the community's concerns about divorce in an educational manner. The news media have consistently been tremendously supportive of the program—especially in highlighting the impact of divorce on children.

The authors made special efforts to reach radio programs that appealed to different audiences. The radio presentations have ranged from talk shows lasting from one to two hours to interviews lasting from 10 to 45 minutes. Several stations ran spots every four to six hours for periods ranging from a week to three months. Radio scheduling ranged from early morning through late evening and on weekends as well as weekdays. The authors were invited to appear on all the local television affiliates at least once.

Each interview held exciting possibilities. For example, one television station adapted materials from the children's section of the workshop and created a two-hour special on the feelings and needs of children in divorcing families. After this program, several high schools polled their students about the experience of divorce and began to deal with the special needs and feelings of students from divorced families. Journalists have continued to use the authors as sources in a variety of issues related to divorce (such as articles on the economic problems of single-parent families, aging alone, and so forth) and have attended not only this workshop but several other programs that the agency offers.[14]

Legal System

The authors approached the legal system (which more than any other deals directly with the conflicts of divorce) by contacting the county bar association. After reviewing the materials, the bar association invited the authors to address that group. Subsequent contacts were made with the district court judges to explore possible ways in which the agency, the authors, and the court system could work collaboratively.

Several plans emerged from this meeting. The first was to design a brochure that will speak to both children and parents about common feelings in divorce and that will offer some suggestions for handling the conflicts that occur. This brochure will be mailed to all parents receiving or making child support payments in this county. The authors agreed to consult with the court on request in divorcing family situations, an agreement that later highlighted the need for the hiring and training of special court personnel to work with such families. The bar association has continued to give the workshop active support, and attorneys regularly consult the authors about issues relating to divorce. Two members of the bar association have volunteered time in the workshop itself, and others have agreed to serve the program in an ongoing advisory capacity. This has proved valuable in helping participants understand the roles of the attorney and the judge in divorce proceedings.

SUMMARY

Many divorcing families do not seek help from social service agencies in dealing with the crisis of divorce. The children in these families thus receive little help in coping with their feelings. By using other helping agencies, volunteers, the news media, and the legal system, the authors were able to reach families that otherwise would not have sought assistance. In a workshop setting, these families were offered an opportunity to gain and integrate skills to cope with their grief. The importance of this for children in developing future life attachments appears to be significant.

Several questions—yet to be answered—have come out of the workshop experience: What are the identifiable strengths in children who have experienced divorce once? in children who have experienced divorce twice? What is the effect of families with a stepparent on children in terms of identity, sense of family history, and the like? Are children younger than six years of age able to integrate the skills taught in this format? Hopefully, future workshops will contribute the answers to these questions.

NOTES AND REFERENCES

1. *See,* for example, **Otto Pollak**, "The Broken Family," in **Nathan E. Cohen**, ed., *Social Work and Social Problems* (New York: National Association of Social Workers, 1967), pp. 321–329; **Richard B. Stuart**, "Operant-Interpersonal Treatment For Marital Discord," in **Tony Tripodi** et al., eds., *Social Workers at Work* (New York: Peacock, 1972), pp. 32–42.

2. **Carol H. Meyer**, "Direct Services in New and Old Contexts," in **Alfred J. Kahn**, ed., *Shaping the New Social Work* (New York: Columbia University Press, 1973), pp. 26–52.

3. The Bureaus of Vital Statistics of the states of Kansas and Missouri cite the following: In Kansas in 1976, one divorce occurred for every 1.9 marriages; in Missouri, the same statistic was one divorce for every 2.2 marriages.

4. One such example is International Parents Without Partners, 7910 Woodmont Avenue, Washington, D.C. 20014.

5. **Jan Fuller**, *Space: The Scrapbook of My Divorce* (New York: Fields Publishers, 1973).

6. The concept of the separation triangle is taken from **Becky Norris**, *New Beginnings for Singles* (Mission, Kans.: The Johnson County Mental Health Centers, 1975), p. 26.

7. **Elizabeth Kubler-Ross**, *On Death and Dying* (New York: Macmillan Publishing Co., 1969).

8. Op. cit., p. 26.

9. **Judith Anne Bridgeman and Beverly Ann Willis**, "Families in Transition— A Divorce Workshop," Unpublished paper accompanying videotape presented at the annual meeting of the American Group Psychotherapy Association, San Francisco, February 6, 1977.

10. **Richard A. Gardner**, *Psychotherapy with Children of Divorce* (New York: Aronson Press, 1976), pp. 20–33; **Gardner**, *The Parent's Book About Divorce* (Garden City, N.Y.: Doubleday & Co., 1977), pp. 53–81.

11. **Virginia Satir**, *Peoplemaking* (Palo Alto: Science and Behavior Books, 1972), pp. 30–112.

12. **Judith Anne Bridgeman and Beverly Ann Willis**, *Pain Games II.* Videotape produced by the Johnson County Mental Health Centers, Olathe, Kansas, 1976.

13. In brief, these games are as follows: "Don't Worry, I'll Be OK"—an emotional game of denial based on the family's attempt to cope with their feelings about the divorce. For example, parents often give false reassurance to their children to avoid facing their own and their children's pain. "The Messenger Game"—family members struggle with their anger about the divorce and the changes that have resulted from it by sending messages to each other through other family members rather than giving straightforward, honest information. "Disneyland Daddy"—the guilt and insecurity of parents are explored as they struggle to relate to their children after divorce. With the changed circumstances, it is tempting to fill visits with activities and gifts rather than talking together. "Cut Down"—focus is on the anger the two parents feel for each other and the difficulty in resolving their disappointment about their marriage. The anger they express, however, is directed toward the child. The game illustrates the devastation such communication wreaks on the child's identity. "I Spy"—illustrates the difficulty parents experience in letting go of the spouse roles; they attempt to hang on by spying on each other through the child. Like "Disneyland Daddy," this game has obvious payoffs in power for the child. "The Friendly Divorce"—examines the struggle divorcing families encounter while severing the loving bond. Each parent begins to look at him- or herself, experiences the loss of the other, and feels frightened about moving ahead independently. Each is tempted to reach out to the other, but the reality of their conflicts continue and appropriately interfere with their attempt to be friends. "I Wish"—a central task for the children to resolve. Children often reminisce about the good times in the family prior to the divorce and hope for reconciliation. Like their parents, to adjust to the divorce, they must recognize their parents' conflicts and the finality of the divorce. The authors have identified "Cut Down" and "The Friendly Divorce" as the two most destructive (to self-esteem and clear communication) Pain Games that families can play.

14. *See,* for example, "Helping the Family Cope with the Changes in Divorce," *The Kansas City Star* August 15, 1976, sec. c, pp. 1–3; "Divorce in Johnson County," *The Squire* February 17, 1977, Vol. 17, No. 3], p. 1; "How Families Cope with Divorce . . . 'Disneyland Daddy,' 'The Messenger,' and Other Pain Games," *The Daily News,* February 25, 1977, p. 3.

Psychiatric Social Work with the Aged: A New Look

HARRY B. SHOHAM

All too often the emotional problems of the aged are neglected, based on the belief that work with them is futile. However, experience with over 100 special problem patients in a geriatric center has led the author to the conclusion that traditional social work methods can be effective in dealing with the special psychological problems of the aged when modified to accommodate the individual's level of comprehension and functioning. It is unrealistic goals that create in the social worker a feeling of hopelessness, that nothing can be done. Rather than setting an abstract goal—such as "cure"—the worker must set a realistic, limited goal—the maximum possible restoration or preservation of function with minimal distress to patient, family, or community.[1]

The feeling that treating the psychological problems of the aged is a hopeless task is probably the major reason why a body of skills and knowledge in this area has been late in developing. A second reason is the prevailing negative attitude toward the aged in our society. It is important that social workers overcome in themselves the beliefs that emphasize youth and useful productivity as the ultimate good. If they do not do so, they may feel their efforts with the aged to be a questionable use of limited social resources.

This paper will reexamine traditional ways of looking at organic brain syndrome, anxiety, death and dying, depression, and delusions and paranoia in the aged. The author's viewpoint, rather than relating the treatment to the diagnosis, focuses on the subjective experience of the individual, with special emphasis on dealing with irrational behavior.

178

ORGANIC BRAIN SYNDROME

It is estimated that at least 50 percent of the geriatric population institutionalized in nursing homes and mental hospitals suffers from organic brain syndrome (OBS). A sizable number of the noninstitutionalized elderly —some estimate as many as 30 percent—have similar symptoms.[2] This condition is characterized by impairment of orientation, memory, and intellectual functioning, and is commonly termed senility. In its chronic form, OBS is assumed to be the result of irreversible, diffuse disturbance of cerebral tissue function.[3]

There is considerable evidence that OBS patients, like the rest of us, do not use the full brain capacity available to them. Much of their confusion and disorientation appears to be reaction formation to isolation and social neglect rather than a result of organic disease. A great deal of the memory loss that is supposedly merely a consequence of brain changes is quite selective and could represent purposeful withdrawal from a painful environment. Senility itself has been defined by some as a form of emotional breakdown in older people resulting from anxiety.[4] Studies seem to show that there is no one-to-one relationship between the degree of brain tissue deterioration as demonstrated by postmortem examination and the patient's functional history. All these factors would tend to point to the importance of influences other than brain damage on the level of functioning.

This should not be surprising. Individuals react differently to other organic conditions—blindness, for example. One individual will learn to function on a totally independent level, while another will become a helpless invalid. Likewise, in the case of two patients with the same degree of memory loss and disorientation, one will be fearful and anxiety-ridden, while the other will drift calmly through the day in a fog of unconcern. The level of functioning that patients with cognitive deficits achieve would seem to be strongly influenced by premorbid personality factors and characteristic lifetime modes of coping.[5] Moreover, psychiatric geriatric patients rarely present discrete syndromes. The typical patient has a clinical picture that is a combination of symptoms. Depression, paranoia, and anxiety states varying in proportion and degree are commonly combined with organicity.[6] It would seem, therefore, that a shift of emphasis from the currently conventional attempt to reorient the patient to reality is called for.[7] Rather, focus should be on the patient's priority problems, the anxiety or depression the patient is suffering.

Although he does not use it in its commonly accepted sense, the author prefers to use the admittedly provocative term *insight therapy* as an appropriate technique for working with OBS patients. This is done to counter the extremely prejudicial feeling that nothing can be done for these patients, that they are completely incapable of understanding and learning. It has been the writer's experience that OBS patients are capable of learning, albeit with great difficulty necessitating extreme patience and endless repetition. In dealing with severe learning disability, it follows that it is important for the worker to allocate his or her effort to those areas of most significance to the patient. For example, teaching a patient who gets into trouble by straying into other patients' rooms not to do this would be a matter of high priority.

"Insight therapy" is used here, not in terms of relating patients to objective reality but rather to their own reality, helping them to become aware of and deal with their feelings at their own levels of understanding. If a patient is racked with fears, depressed, and anxiety-ridden, that patient needs help in coping with these feelings, just as an oriented person does. This can be accomplished only when the worker develops the skill to look past the distortions of reality that tend to serve as distractions and learns to focus directly on the emotional experience of the patient.

It is interesting to note that confused patients are frequently quite adept at this form of insight, at relating on a feeling level. They readily react to the feeling tone of a communication. The most deteriorated patient, who is incapable of making an intelligible verbal response and seems completely unable to understand speech, can perhaps respond to a pat on the back with a receptive smile. That patient may never learn to identify the worker yet still be capable of achieving the insight that the worker is a friend. No one should be denied the attempt to establish human communication or the opportunity to receive help. If we are dedicated to the principle of keeping people alive, must we not also assume the responsibility of providing the opportunity for that life to be as meaningful and satisfying as possible?

ANXIETY

In the psychiatric textbooks, in every clinical disturbance, disordered psychological functioning is ultimately laid at the doorstep of anxiety. Even in patients with organic damage, anxiety owing to feelings of inadequacy is a prominent feature. Anxiety is triggered by stress, which depends not only on the nature of the event but also on the resources and coping mechanisms of the person.[8] The older patient is probably at the maximum point of stress in his or her own life and at the low point of available resources for coping. Environmental manipulation, by mustering all available resources, both physical and psychological, can help maximize coping potential.

Although dependency may be encouraged as one stage in the helping process, the final goal is independent functioning. In work with the aged, the definition of independent functioning must be modified to take into account the irreversible impairments that have occurred. "Independence" is not an absolute concept. An impaired person can learn to be independently mobile with a cane, crutches, a walker, or a wheelchair. Support services, such as Meals on Wheels, special transportation, visiting nurses, or home attendants, can help an individual function independently in the community.

Dependence on the worker can be a resource instead of an obstacle to help. It can be the crutch that enables a mentally impaired person to function in the community as opposed to a nursing home or help the anxiety-ridden patient to remain in the health-related facility as opposed to requiring skilled nursing care.[9] The following case history will serve as illustration:

> Mrs. S is a well-groomed 87-year-old woman in the health-related facility. An attractive woman, she had been a dependent housewife throughout her life and had outlived three husbands. Despite moderate OBS, she would function fairly well until some incident brought on an overwhelming anxiety attack that threw her into a near convulsive state. A frequent precipitating situation was her inability to find money that she thought she remembered having put away.

In recognition of her dependency needs, the worker focused on developing a dependent relationship with Mrs. S in which he would act as the surrogate parent. He informed her repeatedly that he was always available to take care of her. Overcoming her resistance, he took charge of her money, doling out to her only what she needed.

As an illustration of what the author means by relating to the feelings of OBS patients rather than to objective reality, it is interesting to note that although Mrs. S has developed a feeling of trust of and dependence on the worker, in her confusion, she is not quite aware of his identity. Upon leaving her, the worker frequently hears her comment to another confused resident who has inquired who he is, "I think he is my son-in-law." Nevertheless, with the crutch of a dependent relationship to sustain her, she has not had a single repetition of the anxiety attacks that had become a regular pattern in her life.

DEATH AND DYING

Death, being an ever present factor in the lives of the aged, can be a continual breeder of anxiety. Dying has been described as a process with many stages.[10] If a patient is at a stage in which he or she most needs to practice denial, this should be permitted. But if a patient has a need to communicate, the conspiracy of silence that can isolate him or her must be avoided.[11]

However, death frequently occurs suddenly and unexpectedly. Toward the end, many patients are in a comatose or delirious state and unaware that they are dying. It must be remembered that although work with the dying is a time-limited problem, the fact of death is a matter of universal concern in working with the aged. For the aged, it becomes increasingly difficult to continue to practice the denial we practice in our youth; it is so much a part of everyday life. Insufficient attention has been paid to the fact that it is late for the worker to become involved in the critical period when a person is dying. Much can be accomplished earlier to help the patient resolve feelings about death. This should be an important ongoing goal in working with all aged people.

First, it is important for workers to resolve their own feelings about death. Any discomfort they feel about the subject will be transmitted to the patient. Second, the patient should be encouraged to ventilate his or her feelings about death. Life review—reminiscing about the past—can be helpful in reaching some kind of accommodation with inevitability. Third, to keep a person from participating in the funeral services of friends and relatives is a denial of an aspect of living that should be followed in only the most extreme circumstances. For the institutionalized, an opportunity to visit dying friends can serve to alleviate some of their own fear of dying alone, friendless, and surrounded by strangers. Finally, the absolute sense of powerlessness is one anxiety-provoking aspect of dying. Helping a person make arrangements for his or her own funeral and burial is an important symbolic act that enhances a person's sense of power and affirms a person's independence.

DEPRESSION

It is estimated that about 50 percent of all psychiatric disturbances of the aged are functional. Considering the losses they have suffered, it is not surprising that the most common syndrome, both with and without organicity, is probably depressive illness.[12] But a depressive reaction is not the same illness for different individuals. It is a blanket term that encompasses many different kinds of subjective experience depending on the individual's personality, character structure, lifetime defenses, and patterns of coping with loss.[13]

The normal humane response to a depressed person is to provide sympathy, and the conventional therapeutic stance tends to follow this model. However, at times this approach can be inappropriate and even self-defeating. Only by developing the skill to understand the meaning the depression has for the individual can the worker tailor treatment goals and techniques for effective treatment.

Offering consolation and reassurance to a patient wallowing in self-pity can serve to feed into the feeling and reinforce it. The guilt-ridden patient who is full of self-blame for situations beyond his or her control needs help to externalize the guilt. Whereas a patient suffering from a sense of empti- ness and abandonment will benefit from active support and reassurance, a patient whose depression stems from internalized anger can become worse when praised or rewarded. Kind firmness to help the patient express anger outwardly rather than inwardly can help overcome the patient's feelings of no longer caring.[14]

This regimen may seem punitive, contrary to therapeutic concepts, and difficult for the worker to adopt. However, when the patient has a need to focus on something besides misery, it enables the worker to provide that focus. The expression of anger can be encouraged when it occurs and elicited by the skilled worker when it does not.[15]

> Mr. W, a 73-year-old resident in the HRF, suffers from muscular dystro- phy and consequently periodic depression. Because Mr. W loves to tinker, the worker encourages him to keep busy with projects. When Mr. W became particularly aware of his progressive deterioration and weak- ness, he sank into deep depression, withdrawing from his usual activi- ties and threatening suicide. He rejected sympathy and understanding because these could do nothing to change the reality facing him. Food was an important source of gratification for Mr. W, and he frequently complained about the quality of institutional meals. To shift Mr. W's focus from his own misery, the worker continually brought up the sub- ject of food. By a rational explanation of the difficulties of meal prepara- tion in a large institution, he provoked the patient to shift his anger from himself and his failing physique to the institution for not providing him with an adequately nourishing diet and to the worker for defending the institution.

Adult children frequently react to parents' chronic complaints as symptoms of depression. They have to be helped to understand that com- plaining is actually a sign of health. It signifies that the individual cares about her- or himself. It is when the individual stops complaining that the worker should become concerned. Depressive symptoms are not infre- quently a device used by disappointed parents to punish children for "aban- doning" them. The children, frequently guilt-ridden, need help to under- stand the true significance of the symptoms and the appropriate way to react to them.

> Mr. M is a 90-year-old patient in the skilled-nursing facility. Chronic arthritis and general weakness complicated by moderate OBS have caused him to curtail the work activities that lifelong had been his major source of interest. He is chronically depressed. When his only son visits

him, they become embroiled in a violent argument over the son's refusal to take Mr. M to live with him. After one such visit, Mr. M attempted to run to a high floor, shouting that he was going to jump out a window. The son, naturally concerned, called the worker and questioned the advisability of his continuing to visit his father since his visits seemed so disturbing to him. The worker pointed out to the son that the reason for his father's anger was that he wanted more of him, not less. Although the worker appreciated the impracticality of caring for the father at home, it was apparent that Mr. M refused to recognize that fact.

The worker was able to help the son to understand that refraining from visiting would serve to compound the patient's depression and that the son's visits were therapeutic in that they offered his father the needed opportunity to ventilate his anger, seemingly directed at the son, but in actuality at the situation in which he found himself. By helping the son understand the true meaning of his father's symptoms, the worker enabled him to cope with them and to react more appropriately.

DELUSIONS AND PARANOIA

The author has frequently been called on, in crisis situations, to resolve problems caused by irrational behavior stemming from delusions and paranoia. Delusions are conventionally defined as pathology and dismissed simply as symptomology that requires alleviation. It must be remembered, however, that irrational ideas are not impinged on the psyche mysteriously from without but are constructs of the patient's own mind. Instead of pathology, delusions can often be simple adaptive constructions.[16]

A patient, for example, complains bitterly to the author about her disgusting male neighbors who spy on her through her television set as she undresses. What a marvelous device this is to enable this crippled old woman to feel desirable enough to provoke men to watch her disrobe.

Sometimes the delusions are useful to the patient but troubling to those around him or her. Sometimes they can be disturbing to the patient as well. Although entering a patient's delusionary system is regarded by many as antitherapeutic and seen as reinforcing unreal thinking, working with the patient's feelings rather than against them can help resolve deep-rooted conflicts and enable the patient to relinquish maladaptive symptoms. Whatever the reality of the belief system, what the patient is feeling is undoubtedly real and should be the worker's focus of concern. The following can serve as illustration:

Mrs. E is a tiny, 94-year-old resident in the HRF who toddles freely about the institution, busying herself with the various therapies and recreation programs. Despite moderate confusion, she manages quite well except for occasional lapses. On one such occasion, she suddenly decided that her mother had just died, and she wanted permission to attend the funeral. Attempts to reason with her were futile. She insisted that she was 16 years old and, as such, was certainly mature enough to attend a funeral.

There was, of course, no way for her to attend a nonexistent funeral. However, the worker obtained a small stool for her to sit on. This enabled her to practice the Jewish mourning ritual, symbolically sitting close to the earth, in her room. The worker visited her daily, and they spoke of Mrs. E's memories of her mother and feelings about her death. It is interesting to note that despite Mrs. E's extreme confusion, she kept track of the passage of time, counting off the prescribed seven days of mourning accurately. The seventh day over, she relinquished the stool and ended her mourning. The following day, she resumed her former activities and never mentioned her mother's death again.

Delusions can best be understood as metaphorical expressions that, for one reason or another, the patient finds difficult to express directly. Bizarre accusations, for example, may be exaggerated distortions of real events—a metaphorical way of describing hostility the patient senses on the part of some caretaker.[17] A patient who complained irrationally that the room in which she was forced by the nursing staff to sleep was not her own was relating a great deal about her hidden feelings. She was indicating that she was unhappy about being where she was and that she was angry with the nursing staff at the way she was being treated. Insight therapy with this patient did not consist of reorienting her to her room. The obsessive delusion about her room was merely symptomatic of her real problem. Insight therapy consisted of helping her deal with her feelings of unhappiness at being in an institution and of helping her to achieve the understanding that the nurses were really concerned about her welfare. When her feelings were resolved, her delusion could clear up.

The ability to interpret delusions and respond to irrationality naturally and matter-of-factly is a skill not easily mastered. Our everyday language is saturated with idioms that we have learned to accept. Although the literal meaning is bizarre, we recognize as rational such statements as "he is a pain in the neck" or "she swallowed her pride." These are culturally accepted metaphors. However, to understand the metaphorical language of the delusional patient, a reorientation in listening is indicated. The first hurdle the worker must overcome is the conventional tendency to dismiss the entire message as simply "crazy talk." Then the worker must develop the skill to disregard the literal superstructure and concentrate on trying to understand the emotional content of the message. It means learning a foreign language that the patient has invented. By unveiling the metaphorical mask behind which the patient's feelings are shrouded, the worker can help the patient not only to become aware of his or her feelings, but also to try to understand and deal with them.

If it is difficult for professional social workers to learn to understand delusional behavior, it is much more difficult for the untrained. Family members and nonprofessional staff members in institutions frequently find themselves at a loss. There is a simple technique the writer has found most helpful to teach family, staff, and volunteers to react to irrationality. It consists of learning to insert the imaginary phrase *I feel like* in front of the patient's message. The patient's statement "I want to go home" is reinterpreted as "I feel like I want to go home." The appropriate response to "I want to go home" would be "This is your home." This is a response the patient would find difficult to accept. However, an appropriate response to "I feel like I want to go home" could be "You must miss your home." While not reflective of objective reality, this would be truly responsive to the patient's reality. It would enable the patient to ventilate his or her feelings and encourage continuation of the communication process. Unlike the abstract concept of attempting to relate to the patient's feelings, this is concrete and specific—a formula easily understood and readily applied.

CONCLUSION

The author does not pretend to present a definitive guide to psychotherapy with the aged. The author has merely attempted to share his thinking, resulting from analysis of his experiences, and hopefully to raise some provocative questions for further exploration.

If there is a central theme to this paper, it is for the worker to develop the skill to be able to identify people as individuals. We are so accustomed to categorizing and classifying that we sometimes tend to distort individuals to fit them into convenient compartments with appropriate labels. A label can, however, frequently mask more than it reveals. Whether the patient is diagnosed as suffering from an organic or functional illness, anxiety, depression, or paranoia, it is not the label—the diagnosis—but rather the meaning to the person—the feelings the patient is experiencing—that determines the nature of the treatment indicated.

A worker may feel insecure with this, asking: How can one be sure that one understands what an uncommunicative patient in the throes of depression is really feeling? How can one be sure that one's comprehension of the irrational patient is correct or that one is interpreting delusional metaphors accurately when these are disguised even from the patient? Absolute certainty as to another's psyche is too much to expect. The important objective is to respond in a way that touches some responsive chord in the patient and thereby keeps communication open. In the last analysis, the patient will let the worker know whether she or he is right or wrong.

Social workers are not all-powerful, and they must recognize that there are problems that do not offer satisfactory solutions. The concept of realistic, limited goals, however, means that some treatment plan is available for every situation. This does not necessarily mean that treatment will be successful, any more than for a younger population. But it does mean that no individual, no matter what his or her condition, need be given up entirely.

A radical change in the treatment of the psychiatric problems of the aged will occur only when society as a whole undergoes a significant change in its attitude toward the aged, when the aged are not stripped of every useful and respectable role function other than the role of the "sick patient." It is incumbent on social workers individually, in our agencies, and through our professional organizations to exert our influence to help effect that change.

NOTES AND REFERENCES

1. Group for the Advancement of Psychiatry, *Clinical Psychiatry* (New York: Science House, 1967).

2. **Carl Salzman, Bessel vander Kolk, and Richard Shader.** "Psychopharmacology and the Geriatric Patient," in Shader, ed., *Manual of Psychiatric Therapeutics* (Boston: Little, Brown & Co., 1975), pp. 171–184.

3. Group for Advancement of Psychiatry, op. cit.

4. **Muriel Oberleder**, "Emotional Breakdown in Elderly People," *Hospital and Community Psychiatry,* 20 (July 1969), pp. 191–196.

5. **S. H. Cath**, "Functional Disorders," in **Leopold Bellak and T. B. Karasu**, eds., *Geriatric Psychiatry* (New York: Grune & Stratton, 1976), p. 145.

6. **T. B. Karasu and C. M. Murkofsky**, "Psychopharmacology of the Elderly," in **Bellak and Karasu**, op. cit., p. 236.

7. **J. C. Folsom**, "Reality Orientation for the Elderly Mental Patient," *Journal of Geriatric Psychiatry,* 1 (Spring 1968), pp. 291–307.

8. **H. I. Lief**, "Anxiety Reaction," in **A. M. Freedman and H. I. Kaplan**, eds., *Comprehensive Textbook of Psychiatry* (Baltimore: Williams & Wilkins, 1967), pp. 857–870.

9. **A. I. Goldfarb**, "Patient-Doctor Relationship in Treatment of Aged Persons," *Geriatrics,* 19 (January 1964), pp. 18–23.

10. **Elizabeth Kubler-Ross,** *On Death and Dying* (New York: Macmillan Co., 1970).

11. **T. B. Karasu and Stuart Waltzman,** "Death and Dying in the Aged," in Bellak and Karasu, op. cit, pp. 247–278.

12. **E. W. Busse and Eric Pfeiffer,** eds., *Behavior and Adaptation in Late Life* (Boston: Little, Brown & Co., 1969).

13. Group for the Advancement of Psychiatry, op. cit.

14. **W. G. Crary and C. W. Johnson,** "Attitude Therapy in a Crisis-Intervention Program," *Hospital and Community Psychiatry,* 21 (May 1970), pp. 45–48.

15. **James Folsom and Geneva Folsom,** "Team Method of Treating Senility May Contain Seed for Medical Revolution," *Nursing Care,* 6 (December 1973), pp. 17–23.

16. **Leopold Bellak,** "Crisis Intervention in Geriatric Psychiatry," in Bellak and Karasu, op. cit., pp. 175–190.

17. Ibid.

Human Sexuality and the Institutionalized Elderly

LINDA K. FISHMAN

Social workers are employed in nursing homes to assess and meet medically related psychosocial needs of patients; however, patients' sexual needs are often ignored. The literature related to social work in nursing homes either does not mention sexual needs at all or mentions them only in passing, and the literature on sexuality and aging focuses mainly on the noninstitutionalized aged.[1] A base of scientific knowledge, understanding of values and attitudes, and self-awareness is a prerequisite for any social work intervention. After exploring some basic knowledge, attitudes, values, and myths about sexuality of the aged, this paper will provide suggestions regarding modes of intervention for sexual problems of nursing home patients.

FIVE AREAS OF CONCERN

Dr. Alex Comfort has stated, "Old folks stop having sex for exactly the same reasons they stop riding a bicycle: general infirmity, because somebody told them it looks ridiculous, or because they haven't got a bicycle."[2] He might also have added that they may have no place to ride a bicycle or may believe it is immoral to do so! Study of these five areas—infirmity and ability, fear of ridicule, lack of a partner, lack of privacy, and moral prohibitions—is essential to understanding sexuality and the geriatric nursing home population.

Infirmity and Ability

With age there is a general slowing of all physical and physiological processes, including sexual functioning. Slowing or decrease in intensity

189

does not mean cessation of functioning. Sexual interest and activity are present in the aged and can continue throughout life, even into the ninth decade.

Contrary to popular myths, interest in sex and the ability to perform sexually do not disappear in women after menopause. In fact, often interest in sex increases and inhibitions decrease when the fear of pregnancy is removed. The aging female is slower to respond to stimulation, has reduced duration of orgasm, and produces less vaginal lubrication. The latter is the most common functional problem for the elderly female and is ameliorated easily by the use of lubricating and hormonal creams.

As the male ages, he requires more direct stimulation and a longer period of stimulation to achieve an erection and reach orgasm. Ejaculation lacks the intensity of force and the duration of earlier years. These diminutions of sexual function are usually less serious than the psychological reactions, concerns, and preoccupations about them, which can produce more serious problems, including impotence. If the male is aware that these changes are normal and accepts them, he should have no problem remaining active sexually.

Sexuality and sexual behavior involve a great deal more than merely intercourse culminating in orgasm. Sexual activity can be satisfying without being exclusively genital and orgasmic. It involves all sorts of warm, touching, tender, caring, gentle behaviors. With decreased emphasis on purely genital sex, the aged can develop sexual behavior patterns that are meaningful and satisfying.

Intensity, rapidity, and duration of anatomical and physiological sexual responses are reduced with age. However, the most important factor in maintaining sexual functioning among the aged is regularity of sexual activity. Those who have been most active sexually on a regular and continuous basis are those most likely to maintain sexual functioning in their later years. Nursing home patients are not only elderly but also suffer from illnesses that necessitate skilled nursing care; however, physical illness does not preclude sexual interest or ability to function sexually. The elderly nursing home patient can remain sexually active within the limits of his or her physical ability.

Physical therapy, restorative nursing, occupational therapy, and activities programs in nursing homes are aimed at improving or maintaining levels of physical functioning. Remotivation therapy, reality-orientation programs, activities, and occupational therapy provide stimulation to improve and maintain mental functioning. These and other therapeutic programs in skilled nursing facilities are based on the simple principle applicable to functioning at any age: "Use it or lose it." This principle applies to sexuality as well; yet formal programs aimed at preserving sexual functioning for nursing home patients are essentially nonexistent.

Fear of Ridicule

Human beings are social beings and require the acceptance and approbation of others. Discomfort with sexuality often is manifested in nervous laughter and joking, most typically in the "dirty" joke. Such jokes about the aged either focus on reduced sexual ability or on sexual interest that is deemed inappropriate.

Men are allowed an interest in sex until later in life than women and, within our culture, remain sexually attractive until an older age. While male sexual ability is at its peak in the late teens, adolescence is not viewed as the most attractive age for a man. Men in our society are valued in terms of their careers and earning capacities, which tend to peak in the fourth to fifth decade. Lines are thought to give "character" to the aging male face, and graying temples are considered distinguished. Prominent men are accepted and even applauded when they marry women 20, 30, and even 40 years younger than they. At about age 60, men begin to lose this charm, and jokes develop about the "dirty old man" who remains interested but cannot function sexually.

A "double standard of aging" exists in our culture.[3] The female becomes a subject of ridicule much earlier in life and is treated even more unfairly than the male with regard to aging. Women still are viewed in our society as having sexuality primarily in relation to youthful attractiveness and to reproduction. Both the ornamental and procreative utility of a woman begin to diminish in the mid-to late thirties. At this midpoint in life, the female already is seen as aging, although she really is at the peak of sexuality in her late thirties. The added "character" of the lines in a man's face are merely wrinkles on a woman's face.

By the time a woman reaches the age when she is likely to enter a nursing home, she has learned that she is no longer a sex object in our society. Her body is defined as unattractive and her sexuality as inappropriate. We have no concomitant jokes about the "dirty old woman" because the possibility of sexuality for an elderly woman is almost unthinkable. Fear of ridicule is a powerful deterrent to expression of sexual interest among aging women. In fact, there are strong negative sanctions against such behavior.[4]

Lack of a Partner

Among nursing home patients in the United States, "sixty-three per cent are widowed; 22 per cent never married; about 5 per cent are divorced; and only 10 per cent are married."[5] Most of the married patients are male, and there is a ratio of three women to each man within the nursing home population.[6] Among single persons over age 60, either within or outside institutions, the female to male ratio is 6:1. The number of married couples residing in nursing homes is an exceedingly small percentage of the total population.

Not only in numbers but also in options available for expression of sexuality, the male without a partner is at a definite advantage. While no statistics are available, it is likely that masturbation is the most prevalent form of sexual behavior among nursing home patients. In one of the very few studies of sexuality in nursing homes, masturbation provoked the most "discomfort, embarrassment, and denial."[7] The male patient is more likely to have had previous masturbatory experience, and masturbation is a more acceptable behavior for males than for females. Sex therapy with younger preorgasmic women often includes the granting of permission to masturbate and the teaching of techniques for masturbation. Women of older generations may have neither permission for masturbation nor knowledge of masturbatory techniques. They are treated similarly to the cerebral palsied and others who are congenitally handicapped in that it is assumed they are not interested in such sex education or that it is too delicate a subject to discuss with them.[8] Should the female nursing home patient be "caught" masturbating, the sanctions against her are greater than for the male. Dr. Victor Kassel states: "The attitude is that a masturbating elderly woman is a vile, filthy, reprehensible undesirable who contaminates the wholesome living conditions of nice old ladies."[9]

Intercourse, masturbation, and other forms of sexual activity leading to orgasm are valuable for release of tensions and reduction of anxiety. Sexual interaction also is part of meaningful relationships and produces feelings of worth in individuals. The needs for warmth, closeness, and touching are lifelong and are unmet for many nursing home patients without partners. Frequently elderly patients will be found in bed together, engaging in no explicitly sexual behavior but only seeking warmth and closeness to another human being.

Lack of Privacy

Appropriate sexual behavior in our culture is defined as private behavior involving only the participants. At various points in the life cycle, individuals may have no private place for sexual activity and are concerned about being "caught in the act." Adolescents residing in their parents' homes have much of their early sexual experiences in cars and vans. Parents of young children at one time or another find their sexual activities interrupted by a toddler who wanders into their room. As children mature, learn to knock before entering their parents' room, and eventually leave home, couples are ensured more privacy for sexual activity as they age. While residing in his or her own household, the elderly person has enjoyed 10 to 30 or more years of such privacy before entering a nursing home and even more dramatically relinquishing privacy.

Patients' rights are included among the Medicare and Medicaid regulations for providers of skilled nursing care. Among these rights is the assurance of privacy for visits by one's spouse. If both are inpatients, they must be permitted to share a room if they desire to do so, unless this is medically contraindicated. No such privacy is mandated for individuals who are not married. There are few private rooms in most nursing homes; therefore, the majority of patients have one or more roommates and little privacy. Lacking a private place for sex and also being either confused and/or lacking social awareness or inhibitions, nursing home patients may masturbate or engage in stroking another patient's genitals in public areas of the nursing home that are totally inappropriate places for such activity. Such behavior in a nursing home lobby or lounge is offensive to other patients, their families, other visitors, and members of the staff. Most frequently this behavior is totally forbidden rather than channeled to a more appropriate alternate area of the nursing home.

Personnel generally are lax about observing the simple courtesy of knocking before entering a patient's room, which cannot be locked because of fire safety regulations. Some skilled nursing facilities provide a "petting" room for consenting patients with the assurance that no one will enter without knocking first. While no research data are available, patients may refrain from using these rooms because of the embarrassment of having others aware of what they may be doing in them.

The lack of an adequate environment for sex also includes the room's furnishings. Nursing home beds are single beds. Most patients suffer from some physical handicap or general loss of agility that may make sexual activity between two patients on a single bed almost impossible.

Environmental modification recently has gained renewed respect as an important social work technique.[10] In one instance, environmental modification involved arranging a suitable environment for sex for a newly married couple in their twenties, both severely disabled and residing together in a nursing home. The facility had provided a room for them to share, but it took some convincing before their single beds were wired together. Finally, they were provided with a "Do Not Disturb" sign for their door. While this paper deals mainly with the geriatric nursing home population, approximately five percent of nursing home patients are 55 years old or younger.[11] They fare no better than the geriatric population regarding their sexual needs.

Moral Prohibitions

Members of older generations tend to be more conservative and traditional in their moral values regarding sex. They usually are also more religious and thus place more emphasis on religious prohibitions against extramarital sex. The sexual revolution has not influenced them as much as it has younger generations. Negative moral judgments may come not only from peers and staff but also from their children, who are often unable to accept their elderly parents' sexuality.

Living together without benefit of legal marriage is becoming more frequent among senior citizens. The Social Security system penalizes many couples by lowering their combined Social Security income after a marriage late in life. Economic considerations historically have been important to the institution of marriage and can discourage as well as encourage it. Sometimes the middle generation finds itself in the position of defending the morality of marriage to both their parents and their children who are living together without benefit of marriage. Morality remains a strong influence in the older age groups and may precipitate serious feelings of guilt and anxiety.

SOCIAL WORK INTERVENTION

Social work intervention to enhance the sexual functioning of the geriatric nursing home patient may take several forms. These will be covered following a discussion of the preparation required by social workers wishing to deal with this problem area.

Preparation for Intervention

The publication of *Human Sexual Response* by Masters and Johnson in 1966 is a milestone marking the beginnings of scientific knowledge about human sexuality.[12] Descriptions of the various sexual dysfunctions and modalities for treating them were published by Masters and Johnson in *Human Sexual Inadequacy* in 1970.[13]

Most health professionals in practice today had little or no content on human sexuality included in their formal education, since courses in human sexuality are only now beginning to be part of the curricula in medical schools and schools of social work. An increasing number of workshops or short continuing education courses are being developed by medical schools, schools of social work, and gerontology institutes in order not only to present factual material but also to assist the professional in examining his or her own attitudes and values regarding sexuality and in developing the self-awareness required to work in this area.

In California after January 1, 1978, all persons seeking or renewing licenses to practice clinical social work, marriage and family counseling, or psychology must show evidence of completion of training in human sexuality. At the time of this writing, however, there is neither certification nor licensure of sex therapists. It is therefore suggested that the social worker seek training and/or consultation from a sex therapist who is affiliated with an institution of higher education or a known medical institution.

Finally, the social worker should understand the difference between sex counseling and sex therapy. The social worker in the nursing home setting can function adequately as a sex counselor with no further training beyond some continuing education courses or workshops to gain basic knowledge in human sexuality. Sex counseling mainly involves taking a sex history, assessing the basic nature of the problem, and providing help via acceptance of feelings and attitudes, educational information, and the like. It is estimated that approximately 70 percent of patients who seek assistance at a sex dysfunction clinic can be helped by such simple sex counseling techniques as providing permission or validation, offering limited information or education, and making simple specific suggestions. Sex therapy involves a much more intensive therapeutic program using specialized techniques. Training as a sex therapist takes about six months. Such intensive training is not necessary in order to work with most problems of sexuality in nursing homes.

Types of Intervention

Social work intervention to meet the sexual needs of geriatric nursing home patients can take six forms:

1. Casework services can provide an accepting, nonjudgmental, and understanding approach to solving the nursing home patient's sexual problems and concerns. Such problems can be approached using whichever basic therapeutic models and theories the worker generally utilizes. It has been suggested that sexual counseling for the aged can best be introduced within the context of presenting interpersonal problems.[14]

2. Group work services may help patients to deal with common problems related to sexuality and aging in a nursing home setting. The author has observed group therapy sessions with patients in their seventies and eighties, all with severe organic brain syndromes and/or chronic serious psychiatric disorders, talking about their problems of sexuality. At another skilled nursing facility, a discussion group on sexuality was formed for young patients with severe physical disabilities, such as muscular dystrophy, multiple sclerosis, cerebral palsy, and spinal cord injuries. Groups also can be used to provide sex education and information to nursing home patients.

3. Supervision of social work designees in nursing home settings provides an opportunity to assist persons with BSWs or even less formal

education to help patients with sexual problems. In the author's experience, individuals with BSWs have been quite successful in working with patients exhibiting sexually aggressive behavior. Acceptance of sexuality as natural for the aged and comfort in discussing sexual material is perhaps more important for the helping person than the level of education that person possesses.

4. In-service training programs provide an excellent opportunity for the social worker to educate nursing personnel and other staff members of such facilities to help them deal with their own attitudes toward and feelings about the sexuality of their patients.

5. Consultation can be provided to assist the nursing home administrator, medical director, and director of nursing and thus to influence patient care policies. Frequently these individuals will bring sex-related problems to the attention of the social worker. Even when they do not raise such questions, the problems may still be present. Good consultation in a nursing home or any other setting involves not only answering the consultees' questions but helping them to expand their awareness and ask new questions as well.

6. Research must be undertaken by social workers to identify and understand better the sexual needs and problems of nursing home patients. Federal regulations governing the use of human subjects in research present a real problem in this area. In one study only 50 percent of nursing home patients who were approached agreed to be interviewed about sex.[15]

SUMMARY

Currently there is renewed public interest in nursing homes and their obligation to provide high-quality care. Greater emphasis is being placed not only on the right of patients to a clean and safe environment and the highest standards of professional care but also on the right to respect, privacy, dignity, and recognition of the entire range of human needs. The right to express and meet sexual needs must be recognized as a part of this. Social work can play an important role in recognizing, understanding, and meeting the sexual needs of the nursing home patient.

NOTES AND REFERENCES

1. *See,* for example, **Michael J. Austin and Jordan I. Kosberg,** "Nursing Home Decision Makers and the Social Service Needs of Residents," *Social Work in Health Care,* 1 (Summer 1976), pp. 447–456; **Austin and Kosberg,** "Social Service Programming in Nursing Homes," *Health and Social Work,* 1 (August 1976), pp. 41–57;

Lou Ann B. Jorgensen and Robert L. Kane, "Social Work in the Nursing Home: A Need for an Opportunity," *Social Work in Health Care,* 1 (Summer 1976), pp. 471–482; Kosberg, "The Nursing Home: A Social Work Paradox," *Social Work,* 18 (March 1973), pp. 104–110; Lu Pearman and Jean Searles, "Unmet Social Service Needs in Skilled Nursing Facilities: Documentation for Action," *Social Work in Health Care,* 1 (Summer 1976), pp. 457–470; Rose Locker, "Elderly Couples and the Institution," *Social Work,* 21 (March 1976), pp. 149–150; Eugene Baron, "When You're Old, Money is Honey," *Social Work,* 20 (May 1975), pp. 230–232; Irene Long, "Human Sexuality and Aging," *Social Casework,* 57 (April 1976), pp. 237–244; Faye Sander, "Aspects of Sexual Counseling with the Aged," *Social Casework,* 57 (October 1976), pp. 504–510.

2. Alex Comfort, Panel Discussion, American Geriatrics Society, Toronto, Ontario, 1974.

3. *See* Susan Sontag, "The Double Standard of Aging," *Saturday Review of Society,* 55 (September 23, 1972), pp. 208, 211, 221–223.

4. Victor Kassel, "Sex in Nursing Homes," *Medical Aspects of Human Sexuality,* 10 (March 1976), p. 130.

5. U.S., Congress, Senate, Subcommittee on Long-Term Care of the Special Committee on Aging, *Nursing Home Care in the United States: Failure in Public Policy—Introductory Report,* 93rd Cong., 2d Sess., December 1974, Rep. 93–1420, p. 16.

6. Ibid.

7. Mona Wasow and Martin B. Loeb, "Sexuality in Nursing Homes," in Irene Mortenson Burnside, ed., *Aging and Sexuality* (Los Angeles: University of Southern California Press, 1975), p. 38.

8. Robert C. Geiger and Susan E. Knight, "Sexuality of People with Cerebral Palsy," *Medical Aspects of Human Sexuality,* 9 (April 1975), p. 218.

9. Kassel, op. cit., p. 130.

10. *See* Richard M. Grinnell, Jr., and Nancy S. Kyte, "Environmental Modification: A Study," *Social Work,* 20 (July 1975), pp. 313–318.

11. Memorandum from Chief, Long-Term Care Statistics Branch, Division of Health Resources Utilization Statistics, National Center for Health Statistics, Health Resources Administration, Public Health Service, U.S. Department of Health, Education, and Welfare, Table H, March 1975.

12. William H. Masters and Virginia E. Johnson, *Human Sexual Response* (Boston: Little, Brown, & Co., 1966).

13. William H. Masters and Virginia E. Johnson, *Human Sexual Inadequacy* (Boston: Little, Brown, & Co., 1970).

14. Sander, op. cit., p. 510.

15. Wasow and Loeb, op. cit., p. 38.

Enhancing Sexuality: A Humanistic Approach to the Mastectomee

JOANNE E. MANTELL AND CECILY GREEN

In the last decade, increased public disclosure of personal ordeals with cancer has advanced the development of tertiary modes of cancer prevention. A steady stream of information, intended to increase awareness and knowledge of cancer, has flowed from the medical and lay press. Although intervention has traditionally focused on early detection and treatment, the importance of the psychosocial rehabilitation of cancer patients is being more widely recognized by the medical establishment. This trend may be attributed in part to recent medical advances that prolong the lives of cancer patients as well as to greater consumer demand for humanistic care in our increasingly technological and bureaucratic health care system.

Since cancer is now considered to be a chronic rather than an acute disease with a death trajectory, attention needs to be directed not only to living with the disorder, but to maintaining and enhancing the quality of that life. Death education seminars for professionals and the public have gained widespread popularity. Unfortunately, the sexual concerns of the cancer patient still provoke professional resistance.[1] Despite present-day liberalized attitudes and knowledge about sex, the medical community is generally inattentive to the sexual needs of the chronically ill and disabled. The conservatism of health professionals, as well as their reluctance to confront these issues directly, may hamper their ability to deal with the sexuality of cancer patients.[2]

Although the consequences of such professional behavior have serious

198

ramifications for all cancer patients, women who have undergone a mastectomy are especially vulnerable because of our culture's preoccupation with the sexual connotation of the breast. To many women, a mastectomy means not only the surgical excision of a breast, but loss of femininity, physical attractiveness, and sexual desirability. Not only does a woman need to deal with an altered sense of self, she has to learn to cope differently with her network of supportive relationships.

Sexual stereotypes for both men and women are embedded in our value system. There appears, however, to be a sex differential with regard to these stereotypes. While men are typically evaluated on the basis of their role performance, women are often evaluated aesthetically. As a result of the emphasis on physical attributes, a woman who does not fit the ideal may perceive herself as stigmatized.

Women's obsession with having bodies that are congruent with the ideal has promoted the popularity of breast reconstruction. Although such surgery modifies the body's facade, a distorted perception of body-image may remain. "Expecting a surgical procedure to produce a change in another's behavior is a magical expectation which cannot be satisfied by surgery."[3] Rather, a woman's desire for breast reconstruction should be self-motivated if positive changes in body-image are to occur.

THEORETICAL BACKGROUND

Sexuality incorporates not only the physical acts of sex, but also such interpersonal and intrapsychic phenomena as environmental conditioning, social learning, cognitive development, behavioral patterns, psychological traits, and sex-object preference.[4] Sexuality provides a means of expressing affection and communicating with others. As Kirkendall states, "sex in its most satisfying form is more a matter of interpersonal relationships than of simple physical experience."[5]

In addition, sexuality encompasses components of self-concept and body-image. Although self-concept has been used to describe a wide range of cognitive constructs, it often refers specifically to self-evaluative elements of behavior, including attitudinal and emotional concomitants, subsumed under the labels self-esteem, self-regard, self-worth, and self-acceptance.[6] The authors' definition stems from the symbolic interactionist perspective, which views self-concept as a reflexive behavioral process conditioned and reinforced by the attitudes and appraisal of others.

Body-image, which is an integral part of self-concept, involves an individual's mental, emotional, and symbolic representation of the body.[7] Perception of body experience is based on objective physical attributes as well as personal interpretations of these external properties.[8] Cognitive dissonance may result from incongruence between actual and ideal-body image. This discrepancy may produce a distorted concept of body-self and lead to increased anxiety, lowered self-esteem, and impaired social and sexual interactions.

THE PSYCHOSEXUAL WORLD OF THE MASTECTOMEE

Critical to effective rehabilitation is the manner in which individuals respond to permanent physical disfigurement or impairment. The anatomical change caused by a mastectomy can interfere with a woman's judgment of herself and can preclude successful postoperative adjustment. When a woman realizes that she no longer possesses a positively valued body part, she may experience a loss of self-esteem. Consequently, grief for the missing breast may need to be expressed before adjustment to disfigurement can occur and a sense of worth be restored.[9] In this respect, it is desirable for a woman to express herself sexually in whatever manner physically possible soon after surgery.

Acknowledgment of the woman as a sexual being by those she encounters in the hospital—professional helpers, sexual partner, and family—can contribute to reducing anxiety. "Recognition by hospital staff that desire for sexual contact with one's partner is appropriate for the sick as well as the healthy may help relieve tensions not only in patients but also in their spouses."[10] Since a woman is emotionally vulnerable in the postsurgical period, physical contact can be an effective measure to counteract her threatened self-esteem. Touching, tenderness, and genuine warmth are especially important for sensory and emotional stimulation. Sexual partners can be physically affectionate, stroking their mates and making ribald remarks. Such activity may be a better prescription for the woman's recovery than other therapeutic efforts. Nurses can encourage patients to groom themselves and wear attractive lingerie rather than drab institutional garb.

The psychological effects of mastectomy can interfere with interpersonal relationships. Communication may be inhibited and the equilibrium of the family unit and other social relationships disrupted, to the extent that usual patterns of human interaction are curtailed. A woman's reaction to her own body becomes a model for others' attitudes toward her. A woman who feels comfortable with her new body-image will perceive herself as acceptable and sexually appealing, and she will communicate this self-confidence to others. In contrast, aversion to the sight of a mutilated body and fear of rejection can impair sexual responsiveness.[11] Removal of a breast may be interpreted as a loss of sexuality. In extreme cases, depression may ensue. For example, women who prior to mastectomy boast of having a youthful figure suitable for a bikini may be reluctant to be seen in public after surgery.

Even women who have not internalized the prevailing cultural attitude of the breast as a sex symbol are threatened by their perceived asexuality. Loss of feminine identity may be viewed as an emotional menopause, an embarkation toward a "career of androgyny." Consequently, if a woman does not alter her perception of body-image, she may inhibit her sexual expression.

Once a mastectomee has considered the possibility of metastases and the threat of premature death, she is free to concentrate on the quality of her life. A major source of anxiety stems from fear of rejection by a sexual partner. In some cases the fear is a reality, in others, a fantasy. For some women, anticipatory rejection is so overwhelming that they avoid new social relationships and sexual activity or, in the extreme, withdraw from existing relationships. The fear is not imaginary if a sexual partner is turned off at the thought of touching a disfigured body. Nevertheless, sexual unresponsiveness may be precipitated by this expectation.

Apprehension about ability to satisfy a partner may decrease some women's interest in sex. Preoccupation with performance can also interfere with sexual gratification. Anxiety may result from a woman's expectations of failure, which can be mitigated only by changing both parties' perceptions of and attitudes about their sexual responsibilities.

At the same time, it is important to remember that sexual adjustment to disability is often based on the quality of one's prior sex life.[12] A loving and understanding partner is an essential ingredient for continued sexual satisfaction and happiness. Women who have always had warm, nurturant relationships may only experience minor changes in sexual activity following surgery. In contrast, the impact may be severe when sexually incompatible relationships existed prior to surgery.

IMPACT ON THE SEXUAL PARTNER

Although a woman is the target of the surgical assault, sexual functioning can be considered within an interactional context rather than from her singular perspective. Since partners are integrally involved in a woman's concept of sexuality, they often express concerns of equal magnitude. Lack of tact and sensitivity can contribute to a woman's problems by reinforcing her feeling of being a sexually undesirable love object.

Partners are often hesitant to resume sexual activity for fear of hurting the woman. There is concern that lovemaking may cause further injury or complications, such as pain or opening of the incision. Fear of contagion can also lead to impaired sexual interaction since physical contact may be avoided. It is interesting to note that in the late nineteenth century, oral-genital stimulation was thought to cause cancer.[13] In addition, because the surgical site is sensitive, partners often seek to protect the traumatized area.

Some partners are discomfited by their initial view of the incision, the flat or concave chest. The shock of this mutilation may be so startling that there is an aversive reaction. Scarring, particularly after radical mastectomy, can be frightening, and the sudden reality of a less-than-perfect body, traumatic. A partner's verbal acknowledgment of ambivalence toward the scar and willingness to explore these feelings with the woman can accelerate both parties' acceptance of the altered body-image.

Because some women hesitate to examine the surgical site and the remaining breast for detection of new disease, partners can be supportive by sharing the responsibility for monthly breast examinations. In addition to sensual stimulation, such activity can communicate the partner's acceptance of the woman rather than his emotional neutrality toward or rejection of her, and thus enhance her sense of self-esteem.

New daily living habits may be adopted because of changes in body form and function. Postsurgical lymphedema, which often requires a woman to elevate her swollen arm on a pillow, may necessitate reversing her place in bed. Women may choose to wear a sleeping bra to restore their sense of balance and intactness as sexual partners. When breast play has been an integral part of the sexual experience, the partner can add new areas for erotic stimulation. Experimentation with coital positions may also be necessary to maximize comfort. If the rationale for these changes is explained, a sexual partner will not perceive them as barriers to sexual advances. At the same time, a woman may interpret her partner's hesitancy about initiating sexual activity as a confirmation of her unworthiness and sexual undesirability. Thus, candid dialogue, in which both parties share their sexual expectations, conflicting emotions, and uncertainties, is essential for resolving misconceptions, providing an atmosphere of reassurance, and facilitating a growing intimacy.

THE HEALTH PRACTITIONER'S PERSPECTIVE

Although responsibility for sexual problems has traditionally been relegated to the medical sphere, health personnel, including physicians, generally are unable to treat their mastectomy patients' sexual problems because of inadequate preparation in their professional training.[14] In addition, most health professionals have not dealt fully with their own sexuality. Incomplete knowledge about human sexual responses and personal awkwardness and discomfort have caused sexual issues to be devalued or avoided. Approaching sexual matters with patients can be threatening when vulnerability to their own personal experiences is awakened.[15] At the same time, some patients are reluctant to confide for fear of adverse judgment or condemnation. Consequently, a conspiracy of silence is often maintained.

Need for Sex Education

Greater awareness of iatrogenic sexual dysfunction on the part of the health practitioner is needed. Before professionals can realistically be expected to assist women with the emotional turmoil induced by mastectomy, skill, competence, and sophistication in human sexuality are required. In addition, while facilitating an atmosphere of permissiveness, professionals who convey comfort with their own sexuality can serve as role models for patients and help put them at ease. Nonthreatening self-disclosure will not only encourage greater candor, but will help relieve the burden of patients' self-imposed inhibitions.

Professionals need to resolve their own anxieties about human sexuality before they can be effective helpers.[16] Education in sexuality is essential for equipping medical personnel with the information, attitudes, and clinical skills required for an integrative learning experience. The content for any human sexuality curriculum should include treating sexual dysfunction in the acutely and chronically ill, the unabled, and the disfigured as well as in the able-bodied. Emphasis on prevention of sexual dysfunction is also appropriate. Various techniques can be used to accomplish these tasks, including small-group discussion, role-playing, desensitization-resensitization, and audiovisual aids.[17] Unless professionals are provided with an adequate education in sexuality, they will continue to be blinded to patients' sexual problems and thus perpetuate the pervasive inadequacy that is characteristic of the medical model.

SOCIAL WORK'S CONTRIBUTION

Since responsibility for patients' sexual well-being has not been assumed by the medical profession, social workers can make a contribution to patient care by considering this as being within their legitimate domain. With their skills and training in psychosocial diagnosis and assessment, social workers are especially well equipped to play an instrumental role in sexual counseling. Although some social workers are already engaged in this activity, the authors advocate such counseling as integral to social work practice in the health care field. Two avenues of therapeutic assistance that are not mutually exclusive are the prevention and the treatment of psychosexual repercussions of medical problems. The nature of the strategy selected, however, needs to be attuned to the patient's needs.

Evaluation of the sexual implications of a mastectomy for both the woman and her partner is essential. Ideally, counseling should be initiated immediately following diagnosis and prior to surgery. Since many women will not directly confront such issues, it is imperative that social workers assess a patient's emotional status before determining the extent of trauma.

Concerns of the partner need to be addressed in relation to their effects on the sexual relationship. Adjustment to mastectomy is typically affected by the following:

1. Sociodemographic factors
2. Lifestyle before mastectomy
3. Participation in social activities
4. Extent of social network
5. Quality of intimate relationships
6. Psychological well-being and sense of self-esteem
7. Degree of narcissistic investment in the breast and body-image
8. Sexual behavior prior to surgery
9. Congruence between actual and ideal sexual expectations
10. Orientation toward performance as a sexual goal

The stresses of dealing with cancer, whether they stem from the shock of diagnosis, treatment effects, or role adaptation, need to be confronted before specific sex-intervention techniques are explored. For example, during initial conferences, meditation, positive imagery, and progressive relaxation can be introduced and demonstrated for anxiety reduction.

Postoperative Therapeutic Assistance

There is an immediate need for therapeutic assistance in the postoperative setting. Hospital-based social workers can engage in a variety of effective interventions to enhance a mastectomee's sexuality, including the following:

1. *Attendance to cosmetic needs*

a. A Reach to Recovery visit can be ordered through the local American Cancer Society unit. In this program, a medically stabilized mastectomy veteran visits women who have recently had a breast amputated. The visitor serves as an understanding, sensitive listener, sharing only that part of her experience that is pertinent to effecting the patient's recovery. The new mastectomee is presented with a dacron-filled temporary prosthesis that can be worn until her surgeon approves the purchase of a permanent one. Information is provided about the various types of prosthetic devices and bathing suits suited to the mastectomee. In addition, patients are given a booklet dealing with the emotional issues of mastectomy as well as practical suggestions for postsurgical rehabilitation, for example, illustrated exercises to restore physical functioning.

b. It is especially important that patients leave the hospital premises with at least a facade of femininity. If a Reach to Recovery visit is not possible, suggestions for fashioning a temporary prosthesis should be offered. A temporary prosthesis can be constructed from any soft material that, when inserted in a bra cup, will not put any weight on the newly excised area, such as cotton filling from a sanitary napkin, wadded nylon hose, or facial tissue.

2. *Provision for psychological support*

a. In addition to individual counseling, group counseling can be beneficial. Recognition that other women share the same confusion, distress, and pain is especially supportive and may help decrease feelings of uniqueness and isolation. Themes for group discussions might include feelings of bodily assault, fears of disease recurrence and premature death, problems of emotional adjustment to disfigurement, and the impact of mastectomy on a woman's social network. The therapeutic benefits of group support will hopefully include earlier confrontation and resolution of painful emotions as well as increased communication with significant others.

b. If the sponsorship of such groups is not practical, the availability of mastectomy consciousness-raising groups in the community can be investigated.

Community-Based Support Services

The immediate effects of diagnosis and initial treatment present difficulties but are less troublesome compared to those faced months after hospital discharge. Community-based support services are desirable for long-term adjustment to mastectomy.

The first issue for professionals to address is the woman's need to become acquainted with her new body contours. Resistance to looking at or touching the surgical site is common. Reconciliation of the new with the old familiar self is essential for effective interaction with others. In addition to encouraging a patient to fantasize about her new physical appearance, a social worker can offer to be present with the woman during the initial "unveiling." Weeping should not be discouraged, since it constitutes mourning for the lost breast. Women who struggle for self-control often reinforce their denial and only prolong the pain that must eventually be confronted. Although a woman may be reluctant to expose her vulnerability before family and friends for fear of causing them distress, the charade she plays may be costly in terms of emotional energy expended—energy that can be better directed toward the healing process. A sensitive social worker can cope with the resulting countertransference as well as uncover a woman's subtle and often covert concerns. Acknowledging feelings of sadness, anger, and rage may not only facilitate their dissipation but enhance sexual communication with a partner.

A second role for a community-based social worker is teaching the mastectomee a range of experiential exercises geared to restoring her confidence as a sexual being. A variety of individual and group techniques can be suggested, but a combination will be most effective. Some of these exercises are best done in the nude.

Exercises to be done in private include the following:

1. *Water play.* Water play can be used to increase sensory discrimination, stimulate sexual arousal, and release sexual tension. Lying in a warm bubble bath or standing in a shower, gently soaping the entire body surface, is a nonthreatening means of tactile exploration of one's own body and can be less intimidating to those women unaccustomed to self-pleasuring. Altering water pressure with a shower massage to sore or tense areas may be both pleasurable and soothing. Practicing repeated contraction and relaxation of different muscles (thigh, pelvis, abdomen, and buttocks) can be sexually stimulating for some women.

2. *Mirror-image*

a. By posing before a mirror in various gradients of light, ranging from dim to bright sunlight, and regulating the amount of light to the optimal level of comfort, a woman can progressively desensitize her reactions and explore feelings about her altered body-image.

b. Standing before a full-length mirror, preferably a three-paneled one, the woman articulates her feelings about the aesthetics and function of each body part. By this means, she can increase her awareness of positive as well as negative feelings. With each subsequent exposure, disparity between her expectations and reality is reduced.

3. *Role-playing.* By repetitively role-playing her concept of the ideal feminine image, a woman may gradually incorporate some of the admired traits as part of her new self-concept.

4. *Personification.* Holding a two-way conversation with her missing breast, reviewing the significant role her breasts played in her life (for example, wearing her first bra, initial experiences in sex play, and breast-feeding) can facilitate the mourning process.

Group exercises that can be suggested are the following:

1. *Body meditation.* Lying in a comfortable position, fully clothed and with eyes closed, women are instructed to touch, massage, and caress those parts of their bodies that conjure up negative feelings. After completion of the exercise, the support provided by group feedback will contribute to the dissipation of such feelings.

2. *Human-figure drawing.* Women are given a lapboard, colored markers, and paper. Each is instructed to draw her own image. The drawings are then passed to other group members, each of whom writes her interpretation of the feelings expressed by the figure in the picture. The drawing is returned to its creator, who then talks about what she intended to express and her reactions to the group's comments. This exercise is especially effective for those women who are unwilling or unable to articulate their feelings.

3. *Mirror-image.* The body-image exercise done in private before a three-way mirror is equally effective when executed individually in front of

a group. This exercise provides many women with their first socially nude experience and is a prime opportunity for viewing other mastectomees. Looking at others with their explicit permission in a safe, structured setting is beneficial for gaining a perspective of one's body contours in relation to others. Because the affected site is always hidden from others' view, women imagine that their own mutilation is unique and much worse than that of others who have had the same surgery.

When the postoperative site is stimulated, many women experience a strange tactile sensation owing to varying degrees of numbness in the area. If viewed positively rather than fearfully, this unfamiliar feeling can be recognized as creating a new erogenous zone. As a woman becomes more comfortable with herself as a viable sexual being, she will begin to appreciate this new sensual pleasure. Refraining temporarily from coitus can be encouraged to permit concentration on touching and cuddling. The numbness will gradually recede, and new erotic arousal will result in feelings of warmth, affection, and closeness between the partners.

In addition to the interventions previously discussed, counseling for the significant other, either individually or in a peer group, as well as conjoint counseling, needs to be considered. Healthy adjustment to chronic illness is a process that demands the energies and talent of all community resources if quality care is desired. Therefore, it is essential that long-term services be available.

CONCLUSIONS

Regarding self-image, cancer must be seen as a state of being, specifically affecting the physical state of health, rather than as an indelible imprint on one's character or inner sense of psychological well-being. The loss of a breast does not change a woman's value as a person. If not properly dealt with, such mutilation may interfere with self-esteem, impair interpersonal relationships, and precipitate sexual dissatisfaction.

Social workers can make a significant contribution to postmastectomy rehabilitation by offering services designed to facilitate women's acceptance of their altered body-image and worth as sexual beings. In particular, it is desirable that programs aim to increase sexual enjoyment, reduce the focus on performance expectations, explore noncoital techniques, and enhance communication with partners. At the same time, professionals should not be overzealous in attributing sexual concerns to mastectomees since some women can effectively cope on their own.[18]

With increased orientation toward holistic patient care, circumvention or avoidance of the sexual needs of mastectomees can no longer be justified. If social workers are to ease their burden, they have little recourse but to accept the responsibility for sex counseling as a legitimate professional endeavor.

NOTES AND REFERENCES

1. **Mona Wasow**, "Human Sexuality and Terminal Illness," *Health and Social Work*, 2 (May 1977), pp. 105–121.

2. **Jay Mann**, "Is Sex Counseling Here to Stay?" *The Counseling Psychologist*, 5 (1975), pp. 60–63.

3. **Irving S. Kolin, James L. Baker, and Edmund S. Bartlett**, "Psychosexual Aspects of Mammary Augmentation," *Medical Aspects of Human Sexuality*, 8 (December 1974), p. 94.

4. **Daniel G. Brown and David B. Lynn**, "Human Sexual Development: An Outline of Components and Concepts," in **Anne Juhasz**, ed., *Sexual Development and Behavior: Selected Readings* (Homewood, Ill.: The Dorsey Press, 1973), pp. 55–68.

5. **Lester A. Kirkendall**, "Developing Human Sexuality," in **Kirkendall and Robert N. Whitehurst**, eds., *The New Sexual Revolution* (New York: Donald W. Brown, Inc., 1971), p. 154.

6. **Edward L. Wells and Gerald Marwell**, *Self-Esteem: Its Conceptualization and Measurement* (Beverly Hills, Calif.: Sage Publications, Inc., 1976).

7. **Paul Schilder**, *The Image and Appearance of the Human Body* (New York: International Universities Press, Inc., 1970).

8. **Franklin C. Shontz**, *The Psychological Aspects of Physical Illness and Disability* (New York: Macmillan Co., 1975).

9. **Lillian Leiber, Marjorie M. Plumb, Martin L. Gerstenzang, and Jimmie Holland**, "The Communication of Affection between Cancer Patients and their Spouses," *Psychosomatic Medicine*, 38 (November-December 1976), p. 387.

10. **Bernard Schoenberg and Arthur C. Carr**, "Loss of External Organs: Limb Amputation, Mastectomy, and Disfiguration," in **Schoenberg, Carr, David Peretz, and Austin Kutscher**, eds., *Loss and Grief: Psychological Management in Medical Practice* (New York: Columbia University Press, 1970), pp. 119–131.

11. **Helen Singer Kaplan**, *The New Sex Therapy* (New York: Brunner/Mazel in cooperation with Quadrangle/The New York Times Book Co., 1974).

12. **Schoenberg, et. al., op. cit.; Arthur M. Sutherland and Charles E. Orbach**, "Psychological Impact of Cancer and Cancer Surgery, II. Depressive Reactions Associated with Surgery for Cancer," *Cancer*, 5 (September 1952), pp. 857–872.

13. **L. F. E. Bergeret**, *The Preventive Obstacle or Conjugal Onanism* (New York: Turner and Mignard, 1898).

14. **Ira B. Pauly and Steven G. Goldstein**, "Physicians' Ability to Treat Sexual Problems," *Medical Aspects of Human Sexuality*, 4 (October 1970), pp. 24, 30–33, 38, 40, 45–46, 49.

15. **Joshua S. Golden**, "Management of Sexual Problems by the Physician," *Obstetrics and Gynecology*, 23 (March 1964), pp. 471–474.

16. **Herbert Fine**, "Sexual Problems of Chronically Ill Patients," *Medical Aspects of Human Sexuality*, 8 (October 1974), pp. 137–138.

17. **Harold I. Lief and Arno Karlen**, eds., *Sex Education in Medicine* (New York: Spectrum Publications, 1976).

18. **Milton Diamond**, "Sexuality and the Handicapped," in **Joseph Stubbins**, ed., *Social and Psychological Aspects of Disability* (Baltimore, Md.: University Park Press, 1977), pp. 439–450.

Sexual Abuse of Children: Child and Offender as Victims

JO ENSMINGER AND
SUE A. FERGUSON

The physical abuse of children has been a major area of concern for mental health professionals and social service agencies for years. Multitudes of organizations have been developed to aid the battered child, and protective service units have been established on behalf of the abused child and the abusive parent in virtually every state. There is, however, an aspect of child abuse that has been little studied and provided for even less in the development of treatment programs: sexual abuse of children. Only recently have state laws even begun to identify this type of abuse under child abuse statutes. Each year in this country hundreds of thousands of children from infancy through adolescence are sexually assaulted. Generally this abuse has occurred repeatedly before the child is able to tell anyone and receive help. Frequently the child's fears are realized—she is not believed and is punished for lying.[1]

As with rape and the sexual assault of adults, the sexual assault of children is one of the most underreported crimes in this country. Yet it remains potentially one of the most emotionally damaging crimes possible. With increasing frequency mental health professionals are seeing the emotional scars that have resulted from a sexual assault in childhood surface in adulthood as adjustment problems.

The Center for Rape Concern (CRC) is a specialized agency funded through the Philadelphia Office of Mental Health/Mental Retardation. Since 1970, CRC has amassed extensive knowledge on sexual assault and the resulting emotional conflicts suffered by the child and the family. From its research base and the experience of treating hundreds of children, CRC has developed an awareness of the treatment needs of these children and their families.

210

In addition, for more than 20 years CRC has been involved in the treatment of sex offenders, a large percentage of whom are child molesters. In most cases, the child molester is experiencing a great many emotional conflicts and has turned on the child as an expression of his own pain.[2] The combination of CRC's work with child victims of sexual assault and with the child molester has provided an opportunity to use accumulated knowledge to help both groups. This paper will discuss the emotional conflicts and reactions experienced by child victims and by child molesters and the treatment approaches used at CRC.

THE CHILD VICTIM

Any child is potentially a victim of sexual assault. The sexual assault of children differs from the sexual assault of older adolescents and adults in that violence is used infrequently with the child. This difference results from the fact that in almost 80 percent of CRC's cases, the offender is someone the child knows and generally trusts.[3] The offender may be anything from a casual friend of the family or neighbor to a member of the immediate family. In looking at the emotional trauma experienced by the child, it must be remembered that it is someone whom the child trusts and possibly loves who is assaulting her. This is an important factor in the child's perception of and adjustment to the assault.

Although in a majority of sexual assaults against children physical force is not used, verbal force or coercion frequently is used. As stated earlier, the assault may be repeated over a period of time before the child tells anyone. This silence on the part of the child is generally a response to a threat by the offender that either he will punish her if she tells or that her mother will punish her. The child's confusion over what is happening to her then becomes compounded by fear. Another tactic that results in an even more intense fear is the threat that if the child tells anyone, the offender will hurt the child's mother or someone else whom the child loves. Thus the child's fears become the primary target for treatment intervention because they often overshadow any other feelings she may have.

In cases in which the offender is a family member or someone with whom the child has a strong emotional attachment, the offender will often use that relationship both to get the child to cooperate with his sexual advances and to keep her from telling others. The child is made to believe that she is special to the offender and is often given presents and extra privileges because of her special status. This favorable position, coupled with the fear of losing the offender, may persuade the child to keep quiet even though she may not like the sexual activity and may know that it is wrong. In many cases, when the sexual relationship is exposed, the offender will be arrested or the child isolated from him, thereby fulfilling her fear of losing him and leaving her with grief over the loss as well as guilt at having caused the loss.

Family Reactions

Guilt is a feeling frequently experienced by the sexually assaulted child. This feeling can be accentuated by the family's reaction. Parents have a strong need to blame someone when they learn that their child has been sexually assaulted. The appropriate person on which to focus this blame is the offender. Too often, however, the parents place the blame on the child or on themselves. Either way, the child feels guilty. To further compound the problem, the parents may choose to protect the child by keeping her restricted inside the home. This protection is then interpreted as punishment by the child, and her feelings of guilt become confirmed.

The parents' reactions are extremely important in assessing the child's emotional status. Children automatically take emotional and behavioral cues from their parents. If the parents are emotionally overwhelmed by the assault, it is likely that the child will be also. Similarly, activities that take place as a direct result of the assault's being uncovered will also have a direct influence on the child's adjustment. The medical examination and questioning by police officers and other people are in themselves traumatic. Care should be taken to minimize the negative effects of these events. Any punishment or major change in the child's environment is also going to affect her adjustment and must be considered in the psychological assessment.

Professional Intervention

Professional intervention can play a valuable role in decreasing the immediate trauma experienced by the child and in minimizing the long-term effects of the assault and its aftermath. The professional providing the intervention must be aware of the complexity of the situation and be able to assess the child's and the family's needs and to respond accordingly. As with battered children, there is frequently a need on the part of the child and/or the family to deny what has happened. The child may feel a need to protect the offender or the family, and the family may believe that the best way to deal with the situation is not to talk about it. The social worker or psychiatrist must be able to understand the client within these initial restraints.

CRC receives referrals on all reported cases of sexual assault in Philadelphia. In order to expedite contact and to meet the child and family in as comfortable a setting as possible, the social workers operate on a home visit format. The social worker attempts to be in the home within two days after the assault is reported. The first home visit serves several functions. First, the social worker serves as an information resource to the family. There are generally a great many questions that have been left unanswered. Answering these for the family gives the social worker an opportunity to observe interactions among family members and to provide some education to the parents about what the child needs from them.

A second function of the first home visit is to assess whether the child is adequately protected and supervised so that the assault will not be repeated. This is especially necessary if the offender is a family member or if the child was left in the offender's care during the time of the assault. In settings in which protection is not adequate, referrals are made to the Department of Public Welfare Protective Service Unit.

The third and most important function of the home visit is to assess the child's emotional status and to determine what, if any, treatment is needed. It is important in this process to remember that the child has probably had to relate to many strangers in the past few days and that she may be quite frightened by these unknown faces. The social worker becomes one more stranger in this long process. For this reason, the worker must depend heavily on the ability to form a relationship with the child. Much of the social worker's assessment will be based on observation of behavior, especially with younger, less verbal children. The parents' observation of any changes in behavior (for example, in eating and sleeping patterns) is also essential to this assessment.

It is necessary to obtain the details of the assault, if possible, to understand fully the child's experience. Often this information can be obtained from the parents, but it can also be a valuable therapeutic tool to have the child relate the story to someone who will respond in an objective and supportive manner. This will help the child to understand what has happened, why it was wrong, and whose responsibility it was.

The parents are the key to positive adjustment of the child. For that reason, the CRC social worker will spend much time working with the parents in relation to their own feelings and what the child needs from them. The social worker will often encourage the parents to treat the child in the same way that they would if the child has accidentally hurt herself, to show love and support without inducing guilt and fear in the child. It is to the parents' support and understanding that the child looks for reassurance. With younger children who do not really know what has happened, it is not unusual for the social worker to spend the majority of the time with the parents rather than with the child. It is essential to note, however, that throughout CRC's contact with the family, the child remains the primary client.

Experience with adults who were sexually assaulted as children indicates that long-term effects are less likely to develop if supportive intervention takes place shortly after the assault. Generally the social worker's contact with the child and the family is sufficient. In some cases, however, it is necessary to involve a child psychiatrist. Generally this occurs when the child exhibits marked changes in behavior or is not able to verbalize her feelings or when there has been a major disruption in the normal psychosexual development of the child. In the latter case, the child may either regress or accelerate in development. Cases involving homosexual assaults on children nearing puberty may result in sex-role confusion. Child psychiatrists trained in using a variety of techniques to draw out the child can help to resolve the feelings that are creating these problems. The social worker/psychiatrist team can work effectively in dealing with the concerns of the child and the family. For the most part, the purpose of intervention with the child victim of sexual assault is to help the child and the child's family to return to a positive level of functioning.

THE OFFENDER

The stereotype of the "dirty old man" luring children into his car with promises of candy is only one example of the thousands of men across this country classified as pedophiles, or child molesters. The pedophile can be of any race, religion, or economic status. There is no way to identify a pedophile through his physical appearance. The characteristic or group of characteristics that makes him turn to children for gratification is internal.

Joseph J. Peters, MD, the founder of CRC, worked closely with various types of sex offenders for over 20 years. According to Peters, "the pedophile usually manifests a passive-aggressive personality who often has attempted in vain to establish a relationship with an adult female. He lacks the feelings of adequacy and emotional maturity necessary to maintain an adult heterosexual relationship."[4] The pedophile is an insecure individual who sees the child as accepting and nonthreatening. With children the pedophile knows, there may inadvertently be some encouragement by the child because of the attention she receives.

Most adults are able to resist any sexual attraction to a child, but the pedophile is usually an impulsive individual who will act without thinking of the consequences to himself or the child. In approximately 50 percent of the cases treated at CRC, this lack of impulse control is compounded by a drinking problem.[5] Many times the pedophile is able to convince himself that not only did the child cooperate in the sexual activity, she solicited it through her actions. The child is perceived as having the adult ability to make choices and decisions about sexual behavior. The fact that most pedophiles do not have to use physical force tends to reinforce the belief that the child is a willing participant. Indeed, in those cases in which threats of violence are used, they are generally a method of preventing the child from telling what has happened rather than a method of obtaining cooperation in the sexual activity. Often the pedophile is unable to understand the implicit power he has over the child simply because he is an adult.

Treating the Offender

A majority of the men convicted in Philadelphia for pedophilic acts (indecent assault, corrupting the morals of a minor, statutory rape, sodomy, and so on) and given probationary status are referred to CRC for psychiatric evaluation leading to possible inclusion in CRC's treatment program. The primary treatment modality used at CRC in treating these men is outpatient group psychotherapy. Some individual psychiatric therapy is provided for individuals who are not suited for or able to attend groups, but this is minimal. The groups are conducted by a psychiatrist/social worker team containing both a male and a female. In addition to utilizing the skills of both disciplines, this team approach allows the men to interact with both sexes in a positive atmosphere devoid of the pressures incurred in a potential sexual relationship.

On the average, men attend weekly group sessions for a period of one year. Since most of the group members have been convicted of criminal offenses and are attending as a condition of probation, the new member spends his initial weeks dealing with his anger about having to attend the group and with his denial of guilt. Groups are run on an ongoing basis so there is an overlap of new members with old members. This helps to lower the resistance of the newer members because the older members are able to discuss their behavior and life styles openly in an atmosphere of acceptance and support. Even when members are confronted with negative behavior and forced to deal with their ensuing emotions, the group provides the support necessary to enable the member to use the experience in a growth-producing way.

The goal of the group psychotherapy process is to help the individual better understand his internal conflicts and through that understanding learn to control impulsive behavior and to develop more satisfactory social skills. Members are encouraged to develop adult relationships and are given emotional assistance in doing so. The group provides the individual with a place in which to test new skills and to seek advice and support as changes occur.

CONCLUSIONS

The sexual assault of children is an acute problem. The numbers of reported cases are steadily growing. The community has a responsibility to meet the needs of both the child and the pedophile. It must be realized that both are victims in their own right, and therapeutic aims must be directed accordingly. Social workers and social service agencies, as instruments of the community, must become more aware of this growing problem and of the value and methods of early intervention.

NOTES AND REFERENCES

1. The Center for Rape Concern serves male pediatric victims as well as female victims, but the majority of the cases treated are female. Except for introduction of the homosexual component with the male victims, emotional responses are similar in male and female pediatric victims of sexual assault. For that reason, the term *she* is used in the body of the paper, but this refers to both sexes.

2. **Joseph J. Peters and Robert L. Sadoff**, "Clinical Observations on Child Molesters," *Medical Aspects of Human Sexuality,* 4 (November 1970), p. 21.

3. **Joseph J. Peters, Linda C. Meyer, and Nancy E. Carroll**, "The Philadelphia Assault Victim Study" (Philadelphia: Center for Rape Concern, July 1976). Unpublished manuscript research report submitted to the National Institute of Mental Health in partial fulfillment of Grant No. MH 21304.

4. **Peters and Sadoff**, op. cit.

5. **Joseph J. Peters**, "Children Who are Victims of Sexual Assault and the Psychology of Offenders," *American Journal of Psychotherapy,* 30 (July 1976), pp. 398–421.

Treating the Battered Woman

BARBARA STAR

Somehow, it seems, we are constantly "discovering" what has always existed—poverty, racism, child abuse, rape, and now, wife-beating. The past year or so brought a myriad of articles, books, and research studies that flooded the news media with staggering statistics and gory tales of bloodied victims.[1] As is the case with child abuse, wife-battering transcends all socioeconomic boundaries. But the general attitude toward it differs. The sympathy felt for the young child, powerless to escape a cruel adult world, does not exist for the battered woman. Instead, she is often scorned for her reluctance or refusal to leave the abusive situation and labeled "masochistic," "frigid," and "castrating."

Despite social work's relationship with families under stress and with problems that involve destructive behavior, physical abuse among adults has seldom been given serious attention.[2] When the battered woman seeks counseling, some of the stereotypes surrounding the problem can cloud professional judgment. Drawing from the literature, interviews, and the author's own unpublished research with 50 battered women at Haven House, a shelter in the Los Angeles area, this article will examine the psychosocial dynamics of abused women and their marital situation and highlight several aspects of wife-beating that social workers frequently encounter.

WHAT CONSTITUTES ABUSE?

Wife-beating, wife-battering, wife assault, and *spousal assault* are terms variously used in the cases of women who have experienced physical abuse by their husbands or male companions. However, what constitutes abuse often depends on the individual's perception. One woman might consider a slap across the face or a shove against a wall serious physical abuse, while another will not consider herself abused until she requires medical treat-

217

ment. Professionals, too, face the problems of finding appropriate, relevant, and consistent terminology.

Scott provides a useful taxonomy.[3] Falling within the category of "wife" is any woman who lives with a man, whether in a legal, common-law, or de facto spouse relationship. In contrast to a mild, isolated blow, such as a slap or kick once or twice during a protracted time period, battering implies repetition or thoroughness. A battered wife, then, "is a woman who has suffered serious or repeated physical injury from the man with whom she lives."[4]

The abuse and injuries battered women receive range from mild (for example, being pushed or shoved with resultant slight discoloration) to moderate (being kicked, punched, or choked to the extent of producing definite bruises and black eyes) to severe (beating, stomping, or knifing with resultant cuts and/or fractures) and finally, to fatal (death resulting from pummeling, knifing, or shooting). Slapping, punching, and kicking represent the usual forms of attack, with fists and feet the primary weapons. Each assault tends to be more severe than the preceding ones. Over time, battered women sustain an enormous array of injuries: black eyes, bloody nose, hair pulled out, lacerations, bruises on throat and upper arms, concussion, fractured ribs, miscarriage, and irreparable eye damage.[5] Said one five-foot three-inch, 90-pound Haven House client of her six-foot four-inch, 240-pound husband:

> He's taken a knife to me, pointed a shotgun at my stomach, beat me with his fists and his belt, thrown me down, dragged me on the ground, pulled me around by my hair, and thrown me against a wrought-iron fish tank. Once I was in the hospital for two weeks. My kidneys were bruised, my whole back was black and blue, I had lumps on my face, and I still have a scar on my leg where I hit the metal rod on the fish tank.

PSYCHOSOCIAL DYNAMICS

Although no two battered women are the same or share the same experiences, certain themes do recur on the research tests and in the interviews. Generally the women (1) come from emotionally restrictive families, (2) tend to be loners and withdrawn, (3) have not seen or witnessed abuse in their homes, (4) have not had many in-depth relationships with men prior to marrying the abusive spouse, (5) have low self-esteem, (6) were not abused prior to marriage, (7) married men who have witnessed or experienced abuse at home, (8) married excessively jealous men, (9) are not often sexually satisfied by the husband, and (10) do not have a large support system of friends and relatives. The following case example illustrates several of these themes.

Mary and Jim

Mary, a 27-year-old Caucasian mother of two, arrived at Haven House shortly after another of her husband's batterings. It was the eighth or ninth (she had lost count) during their four-year marriage. He had punched her on the side of the head, bruising her face and scalp and pulverizing her ear until it turned black from the bruising. Even after three weeks she still felt dizzy and had headaches.

It had not always been that way. During their courtship, when she was 21 and he was 27, everything was wonderful. "He was gentle and considerate. He seemed so strong and secure; like he really had it together. It made me feel secure too." Despite the objections of her parents, Mary and Jim lived together for a year before getting married. He was a cement mason and earned a good salary.

During that time the only abusive incident occurred when he shoved her out of the way after he had a little too much to drink. The real abuse did not start until after their first child was born, a year after they were married. Mary wanted the child, and Jim claimed to also. But he could not stand it when the baby cried. One night he came into the child's room while Mary was holding the three-week-old infant, trying to stop its tears. Jim tore the child out of her arms, threw it into the crib, and slapped Mary across the face, saying she was spoiling the child. At the time, Mary's mother was staying with them to help Mary and heard the whole incident. But neither she, Mary, nor Jim ever mentioned it.

Following the incident, there were many arguments about the best way to raise the child. Jim was a strict disciplinarian and expected complete compliance from both the child and his wife. "It was as though he had certain ways he wanted us to act, and if we didn't do it just so, he got angry. Like he didn't want me to wear makeup, and things had to be done just the minute he asked, and I could never talk to another man. Everything I did seemed to be wrong according to him. He was always criticizing me."

At first Jim handled his frustrations by yelling, pounding tables, and occasionally smashing ash trays against a wall. Once after an arguement, he smashed his fist through a cupboard door, saying, "Just look out, that could be you." Mary cringed but did not take him seriously. Then one evening after returning from the movies, Jim accused her of flirting with a man in the lobby. Mary's protests were met with a fist to the mouth. He apologized and said he did not know what had come over him. She realized then that he had the power to hurt her, and it frightened her.

During a temporary layoff from work, Jim started drinking large quantities of beer. Mary wanted him to stop. He did not like her nagging and blackened both of her eyes. This time he did not apologize. When he was drunk, Jim was unpredictable, and little things could arouse his anger. Mary began weighing every word she spoke and stayed out of his way. When those tactics did not succeed, she suffered a barrage of cursing and more physical abuse.

She became pregnant again. Jim claimed it was not his child and wanted her to have an abortion. She refused. He became furious and beat her severely in a fight that left her badly bruised and bedridden for three days. Their 18-month-old son watched the beating wide-eyed from the doorway and then ran back to his room, where Mary later found him whimpering in his sleep.

Never had Mary experienced such treatment as part of her upbringing. She was the oldest of three children in a Catholic family. Her father was a carpenter and occasionally taught adult education at the local high school. He was a no-nonsense type of person, interested in her activities but not very demonstrative. Her mother was a quiet woman not given to spontaneous gestures of affection. Her mother cashiered at a nearby drug store off and on to earn money. During those times, Mary was in charge of the household and took responsibility for the housework, child care, and meal preparation. She was a quiet, serious girl who kept to herself because there were so few children her age in the neighborhood. Her father did not want her "getting in trouble," so he prevented her from dating until she was almost 18. Her performance in school was only fair, and, much to the delight of her parents, who believed girls only went to college to meet men, she quit school before she graduated and began waitressing. Jim was a customer in the restaurant where Mary worked.

Jim also came from an intact Catholic family in which he was the second of five children. His father was a welder, a large boisterous man who drank too much and beat the children when they did not do as ordered. Jim's parents bickered constantly, his mother nagging and finding fault with her husband, who frequently exploded with rage and smacked her across the room. Jim eagerly left home when he was 18 and enlisted in the army. Afterward he went to trade school on the GI Bill and learned masonry skills.

During her second pregnancy, Mary found herself withdrawing more and more, saying less to Jim. He called her a fat, stupid cow. She contemplated suicide. Several months after the birth of the second child, she realized how removed from other people she had become. She wanted to return to school or to work. Jim would not permit it. She was a mother, and mothers stayed home with the children. It became an ongoing bone of contention that finally culminated in the fight that brought Mary to Haven House.

Marital Interaction

Marital interactions like Mary and Jim's are common among abused women. Initially the women see in the men strength and an opportunity to gain the warmth and affection that were lacking in their relationships with their parents. The men find the women ready listeners and willing to acquiesce to their demands. There is little flexibility between the partners. Each has his or her own traditional roles to play, and deviations upset the delicate balance. What were once considered secure boundaries have, over time, become unyielding walls. Both partners perceive the other as critical and ungiving.

The batterings indicate a learned pattern of emotional expression among the men, in part representing displaced anger toward their own parents (who are often seen as cruel), and are viewed as a means of maintaining themselves as head of the family. For the women who came from abusive families, it represents an expected and integral aspect of married life. For others it is the price they pay to maintain the marital and family unit.

The initial shock of a violent episode soon fades for both parties. The men, unable to control their own rage, look to the women to set limits. The women's lack of physical resistance lends tacit approval to the abuse, legitimizing future abuse. With neither person able to set effective limits, the abuse accelerates in frequency and intensity until the threat to life and limb forces action, usually some form of separation.

Why Do Women Stay?

What motivates women to remain in abusive situations? At one level, economic realities loom large as barriers to effecting change. At a different level, emotional factors loom even larger. Most battered wives are also mothers concerned about the well-being of their children. Leaving the husband usually means plunging into the lowered living standard imposed by the minimum wage or welfare. Only 20 percent of the Haven House clients had technical or professional training. The rest were either unskilled or had never worked. Weighing the choices of perpetual poverty or occasional abuse, many women decide to remain at home.

What makes the choice even harder is the realization that even a bad situation has some redeeming features. Abusive husbands are not abusive all the time. Some attack only when drunk, others once or twice a year. Milder forms of abuse are annoying but tolerable. Although approximately 25 percent of the husbands also abuse the children, many love the children and treat them well. And every apology or act of kindness toward the woman counteracts the memory of pain.

Underneath the real concerns for physical survival lurk the unspoken fears about emotional survival. "I'm afraid to be alone" is a common plea. The woman pictures an empty apartment, having no one to talk with, being alone in the world. Even though, for all practical purposes, her marital world is equally empty, the fact of marriage or living with someone creates the illusion that she is being cared for and cared about.

Loneliness is even more devastating when accompanied by the belief that one has nothing to offer anyone else. After years of negative feedback, a battered woman comes to believe that she is incompetent, physically unattractive, and intellectually inferior. Thinking she might never be able to do any better, the woman stays.

TREATMENT CONSIDERATIONS

Effective intervention requires an understanding of the attitudes and concerns battered women bring with them when they seek help. This section presents some of their major reactions to the helping process and offers suggestions for dealing with them.

A recent study of people seeking help with problems involving violence found that clients overwhelmingly expressed their concern about violence at the point of intake rather than in later sessions.[6] People come to agencies ready to talk about violence, yet too often the issue is not dealt with. Several factors may account for this phenomenon. One involves agency practices. Unless trained to understand the impact of violence on client functioning, both the intake and ongoing workers may diminish its importance, placing the focus on some other aspect of the situation.[7] The client, believing the worker knows best, quickly follows the worker's lead and does not speak of it again.

But factors operating within the client also play significant roles. First, the primary career of most women still remains that of wife and mother. In the minds of many, physical violence signals marital failure. And, to battered women, it means that they have not fulfilled their role properly. Shame, guilt, and humiliation combine to diminish their willingness to talk about the full extent of the violence to which they have been subjected.

Second, the women coming for counseling usually feel ambivalent. They want the relationship to change but not to end. They are not certain of their ability to survive on their own. Focusing on the abuse means the women may have to decide whether to remain or leave, a choice many do not wish to make.

Finally, the mechanism of denial quickly snuffs out any talk of violence. Basically the relationship is sound, they claim. Nothing is really wrong, nothing a few minor changes cannot correct.

Many of these problems could be overcome if the worker took an assault history, that is, asked about such things as these:

1. Witnessed abuse between parents, guardians, or relatives while growing up.

2. Sexual or physical assault from parents, relatives, neighbors, boyfriends, or strangers.

3. Experience of *any* form of physical violence from a spouse.

4. Use of physical violence on a spouse or child.

If the worker takes the abuse seriously, in all likelihood so will the client.

Additional Problems

Once abuse emerges as a viable marital issue, the worker will be confronted with other problems, among them the following:

Emotional emptiness. Most women talk more about their husband's behavior, feelings, and motivations than about their own. This reflects the fact that battered women usually are not in touch with their own feelings. It is as if taking the focus away from *him* removes the core of *her* being, leaving an empty cavern inside. Constantly shifting the focus back to the women and reawakening their sensitivity to their own needs and wishes is the first step. But in large measure, the emptiness reflects the women's own feelings of self-worth. A major treatment effort involves negating years of negative feedback that have been incorporated into the self system by helping the women gain a realistic sense of their intelligence and their abilities. In conjunction with individual counseling, this may also involve having them take such concrete steps as enrolling in a class, performing volunteer work, or obtaining employment.

Denial. Most battered women underplay rather than overplay the violent episodes. Part of their denial includes a refusal to acknowledge the potential seriousness of the situation. With almost blasé nonchalance, a woman will report the way her husband takes a gun from a closet and waves it at her and the children when he has been drinking. It is unrealistic to rely on the men's tenuous control. Unless the real threat to life is reinforced, battered women lapse into a sense of false security produced by their denial.

Isolation. Not only are battered women emotionally isolated, they are often physically isolated as well. Since they tend not to belong to clubs or organizations, such women have only a small circle of acquaintances upon whom to draw. If the husbands drink heavily or abuse the women in public, their friends are further alienated and feel uncomfortable about coming to visit. Shame frequently prevents battered women from telling anyone, including relatives, about the abuse. Even when the women do confide in others, most people do not want to risk involvement. The limited interaction with the wider world keeps such women virtual prisoners of their own fears. Helping the women to build a firm and expanded support system, especially through group interaction, not only breaks the isolation but gives them the courage to explore new avenues for change.

Anger. Pent-up anger lies buried deep within the recesses of the psyche. Battered women are so adept at submerging anger that they often fail to recognize that they possess the emotion. Throughout their childhoods, anger was suppressed, and during their marriages, expressing anger has painful consequences. Most often battered women turn their anger inward, creating large pools of guilt. Sometimes this emerges as mumbled resentment or petty grievances. The women harbor as much anger toward themselves for being in the abusive situation as they do toward their husbands. But they fear that bringing the anger to light will undam a flood of uncontrollable destructive behavior. They need to learn nonhurtful techniques for releasing anger (for example, hitting a pillow) as well as to have a safe environment in which to verbalize anger.

Depression. Years of verbal put-downs, years of feeling like a failure, and years of feeling trapped in a turbulent relationship produce a deep and constant depression. Over 25 percent of the women in the Haven House study tried to commit suicide at some point during the marriage. The risk of suicide is an ever present danger. Monitoring suicide potential is extremely important until the women gain some mastery over the situation.

Passivity. Perhaps the most damaging stereotype concerning wife-beating is the belief that battered women are masochistic. Wife-beating is an international phenomenon affecting millions of women throughout the world. It seems highly unlikely that all these women are seeking punishment. Undoubtedly a small percentage are, but the Haven House research findings suggest another alternative. The personality profiles of the women show timidity, withdrawal, and apprehension—signs of passivity rather than masochism. Passivity may explain why physically abused women do not defend themselves when attacked. Passivity coupled with low self-esteem creates the ideal victim. Many women report temporary abatement from abuse when they do assert themselves. Exposure to basic assertiveness techniques may expand such women's ability to resist the threat of violence and thereby reduce it.

Frustration. Working with battered women is not without its frustrations. Almost everyone can feel compassion for a victimized person, but few can tolerate the perpetual victim. People providing services for battered women often feel compassion turn to annoyance and annoyance to anger when their client fails to take action immediately. Their own tendencies to superimpose a value system and set of expectations foreign to the women can only result in failure. As with most chronic conditions, the road to change in the area of wife abuse is often slow and halting. Desire for speedy progress is seldom satisfied. Setting realistic goals may prevent undue frustration for both client and worker.

CONCLUSION

As a social issue, wife-beating is a problem whose time has come. But as a treatment issue, it is just emerging. Practitioners are beginning to realize that wife-battering is not only a widespread phenomenon but a complex one as well. It varies along several dimensions including the frequency and severity of abuse, the motivations that lead to abuse, the role expectations that influence marital interactions, and the reasons that both parties remain in the situation. A willingness on the part of social workers to confront and overcome outworn conceptions of marital functioning can go a long way toward producing a greater depth of understanding about the problem of wife-battering and its treatment.

NOTES AND REFERENCES

1. *See,* for example, **Roger Langley and Richard Levy**, *Wife Beating: The Silent Crisis* (New York: E. P. Dutton & Co., 1977); **Del Martin**, *Battered Wives* (San Francisco: Glide Publications, 1976); **Murray Straus**, "Normative and Behavioral Aspects of Violence Between Spouses: Preliminary Data on a Nationally Representative USA Sample" (Durham: University of New Hampshire, 1977) (mimeographed).

2. **Margaret Ball**, "Issues of Violence in Family Casework," *Social Casework,* 58 (January 1977), pp. 3–12; **Beverly B. Nichols**, "The Abused Wife Problem," *Social Casework,* 57 (January 1976), pp. 27–32.

3. **P. D. Scott**, "Battered Wives," *British Journal of Psychiatry,* 125 (May 1974), pp. 441–443.

4. Ibid., p. 434.

5. *See,* for example, **J. J. Gayford**, "Wife Battering: A Preliminary Survey of 100 Cases," *British Medical Journal,* 1 (January 25, 1977), pp. 194–197; **Richard Gelles**, *The Violent Home* (Beverly Hills, Calif.: Sage Publications, 1972); **Sue Eisenberg and Patricia Micklow**, "The Assaulted Wife: 'Catch 22' Revisited" (unpublished Ph.D. dissertation, University of Michigan Law School, 1974).

6. **Ball**, op. cit.

7. **Ball**, op. cit.; **Nichols**, op. cit.

Hidden Victims: The Effects of Disaster on Caregivers

LINDA MILLER, DONNA JOHNSON, AND MARILYN La CELLE

Every disaster, whether natural or human caused, is unique and requires a correspondingly unique response from professional caregivers. The body of knowledge pertaining to crisis intervention theory and specifically to human response to disaster is helpful in providing human services professionals with principles and guidelines for effective intervention.[1]

This article examines and discusses disaster intervention services performed by the staff of the Larimer County Mental Health Center during the week following Colorado's Big Thompson flood of July 31, 1976. It is intended to add to the small but critical body of knowledge that relates specifically to the responses of *caregivers,* with recommendations for a comprehensive educational approach that includes experiential, theoretical, and self-awareness components.

Objective assessment of the Larimer County Mental Health Center staff's reactions were derived from three questionnaires that were distributed sequentially, one month, seven months, and eleven months after the flood. In addition, information was gathered from two staff debriefings that were held two weeks and four weeks following the flood and from continuing personal reflections of staff.

DISASTER STRIKES

The Big Thompson River is normally a tranquil, picturesque river that meanders through the Big Thompson Canyon west of Loveland, Colorado. Normally about 15 feet wide with its deepest pool at about eight feet, the river has cut a narrow gorge through the canyon, which has walls that frequently reach a height of six stories. On the evening of July 31, 1976, a torrential rainfall sent an estimated five million tons of water raging through the canyon, destroying nearly everything in its path. Although flash flood warnings had been issued, many of the estimated 4,000 residents and vacationers in the canyon either never heard or did not heed the warnings. The water in the river rose swiftly and formed a wall of water estimated to have been 19 feet high by the time it reached the end of the canyon, leaving 139 persons dead, hundreds missing and homeless. Most survivors were stranded in the canyon. Property damage was estimated at more than $20 million.

Immediate Response

Staff from a variety of human services agencies were involved in the rescue efforts and the aftermath of the tragedy. The staff of the Larimer County Mental Health Center was among those responding immediately. Staff members arrived on August 1, the morning after the flood. Twenty-seven staff members—including eight clinical social workers, six psychologists, three mental health assistants, two psychiatric nurses, one psychiatrist, one occupational therapist, and six clerical workers—were involved in the disaster intervention. Several staff members who arrived had been hired the previous month and were reporting for their first day of work.

To assess the need for mental health services, five teams were sent to the disaster centers: the helicopter port where evacuees arrived and received medical first aid after being flown out of the canyon, the evacuee center at a high school, a funeral home where initial receiving and preliminary identification of recovered bodies was taking place, the new community hospital, and the makeshift morgue in the recently vacated old hospital. Volunteer medical personnel arrived quickly and in large numbers from neighboring communities. However, the people in the canyon had either perished in the waters or survived relatively unharmed, and the medical volunteers returned home after the first day.

The mental health center staff expected its task to be that of providing therapeutic support to survivors. But the survivors were generally calm and were providing support for one another. Their practical needs, such as food, clothing, and lodging, were met rapidly by the community. The remaining and overwhelming need was to locate the missing and identify the recovered bodies of the dead. Until this task was completed, the survivors were emotionally immobilized.

Primary Focus of Efforts

Although the mental health center staff provided services at several of the disaster recovery centers from the first day through the week after the flood, the primary focus of staff efforts was at the morgue in the old hospital.

Friends and relatives of the missing assembled there, wondering whether their loved ones were among the dead.

Ground travel into the canyon and communication from the canyon to the outside world were virtually nonexistent for two days and limited after that. Many unevacuated survivors were gathered into small, isolated groups, waiting for the helicopters to find them. Because of this and the fact that many vacationers thought to have been in the area of the canyon were reported as missing by relatives from all over the country, there were over 900 names on the missing list the second day after the flood and only 55 recovered bodies.

Death in the flood was violent, the result of drowning and merciless battering among boulders and debris. The dead were often unrecognizable, and all were without clothing or other identifying personal effects. Because of the condition of the bodies and the rapidly increasing number of them, it was decided that relatives would not be allowed to view them unless identification had been tentatively established. Some orderly identification process had to be formulated quickly, and the waiting relatives and friends needed emotional support and sensitive explanations. The small morgue and remaining medical staff could not begin to tackle the tasks involved alone, so the mental health center staff, along with other caregivers from churches and human services agencies, quickly became an integral part of the morgue operation.

The center staff was deployed to specific tasks based on skill areas. The center's own hierarchical structure was superimposed on the disaster activity. This structure facilitated clear communication and a task orientation. The director assumed a leadership role and assigned duties. Psychologists with computer programming skills streamlined data-gathering. The psychiatrist and nurses became assistant pathologists. Male staff became body handlers. For other staff members the focus of activity became confirming reports of the missing and eliciting more information about them from anxious friends and relatives. Data files were kept on the bodies and on persons listed as missing. A match of the two was the goal.

Staff Reactions

The frustration and anger of friends and relatives increased because of the waiting period and was matched by the caregivers' anger and frustration. A body match was a victory. Staff members would accompany relatives and friends into the identification room only when the computers and those who examined the bodies were reasonably sure of a match. This was an exceptionally difficult task for caregivers and a horrendous experience for the families owing to the condition of the bodies. Often relatives would make an identification, then not be sure. The caregiver mirrored the relatives' experience. Staff members also needed desperately to make a positive identification, especially in the case of children. Staff members' own horror, anger, and frustration culminated in feelings of inadequacy that had to be set aside while support was given to families and friends. Typical staff remarks were "The bodies just kept coming and coming," "I felt so help-less," "I wanted to see just one that looked like a real person," "I've never dealt with anything like this before."

The initial phase of panic and/or disorganization as the caregiver assessed the scene was relatively brief as the mobilization of efforts became task-centered—body identification. Working with colleagues provided emotional support. Reactions of staff during the first few days of intense involvement were varied. Some felt curiosity about the corpses and then guilt because they were curious. Some felt repulsed, and that feeling of repulsion was mixed with guilt too. Some were furious at the bodies: "Damn it, you look like a sensible man! Why didn't you get to higher ground?" But thoughts and feelings were shared with and accepted by fellow staff members. They were protective of one another. If unable to deal with a task, staff members were able to accept their own limitations and switched tasks, took time out, or went home. There was security in the knowledge that one's feelings were accepted and that one could ask for support when it was needed.

Laughter was an important release for many. While the morbid humor and laughter were a way of coping for some, other staff members were uncomfortable with this and thought it irreverent to the dead.

By the fourth day, the mental health center staff was phasing out. Most of the bodies had been identified, and friends and relatives no longer waited in the halls. The staff trained volunteers to carry on the identification process, which at this point was slow and tedious. Skilled military personnel aided in the examination of bodies for identification clues. One week after the flood, the staff was back at the mental health center, performing its normal tasks. But staff members' feelings were churning, and they were ventilating, rehashing, reliving. There were sleep disturbances, loss of appetite, and some disorganization of family life. Staff, in a unanimous, informal decision-making process, decided that help was needed.

ASSESSING THE EFFECT ON CAREGIVERS

There appeared to be three expressed needs of staff members: (1) ventilation, (2) assessment of their performance, and (3) positive reinforcement. There were also some decisions to be made. How would the staff continue to serve canyon residents who were now refugees? How would outside news media, researchers, and disaster consultants who were making requests and offering services be handled?

First Debriefing

In an attempt to meet these needs, a meeting time was set for a debriefing for all staff. The setting had to allow maximum sharing of feelings and concerns. A time was chosen that allowed all staff members to attend, but attendance was optional. The meeting was held in a comfortable group room, away from the center, to minimize staff roles and hierarchy. The center psychiatrist volunteered to facilitate the session.

During the meeting, the sharing was spontaneous and at times openly emotional. The meeting began with anecdotal material and shifted to self-disclosure and introspection. There was a gradual realization that involvement in the disaster resulted in a resurfacing of unresolved grief. The disaster also represented a confrontation with people's own helplessness in the face of such powerful natural forces. Preoccupation with thoughts of morbidity and the inevitable death of self and loved ones was found to be the rule rather than the exception. Anger was expressed toward unsolicited advice from "outsiders," many of whom were seen as opportunists attempting to advance their professional standing through attachment to the disaster. In retrospect, this anger seems to be part of a territorialism the center staff felt about its being "*our* disaster." The debriefing provided a release for emotions. There were some good, warm feelings and a positive attitude about the staff's involvement.

First Questionnaire

The first questionnaire was distributed shortly after the first debriefing and was prepared by the center's administrative staff to evaluate further staff opinions regarding the center's response to the disaster. Twenty-one of the 27 staff members involved in disaster assistance completed this questionnaire, which consisted of 11 open-ended questions.

Overall, the staff members indicated a feeling that they had inadequate professional and educational preparation for performing the duties required of them. There was agreement that the duties they performed were necessary; however, the need for clearer lines of responsibility and communication in the overall disaster effort was specified by eight of the respondents. One staff member noted, for instance, that the caregivers at the temporary morgue used the word *found* to mean "found safe and alive," whereas the sheriff's office used the same word to refer to those found dead. This resulted in agonizing confusion for the surviving relatives and friends.

The staff rated the first debriefing as helpful. They commented positively on the opportunity to ventilate and at least partially resolve stressful feelings, being comforted that many of their reactions were shared by others. There appeared to be general agreement, however, that the debriefing was too large (involving about 22 people) and that a second debriefing would be helpful for some.

Second Debriefing

Eleven staff members attended the second debriefing, which was held during working hours at the center. Three of the participants had been unable to attend the first debriefing. Several staff members who did attend the first debriefing reported that they felt no need for a second debriefing, while others did feel a need to participate but were unable to fit it into their work schedules.

Although the mood of this second meeting was more reflective and resolved than at the first debriefing, ventilation of feelings related to the disaster was still predominant in the interaction. Staff members present who had also attended the first debriefing generally expressed a greater degree of personal comfort and emotional closure than those who were debriefing for the first time, and they were able to serve as a support system for the newer participants. Comments by participants in general indicated that resolution of perceived conflicts between their professional role expectations for themselves and their personal experiences and reactions was significantly enhanced by the sharing and support experienced in the debriefings. The prospect of a third debriefing was discussed. However, the felt need for it appeared to be minimal, and there seemed to be general agreement that further debriefings could be arranged as needed by small groups of staff members.

Second Questionnaire

The second questionnaire was designed and analyzed by Ron Ilinitch and Martha P. Titus, graduate students at Smith College School for Social Work, and was the basis of their thesis.[2] This 12-page questionnaire contained 41 semantic-differential questions that measured depressive, psychological, and somatic symptoms; interpersonal relations; self-image; and sense of community. Staff members retrospectively self-rated themselves before, during the week of, and after the flood. The questionnaire also gathered demographic information on respondents and contained a checklist of emotional, physiological, and somatic aftereffects, as well as short essay questions.

The analysis of responses in the questionnaire confirmed information gathered in debriefings and from the first questionnaire. The most stressful time period for staff was during the week of the flood, and psychological and psychophysiological difficulties experienced by staff were similar to reports in the literature of difficulties experienced by those more commonly defined as victims. Those staff members with formal disaster training and previous crisis experience reported fewer disruptive psychological and psychophysiological symptoms than those without such training or experience. Most of the respondents who commented on what effect their involvement in the disaster had on their personal lives reported that the effect was positive, with increased recognition of the importance of life and loved ones. Personal and professional self-images were reported to have decreased during the week of the flood, but overall appeared to have returned to predisaster levels.

Third Questionnaire

A third questionnaire was composed and tabulated by the authors. It was completed by 23 staff members 11 months after the flood and was designed to confirm and/or compare the findings of earlier questionnaires and to assess possible lingering effects of the disaster-intervention experience. The questionnaire consisted of 11 items on one page: demographic information, multiple-choice and short essay items, and three semantic differential items.

The analysis of this last questionnaire indicated that all respondents felt their experience would have a positive effect on their professional competence in another disaster. When asked to rate the types of professional training that would have a positive effect on involvement as a caregiver in another disaster, the order of choice was (1) personal reactions of caregivers, (2) therapeutic techniques applicable to disaster victims, and (3) crisis intervention theory and disaster planning and organization. Consistent with the second questionnaire, personal and professional self-images were reported to have returned to predisaster levels, with only mild increase in anxiety, depression, and concerns about death.

Results of the questionnaires were consistent. However, because of the small size of the sample, the fact that not all staff responded to the first and third questionnaires, and the effects of intervening variables over the 11 months, generalization of results to other caregiver reactions in crisis intervention is not reliable.

IMPLICATIONS OF THIS EXPERIENCE

Both the independent research project by the graduate students from Smith College and the center's own questionnaires and debriefings result in the conclusion that caregivers are hidden victims. Staff members experienced many of the reactions that are delineated in crisis intervention theory. They also experienced dynamics that are now being labeled as "burnout."

The data also indicate that crisis intervention experience and previous disaster experience contribute significantly to level of function while providing assistance in a disaster. The authors accept the premise that good self-image, a sense of community, good personal interactions, and minimal signs of depression are indicators that correlate with an individual's maximum performance. The implications for training fall into three categories: (1) experiential, (2) theory, and (3) self-awareness.

Experiential Training

Experiential training is the cornerstone of social work education. The field instruction placement component is an integral piece of training that provides the student with a setting in which to apply content learned in the classroom. The integration process—learning by doing—is basic. Center staff members who regularly rotated on the center's 24-hour emergency service had all served in crisis situations. It is recommended that social work placements in direct service include crisis intervention experience. Obviously, a disaster experience cannot be provided, nor would disaster teams moving in and out of disaster areas supplant the need for local intervention. Just as the therapist builds from the client's own system, communities grow stronger as they use their own strengths in the reconstruction process.

Theory

Crisis theory is currently included in social work curricula. It was striking that an overwhelmingly expressed need by staff after the disaster was for a course in death and dying. Facetiously, this was looked upon initially as a professional propensity to intellectualize—the stock solution to emotions is to take a course on *it,* whatever *it* may be. But theory is valuable, and facetiousness is there to guard against a denial of emotions or a philosophy that puts an unreal expectation on caregivers if it implies that well-trained caregivers are always in control of their emotions.

Self-Awareness

Caregivers have a whole range of emotions that come into play when faced with crisis and disaster. The authors propose that self-awareness of the caregiver as a hidden victim is essential for staffs in human services agencies. Although the authors' own exposure to a disaster situation made the issue clear, victimization of caregivers in their routine activities has also been noted by Christine Maslach.[3] The concept of caregivers having rights, including the right to feelings, is new—if not controversial—to some professionals.

APPLICATION OF CRISIS INTERVENTION THEORY

The authors would like to offer an application of basic crisis intervention theory as a tool for understanding the caregiver as a victim. Drawing from Erich Lindemann and Gerald Caplan's work on crisis intervention, we see the caregiver as facing a crisis in role identity. In a disaster, the caregiver is placed in a role that is undefined. The immediate first stage is chaos. Although the caregivers' perception is not that the event is threatening their lives, the event is threatening their role as caregivers. The expectations are the caregivers' own, as they cast themselves in the role of a superhuman. Thus the total stress-crisis sequence is present: (1) a specific and identifiable stressful event, (2) the perception of the event as meaningful and threatening, (3) the disorganization or disequilibrium response resulting from the stressful event, and (4) the coping and interventive tasks that are involved in an adaptive or maladaptive resolution.[4]

It is essential to recognize that anxiety, self-doubt, fear, and excitement will all be present during the first stage. The second stage must be one of direction and structure. Just as the caregiver in crisis becomes more directive in his or her therapeutic approach with a family in stress, the caregiver must compartmentalize his or her own emotional reactions and assess his or her own strengths and weaknesses to decide in what capacity he or she can act effectively. The center staff's experience at the Big Thompson disaster demonstrated that having a previous hierarchical structure allowed the staff to assume an orderly functioning in a new setting quickly. Staff members were flexible in matching needs to skill areas. Ability to shed superhuman roles is vital. The staff became body handlers, data specialists, and identification experts.

The third stage must allow catharsis of pent-up feelings. Much to the staff's surprise, the use of humor was essential during this phase. For example, bodies were put in large plastic garbage bags, and at one point a sheriff's deputy crawled into one to play a joke on the pathologists. Jokes about bodies and body descriptions bounced back and forth. However, several staff members were uncomfortable with this vital safety valve and guilt feelings cropped up. Anger was another dominant feeling—anger at the bodies, anger that the dead victims had not climbed to higher ground, anger that lists of missing persons and bodies did not match. Guilt was expressed about other human needs and reactions. Caregivers must give themselves permission to rest, eat, talk, be curious, touch, laugh, cry, scream, and ask for help. Maslach says that one will not treat people as objects if one does not treat oneself as an object.[5] It is important to recognize that caregivers will experience the whole gamut of emotions and need to accept those emotions without guilt. An important part of this stage is also to take care of those emotional needs. Caregivers must give themselves permission to be human.

The fourth stage is resolution. As all caregivers know, crisis situations are exhilarating and taxing. There is a letdown when the caregiver moves on and goes back to a regular schedule. The caregiver does not want to give up the high pitch of activity and emotion. An attempt was made to resolve this crisis with therapeutic debriefing sessions. A portion of closure was also achieved when the center submitted a proposal for and received a contract with the federal government to provide mental health services to the victims of the Big Thompson disaster to supplement the center's own services. Now, a year later, the contract has terminated and the needs of canyon residents have been reintegrated into center services. For most of the staff there is resolution, integration, and closure. But not for all. For true to crisis intervention literature, each person has an individual timetable based on interacting variables, and a degree of resolution continues for some.

SUMMARY

It has been the authors' intention to add to the body of literature on crisis intervention by assessing one staff's reactions to a disaster. The staff members were seen to be victims of the disaster. The staff's strategies for self-help appear to have been therapeutic. All staff members reported a professional growth as a result of the crisis intervention, and there has been no report of any major personal disruption. The authors hope that other human services agencies will see caregivers' reactions to disaster as an essential area for continued investigation and research.

NOTES AND REFERENCES

1. *See,* for example, **Kai T. Erikson**, "Loss of Communality at Buffalo Creek," *American Journal of Psychiatry,* 133 (March 1976) pp. 302–305; **Calvin Frederick**, "Crisis Intervention and Emergency Mental Health" (Bethesda, Md.: National Institute of Mental Health) (mimeographed); **Christine Maslach**, "Burned Out," *Human Behavior,* 5 (September 1976), pp. 16–22; **Leo Rangell**, "Discussion of the Buffalo Creek Disaster: The Course of Psychic Trauma," *American Journal of Psychiatry,* 133 (March 1976), pp. 313–316; **Lydia Rapoport**, "Working with Families in Crisis: An Exploration in Preventive Intervention," *Social Work,* 7 (1962), pp. 48–56; **James L. Tichner and Frederick T. Kapp**, "Family and Character Change at Buffalo Creek," *American Journal of Psychiatry,* 133 (March 1976), pp. 295–299.

2. **Ron Craig Ilinitch and Martha P. Titus**, "Caretakers as Victims: The Big Thompson Flood, 1976" (Northampton, Mass.: Smith College School for Social Work, 1977). (Mimeographed.)

3. Op. cit.

4. **Gerald Caplan**, *Principles of Preventive Psychiatry* (New York: Basic Books, 1964).

5. Op. cit.

The Work Environment and Depression: Implications for Intervention

JANICE WOOD WETZEL

Social work practitioners have traditionally used a problem-person-situation model in approaching their clients' concerns. The situation component of the paradigm has usually been that of the family. Such a focus has been reasonable, since the family has long been considered the most influential environment in our culture. Recent research conducted by the author indicates that such a perspective may be inadequate in this transitional era.[1]

PERSON-ENVIRONMENT DEPRESSION RESEARCH

Fifty depressed and 50 nondepressed white women between the ages of 21 and 67, who had families and worked outside the home, were investigated. First, the presence or absence of depression was diagnosed by means of the Feighner Criteria for Primary Affective Disorder, Unipolar Type. To date, this is the only known criterion for depression that has been validated in a follow-up study (interview reliability was 94 percent in a five-year follow-up study of 115 patients hospitalized for psychiatric disorders).[2] Hypotheses Each woman's predisposition to dependence or independence was appraised in regard to her propensity, prior to the onset of depression, to be influenced easily, her interest in the world and in her own self-development (or the lack of such interests), and her general self-reliance, her tendency to take risks and assert herself. Next, the family and work milieu of each woman was assessed in terms of her long-term personal perception of that environment. It was predicted that there would be significant personality predispositions (dependence attributes) and environmental dimensions (controlling factors) that would correlate highly with the prediction of depression or well-being.

It was further hypothesized that the investigator's person-environment incongruence model of depression would be supported. This model posits that dependent and independent people require different environments to support their differential needs. For example, dependent persons require family and work environments in which they are relieved of decision-making, problem-solving, and risk-taking. Independent persons, conversely, require social climates in which they are free to make decisions, solve problems, and take risks.[3] In both cases, the absence of sustaining environments increases one's vulnerability to depression. Note, however, that one's needs at work may be quite different from one's needs at home. Dependence and independence, like other personality traits, are not necessarily stable across environments.[4] It was posited that the interaction between a person and her environment were crucial elements.

Results

A beginning case was made for the investigator's hypotheses. While the incongruence hypothesis was especially evident in the family environment, the significant results relative to the work environment also clearly differentiated depressed and nondepressed samples. Contrary to expectations, the work environment was found to be of far greater consequence than the family environment in predicting the presence or absence of depression. Fourteen out of 18 dependent variables, significant at the .05 level (with a highly significant multivariate F-test on the discriminant function, $p = <$ .0001) were concerned with the work environment. Since depression is the nation's leading mental health problem, such findings relative to women, the significant high-risk population, have serious implications for social work practice.[5] While the family environment was also found to be an influential factor, the overwhelming importance of the work environment in the lives of today's women is of special concern, considering the ever increasing participation of women in the work force.[6] While investigators have noted that traditional housewives are more prone to depression and are likely to be more seriously impaired than are working women, there have been no empirical data to compare the impact of both family and work environments on depressed and nondepressed women.[7]

SIGNIFICANT FINDINGS

In order to apply preventive measures as well as interventions to depression, the most significant findings of this study relating to the world of work will be described. Implications for interventions with both the environment and the person will be discussed. By so doing, the problem-person-situation model will be put into operation both theoretically and pragmatically. Psychosocial assessment of depression, long endorsed by social workers, can begin to be a realistic measurable construct within the limitations of science. This point must be emphasized. Since there is no cause-and-effect knowledge in the annals of physical or social science, we can only extrapolate.

Main Effects at Work

The variable that most significantly discriminated between depressed and nondepressed samples (the main effect) was control in the work environment. It was found that in the work environments of depressed women, management tended to use rules and pressures to control their workers. Such was not the case for nondepressed women. This finding is in keeping with theoretical constructs reflecting the need for personal control, mastery, and effectiveness espoused by social scientists and investigated empirically within a variety of conceptualizations.[8] It can be concluded, therefore, that control at work is not desirable, much less functional, regardless of whether a woman is dependent or independent.

A second major environmental factor at work was found to be suppor-tiveness by the managerial staff. Depressed women were less likely to report experiences of supportiveness by management in their work environments than were nondepressed women. That is, the depressed women reported that they were not likely to be treated with respect, to be given credit openly for their contributions, or to be encouraged to communicate to manage-ment. The employer's expectations were not likely to be considered reason-able, and supervisors did not "stand up" for their employees. The women did not feel that they were encouraged to be self-sufficient and to make their own decisions. The opposite was true for nondepressed women. Clearly, lack of managerial staff supportiveness closely parallels the control dimen-sion. Suggestions for intervention are, therefore, similar. This variable, in addition, provides richly referenced detail, for the factors to be modified are clearly delineated.

The crucial importance of managerial staff supportiveness was further reinforced by the only single significant personality factor that emerged as a main effect in the work dimension. That variable was dependence, charac-terized by women who are easily influenced by others. Vulnerability to persuasion as a dependence factor has been empirically validated. Such women have low self-esteem and feelings of insecurity concerning their own knowledge and reasoning powers.[9] In the present study, not surprisingly, the depressed women were much more likely to be easily influenced at work than were nondepressed women.

Significant Interactions at Work

All three significant person-environment interactions included self-reliance as a critical personality variable. And all three interacting environmental variables also dealt with lack of supportiveness and control. It can be concluded that distressing factors to be considered for treatment intervention cluster around controlling, emotionally unsupportive work environments. Personal predispositions chiefly characterize women who are dependent in that they are easily influenced and lack self-reliance. These women also lack interest in the world and in their own self-development and tend to be nonassertive, despite the fact that they work outside the home.

While the very act of going out to work creates the possibility for growth, it clearly does not ensure it. The socialization of women to dependence, submissiveness, and the family (a different dynamic from family interest plus outside commitment) is deeply ingrained.[10] Maturational processes are not sufficient for the development of independence, for independence appears to be acquired through learning and must be nurtured.[11] While task mastery is an essential ingredient in the development of independence, increasing client motivation is crucial as a change scheme. Consciousness-raising as a basic motivational strategy is of primary importance, for many women are not aware of their predisposition to dependence, nor are they aware of the negative impact their environment has on their lives.

Independent depressed women appear to require similar training. They perceived their environments as noncontrolling and saw family, peers, and staff as being supportive in the absence of information that confirmed these views. Informal interviews with these women indicated that they were fully responsible for their homes and families as well as working in the community. While they deeply resented their partners' (usually a husband) refusal to share responsibility in the home, they still considered their partners to be supportive and noncontrolling. Similar examples of apparent misperception by women have appeared in other studies.[12] Such women's lack of awareness of their real environments may represent a gap in the maturational process.

The final emerging variable, peer supportiveness, is an expression of the extent to which employees are friendly and mutually supportive, characterized by a warm group spirit. A friendly personal interest is taken in one another, with relationships extending beyond working hours. The fact that dependent depressed women typically experienced low peer support provides fuel for programming of peer relations activities in the work environment.

INTERVENTIONS IN THE WORK ENVIRONMENT

Social workers, whether caseworkers or administrators, who are in positions that can influence social policy and planning, can apply these findings to constructive environmental engineering, both in their own work environments and in those in which they are management consultants. When the case is made that restrictive rules and pressures are dysfunctional to employees and, consequently, to their productivity, employers may be convinced to find more rational work incentives.

Catalytic Change Model

An adaptation of the catalytic change model for community action and mental health is the recommended change strategy.[13] In such a model, high-risk groups are identified, along with relevant environmental "structures" and "sentiments." In the case of a work environment, structure refers to staff and peer groups and their informal and formal networks and hierarchies. The sentiments involve shared feelings, opinions, values, and attitudes that govern behavior within the structure. Following group assessment of the needs of the management and employees, identification of those concerns that are most amenable to change and that influence high-risk, depression-prone persons are targeted. In this case, the need of management to control and the needs of employees for emotional support and self-control must be addressed. Management may also be influenced to encourage formal collaborative efforts, as well as to provide time and physical space for informal peer interaction. The discouragement of personally threatening competitiveness, leading to alienation and discord, is also an appropriate strategy.

Note that as facilitators, the social workers do not take charge of the group. They simply act as catalysts for change, withdrawing when the members of the organization have mobilized their goals. By so doing, they are free to address new high-risk situations because they have not acted as protagonists.

Depressed clients who are not in such cooperative work milieus or in positions of power should be counseled to find healthier work situations whenever possible. When such moves are unrealistic, possibilities for creating areas of self-control within the job situation should be explored. There may be components of a client's job description that are open to personal control and can be enhanced. Encouragement of avocational interests, whereby a client can establish control in an alternative environment, may also help to provide a positive balance in the lives of these clients.

PERSONAL INTERVENTIONS

When social skills are lacking, the social worker can aid the client in developing such attributes. For example, communication skills as outlined in now-classic assertiveness training are essential.[14] They will not be detailed here, since they have been thoroughly explicated elsewhere. Such skills tend to encourage the supportiveness of others as well as to decrease the original need for such support.[15]

Motivation Training

A major step toward developmental maturity is awareness of the need for such growth. The Origin-Pawn Game is designed for such a task, experientially dramatizing one's dependent, externally caused (Pawn) orientation.[16] The following modified version of the exercise can be adapted to a group of clients who have been briefed concerning the fantasy nature of the game. The initial activity involves asking the group members to play the role of sixth-grade children who are being given the opportunity to do something creative with paper and pencil. They are told that they are free to do anything they wish to do; if they prefer, nothing at all. The activity continues for 15 minutes, at which time the social worker makes an excuse to leave the room.

After a few minutes, the worker returns, introducing herself as the substitute leader. "Now, children," she says in a loud, authoritative tone, "take everything off your desk but a pencil or pen." If there is any retort, she responds with "No more talking. Raise your hands if you want to say something!" Handing out blank paper, she asserts, "The key to this exercise is being good and doing exactly what I tell you. Raise your right hand. Now put your hand in your lap and sit up straight." The leader will reprimand behavior, finally explicitly directing the group to draw certain lines and figures step by step, controlling every movement, keeping the group constantly under surveillance. Following a few minutes of this controlling behavior, she returns to her original role, supportively suggesting exploration of the anger, hurt, frustration, and lack of control about which the clients are now becoming explicitly aware. The exercise and follow-up discussion provide rich insights in which clients get in touch with subservient, dependent feelings in a short time It is clear from the description that this exercise must be engaged in with discretion. Only well-trained therapists and nonpsychotic clients should take part, for the emotional affect can be as intense as it is effective.

World Interest and Self-Development

A further dimension of awareness training that addresses the issue of interest in the world and self-development is one used in a variety of therapeutic situations. The group members choose topics of potential interest, however peripheral, that they agree to investigate and report on to the group. Topics may include such areas as current events, culinary arts, literature, theater, dance, sports, and so on. Each person shares her infor-

mation with the others and is encouraged to plan group activities around
the reported interest area whenever appropriate. Interests are thus reinforced through positive group experience, which then may be generalized
to the larger community.

Self-Esteem via Task Mastery

Treatment for depression focusing on the development of self-esteem
through experiencing mastery of the environment as well as cognitive learning through reeducation are appropriate interventive methodologies.[17]
These strategies focus on task mastery on the part of depressed clients and
have been found to boost low self-concept, which in turn positively counters
depressed affect.

One must remember to "begin where the client is" and to be certain
that first efforts, however minimal, are chosen by the client and are likely
to result in success. The social worker can then contract with the client for
more extensive accomplishments. Eventually, through personal experience,
the client learns that she is an effective person who has control over her own
well-being and is not dependent on others to sustain her feelings of self-
worth. When she trusts her own knowledge and reasoning powers, external
influence is of less import. Another way to express this development is to
conclude that she has developed a sense of responsible independence and
need no longer live vicariously through others.[18]

The importance of such development to the well-being of human beings has been theoretically maintained by leading social scientists for many
years.[19] Supported primarily by clinical observations, the present study also
provides empirical support for their position.[20] This information may be
shared with the client. The client should be assured, of course, that the
social worker will provide the interim environmental stability that is congruent with the client's present state of dependence. In the meantime, the
world of work is just one environment in which these new interests and
personal development can be applied.

SUMMARY OF APPLIED INTERVENTIVE STRATEGIES

Treatment can be approached from both social policy (macro) and
direct practice (micro) points of view. Ideally, the two focuses are not
mutually exclusive but interact. From the macro vantage point, when more
than suggestion to employers is required, a catalytic change model has been
recommended. In such a schema, social workers facilitate a meeting of
management and employees in an open exchange, discussing differential
needs in order to ameliorate the problems of high-risk depressed personnel.
Control and staff and peer supportiveness in the environment are the major
relevant focal points of concern. When the cooperation of management and

peers to modify the work environment is unrealistic, focusing on segments of possible vocational and avocational control or total environmental change—changing jobs—is to be considered.

At the micro level, the tendency for depressed women to lack self-reliance is of foremost concern. Among the attributes of a dependent person are being easily influenced and nonassertive and having little interest in the world and one's self-development. Such women are especially vulnerable to external control and inadequate support from management and peers. Interventive strategies focus on motivation-training. Beginning with consciousness-raising (the Origin-Pawn Game described earlier), task mastery forms a core for the development of self-esteem and belief in one's own reasoning powers and ability. Increasing interest in the world and in self-development are worked on through group activities. Assertiveness training communication skills are integrated into the program, enhancing self-reliance and staff and peer relationships.

Independent clients, too, must be made aware of the reality of their environments. Only then can they freely exercise their prevailing independent predispositions and remain free from depression. As for dependent clients in treatment, social workers must provide congruently supportive environments because of the absence of these in the larger community. It must be remembered that dependent individuals have the greatest need for nurturance.[21] It is ironic that women, socialized to dependence, are also socialized to be the nurturers rather than the nurtured. This traditional person-environment interaction is clearly dysfunctional. It is not surprising, given this perspective, that women are up to three times more likely to become depressed than are men.[22]

The author is presently involved in a cross-cultural extension of this study. Three hundred white, black, and Mexican-American men and women are taking part in the research. Generalizations to larger populations can only be made when the results provide empirical support. In the meantime, it must be emphasized that the present findings and applied interventions are limited to white females. The author, however, has no reason to predict different results in the extended study.

NOTES AND REFERENCES

1. **Janice Wood Wetzel**, "Depression and Dependence upon Unsustaining Environments," *Clinical Social Work Journal,* 6 (Summer 1978), pp. 75–89.

2. **George Murphy** et al., "Validity of the Diagnosis of Primary Affective Disorder," *Archives of General Psychiatry,* 30 (June 1974), pp. 751–756.

3. **Janice Wood Wetzel,** "Dependence upon Unsustaining Environments as an Antecedent Variable of Depression," Chapter IV, "Preliminary Study: Development of Independence-Dependence Measures," pp. 49–65. Unpublished doctoral dissertation, Washington University, 1976.

4. **Walter Mischel,** *Personality and Assessment* (New York: John Wiley & Sons, 1968); **Janice Wood Wetzel,** ibid.

5. *See* **James Schwab,** "A Rising Incidence of Depression," *Attitude,* 1 (January/February 1970), p. 2; and **Steven K. Secunda** et al., eds., *Special Report on the Depressive Disorders* (Bethesda, Md.: National Institute of Mental Health, 1973).

6. **Martha N. Ozawa,** "Women and Work," *Social Work,* 21 (November 1976), pp. 455–462.

7. *See,* for example, **Pauline Bart,** "Depression in Middle-Aged Women," in **Vivian Gornick and Barbara K. Moran,** eds., *Women in Sexist Society* (New York: Basic Books, 1971), pp. 99–117; **Myrna Weissman and Eugene Paykel,** *The Depressed Woman* (Chicago: University of Chicago Press, 1974); and **E. Mostow and P. Newberry,** "Work Role and Depression in Women: A Comparison of Workers and Housewives in Treatment," *American Journal of Orthopsychiatry,* 45 (July 1975), pp. 538–548.

8. *See,* for example, **Henry L. Minton,** "Power and Personality," in **James T. Tedeschi,** *The Social Influence Processes* (Chicago: Aldine-Atherton, 1972), pp. 100–150; **Julian Rotter,** "Generalized Expectancies for Internal versus External Control of Reinforcement," *Psychological Monographs,* 80 (1966), pp. 1–28; and **Aaron Beck,** "The Development of Depression: A Cognitive Model," in **Raymond J. Friedman and Martin M. Katz,** eds., *The Psychology of Depression: Contemporary Theory and Research* (Washington, D.C.: V. H. Freeman & Co., 1975).

9. *See,* for example, **Carl Hovland and I. L. Janis,** eds., *Personality and Persuasability,* Vol. 2 (New Haven: Yale University Press, 1959); and Arnold Lazarus, "Learning Theory in the Treatment of Depression," *Behavioral Research Therapy,* 6 (February 1968), pp. 83–89.

10. *See,* for example, **Clara Thompson,** "An Introduction to Minor Maladjustments," in Silvano Arieti, ed., *American Handbook of Psychiatry* (New York: Basic Books, 1959), pp. 237–244; **Karen Horney,** *Feminine Psychology* (New York: Norton, 1973); **Julia Sherman,** *On the Psychology of Women: A Survey of Empirical Studies* (Springfield, Ill.: C. C. Thomas, 1971); and **Jean Baker Miller,** ed., *Psychoanalysis and Women* (Baltimore, Md.: Penguin Books, 1973).

11. *See* **James Alexander,** "On Dependence and Independence," *Bulletin of Philadelphia Association of Psychoanalysis,* 20 (1970), pp. 49–57; and **Robert W. White,** "Motivation Reconsidered: The Concept of Competence," *Psychological Review,* 66 (1959), pp. 297–333.

12. *See,* for example, **Edward L. Deci,** *Intrinsic Motivation* (New York: Plenum Press, 1975); and **Jean Curtis,** *Working Mothers* (New York: Doubleday, 1976).

13. **Victor G. Cardoza, William C. Ackerly, and Alexander H. Leighton,** "Im-

proving Mental Health Through Community Action," *Community Mental Health Journal,* 11 (Summer 1975), pp. 215–227.

14. *See,* for example, **Robert E. Alberti and Michael L. Emmons,** *Your Perfect Right: A Guide to Assertive Behavior* (San Luis Obispo, Calif.: Impact, 1974); **Patricia Jakubowski-Spector,** "Facilitating the Growth of Women Through Assertive Training," *The Counselling Psychologist,* 5 (1973), pp. 75–86; and **Stanlee Phelps and Nancy Austin,** *The Assertive Woman* (San Luis Obispo, Calif.: Impact, 1975).

15. **Richard B. Stuart,** "Casework Treatment of Depression Viewed as Interpersonal Disturbance," *Social Work,* 12 (April 1967), pp. 27–36.

16. **A. Kupermen,** "Relations Between Differential Constraints, Affect, and the Origin-Pawn Variable." Unpublished doctoral dissertation, Washington University, 1967. Concepts are based on **Richard de Charms,** *Personal Causation: The Internal Affective Determinants of Behavior* (New York: Academic Press, 1968), pp. 319–353.

17. **Beck,** op. cit.; and **Seligman,** op. cit.

18. **Alexander Lowen,** *Depression and the Body* (New York: Coward, Mc Cann & Geoghegan, 1972).

19. **White,** op. cit.; **K. A. Adler in H. L. Ansbacher and R. R. Ansbacher,** eds., *The Individual Psychology of Alfred Adler* (New York: Basic Books, 1956); **Gordon Allport,** *Becoming: Basic Considerations for a Psychology of Personality* (New Haven: Yale University Press, 1955); de Charms, op. cit.; **Robert Woodworth,** *Dynamics of Behavior* (New York: Holt, 1958); **Abraham H. Maslow,** *Motivation and Personality* (New York: Harper & Row, 1970).

20. *See also* **Beck,** op. cit; and **Seligman,** op. cit.

21. **Peter Lewinsohn,** "A Behavioral Approach to Depression," in **Friedman and Katz,** eds., op. cit., pp. 157–185. *See also* Lowen, op. cit.

22. *See,* for example, **Charlotte Silverman,** *The Epidemiology of Depression* (Baltimore: Johns Hopkins University Press, 1968); **Weissman and Paykel,** op. cit.; and **Myrna Weissman and Gerald Klerman,** "Sex Differences and the Epidemiology of Depression," *Archives of General Psychiatry,* 34 (January 1977), pp. 98–111.

Consultation in Group Homes for Adolescents

CARLTON E. MUNSON

In recent years there has been a trend toward shifting rehabilitation efforts for acting-out adolescents from large institutional settings to small group homes.[1] This change in focus is in part the result of a belief that the group home approach is more humane, more effective therapeutically, and less costly than large institutional programs.[2] However, some have questioned the group home approach because it utilizes mostly paraprofessional staff.[3] The view presented in this paper is that cost can be reduced and effectiveness maintained when good professional consultation is provided to paraprofessional staff.

Social workers are increasingly serving as professional consultants to group homes and need models to guide their activities in such settings. Little conceptualization of the role of the consultant in group homes has appeared in the literature, and the entire criminal justice system has been described as in disarray, in part owing to failure to use sound management models.[4] This article uses role theory as a model for guiding consultative services in group home settings. Since most group homes use an informal approach to organizational structure and functions, there is an acute need for new conceptualizations of consultation because most professionals are accustomed to providing such services in more formal and traditional organizational settings.

CONVENTIONAL AND INTERPERSONAL ROLES

In role theory, roles have been distinguished as *conventional* and *interpersonal*.[5] Conventional roles are based on routine responses to human situations and regularized structures. Interpersonal roles develop out of unique interactive situations, and repeated interaction leads to creative role

246

performance and expectations. Consultants to group homes have inadequate conventional role models or expectations to guide their performance and must use the interpersonal model.

Conventionally, no distinction has been made between consultation and supervision. Supervision implies exercising authority, while consultation implies giving advice and making recommendations. Comments by workers suggest that simply to label supervision consultation can lead to conflict, gradual isolation, and lack of interaction when the worker learns that the freedom to act independently is not recognized or accepted.[6] In group homes, the social work consultant should make clear to all involved that consultation is different from supervision and that interaction with the staff does not involve administrative responsibility. Most group homes have a director who carries this authority, and the roles of director and consultant should be differentiated and clarified. Clarity of responsibility is essential, since it has been shown that an effective, forceful director of a correctional program can have a positive impact.[7]

Conventional use of the term *consultation* in relation to role function can create problems. In some group homes, the term *consultation* has been used to describe treatment services provided by professionals—by psychiatrists, psychologists, social workers, and educators. The functions of such professionals may accurately be described as fee-for-service functions. When such services are provided by outsiders, there is little motivation to develop these services within the organization, and regular staff members tend to shy away from direct helping activities for fear of intruding on the activities of the service-providers. This model severely limits the total program offered by the staff of a group home and restricts its contribution to the rehabilitation process. This is paradoxical, since staff members in most group homes view their programs as heavily milieu oriented. Certain fee-for-service functions are essential to adequate programming, but they need to be integrated with regular staff functions.

The interpersonal role model of the consultant focuses on this integrative function rather than simple provision of clinical social work services. The consultant engages in enhancing the helping skills of the regular staff and interpreting the roles of outside professionals who provide services, as well as integrating these roles and relationships. The importance of coordinating staff roles and service-provider roles cannot be overemphasized, because residents of group homes will often attempt to manipulate the system at any points of potential lack of understanding or agreement. The consultant must help to focus the theoretical treatment approaches of service-providers in relation to change efforts of full-time staff. With no means of coordinating and providing consistency of total program efforts, confusion and weak outcome will result.

In carrying out this role, the consultant needs skill, a clear understanding of how the group home operates, and a great deal of knowledge regarding the disciplines of psychiatry, psychology, social work, counseling, and education. The consultant must go beyond merely answering questions and asking the staff members what they think about their efforts.[8] Staff members need to be encouraged in their own efforts to help residents. Crises and conflicts occur frequently in such settings, and if the staff is merely control and rule oriented, this limits its opportunities to be helpful to residents.

PROFESSIONAL ROLE DISTANCE

Goffman has developed the concept of *role distance* to describe the degree to which a person embraces a given role.[9] Role distance has many implications that can be applied to the role of the consultant. In most group homes, the usual physical trappings that suggest role distance—such as private offices, large desks, degrees displayed on the wall, and manner of dress—are conspicuously absent. The consultant who is used to such surroundings can frequently feel overwhelmed working in a group home. Interactionally, the consultant is denied verbal forms of role distancing, such as nodding, remaining silent, responding to questions with questions, and using the third-person singular and plural to objectify relationships. A consultant using such role-distancing techniques may quickly be isolated from and rejected by both residents and staff.

Participation in the program of a group home demands, in Goffman's terms, high-level involvement and total role embracement. The consultant must develop a delicate balance between subjective involvement at an experiential level and objective professional composure appropriate to the situation. There must be an assessment of the necessary and sufficient conditions for acceptance by residents and staff, and at the same time respect for the consultant's knowledge and skill in making judgments regarding the handling of troublesome situations. This can be achieved through involvement of the consultant with staff and residents on both a formal and informal basis. Initially the consultant needs to get a feel for the group home through participating in such ordinary, unstructured or low-structure activities as meals, watching television, field trips, and shopping trips. Participation in such informal activities must be blended with participation in more formal activities, such as staff/resident meetings, evaluations of prospective residents, and community meetings.

While the nature of structured and unstructured activities varies for different group homes, it is important that balanced interaction take place to allow the consultant and residents to develop role-performance expectations. Residents frequently deal with new residents, new staff, and consultants by denying them status in the group. If the consultant initially becomes thoroughly familiar with staff/resident relationships, resident cliques and systems of collusion, and house rules, devaluation of role performance capability can be avoided.

Certain efforts to overcome role distance to develop a positive relationship with residents and staff can have the opposite of the desired effect. The consultant who attempts to adopt the dress style and colloquial and specialized vocabulary and jargon of the residents creates an artificiality that can deter development of an effective relationship. Instead, the consultant should use his or her natural language and style of dress. Language should be free of technical and professional terms that might be meaningless to residents and paraprofessional staff.[10]

There are indications that natural role distance contributes to the change process at the worker or consultant level. Halmos calls attention to this aspect of change-agent relationships through citing research supporting Homans's hypothesis that interacting individuals tend to become more alike as time passes.[11] Over time, the role distance between the consultant and the residents and the staff lessens, and change occurs on the part of all the participants, including the consultant, but this is a natural evolutionary process rather than a contrived effort. From the consultant's role perspective, if there is to be conscious use of the professional self to promote change in residents and staff, then the consultant must provide a differential model for identification at given points in the consultation process. Support for this view is provided by the research of Tessler and Polansky, who consider their own findings paradoxical in that dissimilarity led to greater verbal accessibility.[12]

To achieve this, the role of consultant must be performed in full view of staff and residents. A consultant who has sessions only with the house director or who meets only with the staff and excludes residents must deal with problems and behavior that is once removed and in verbally abstract form. The consultant who performs in this manner is creating a role distance that can inhibit effectiveness, produce isolation, and ultimately result in rejection.

ROLE-TAKING AND ROLE-MAKING

Group home consultation does not involve just the assumption of the conventional role of consultant but instead necessitates a role-making process. In actual practice, the consultant engages in a process of role-taking and role-making at the same time. The role enactment of the consultant is oriented to two differentiated groups—staff and residents. The staff members usually have some vague conventional role expectations of the consultant, such as teaching them how to handle problems better, improving staff/resident relations, and telling staff what they are doing right or wrong. Residents are less likely to have conventional expectations of the consultant, but when they do, these are related to helping them with psychological adjustment and interpersonal functioning. This is based on their past experience with court counselors and treatment-oriented services.

In such a situation, the consultant is in role conflict because of differing expectations, and unless some selective process is used to define the initial role-taking, confusion will result. The initial role-taking must anticipate future role-making as much as possible. The consultant can avoid confusion through giving the role a central focus. This focus of the consultant's role must be defined in relation to other roles. It has been the writer's experience that three sets of role relationships are generally viewed by the participants as creating problems: (1) residents' interpersonal relationships, (2) staff relationships, and (3) staff/resident relationships. The consultant can designate these three areas as the focus of a dynamic consultation that is carried out in house meetings involving all staff members and residents, with the consultant taking full responsibility for conducting the meetings. When the consultant takes responsibility for these meetings, the staff members, and especially the director, can move out of defensive and authoritarian positions and share some of their own personal feelings and attitudes toward residents' behavior.

Residents' Interpersonal Relationships

When aggressive, acting-out adolescents with deficits in social skills are placed together in a close, semistructured living situation, interpersonal conflicts are a natural result. Emerging collusive systems, cliques, leaders, instigators, and victims crystallize interpersonal conflict over such issues as racism, sexual relationships, theft, drug use, profanity, and physical fights. The group meeting becomes an arena for dealing with specific instances of interpersonal difficulties. Staff members often respond to conflicts through confrontation, issuance of demerits, and physical intervention. The staff lives with the constant fear that interpersonal conflicts will escalate out of hand.

When the skilled consultant takes over responsibility and works through a resident problem, the staff may be surprised to see that the conflict reaches a natural height and can be brought to resolution by the residents themselves with indirect guidance, support, and encouragement from the consultant and staff. Confrontation and direct intervention are sometimes necessary and appropriate but should be a last resort used only when there is a potential threat to the functioning of the larger system.

For this strategy to be successful, interaction must be specific and focus on the goal of conflict resolution. Goal attainment is basic to the group's functional integration, and when the goal becomes conflict resolution, residents will abandon cliques and collusive subgroup orientations to identify with the safer norms of the total group home.[13] The consultant should work directly to influence goal attainment through resolution of a specific conflict situation and indirectly to shift group members from a subgroup normative identity to a total group normative identification that supports the group home's objectives. To accomplish this, the consultant must be thoroughly familiar with the existing subgroups and must be able to interpret the goals of the interaction to staff.

Staff Relationships

Generally full-time staff members in group homes are paraprofessionals. Professional treatment services are provided on a part-time basis by outsiders. The paraprofessionals view themselves as on the front line, working in the trenches, while professionals are depicted as aloof and having limited involvement. Staff members, especially new employees, see themselves as being under attack by residents for their efforts to be helpful. Residents have values and behavioral norms that staff find alien and sometimes offensive. Residents are often verbally abusive toward staff and rarely express appreciation. Staff members develop a sense of a common bond in a system in which professionals offer little or no support and residents show no respect or appreciation. Roles of this nature, which do not have collective approval, tend to result in tension, insecurity, uncertainty, and frustration.[14]

The consultant can function as a mechanism of gratification for the staff. Frequent reinforcement of staff efforts is important. Regular meetings with staff members that emphasize their achievements as much as exploring staff/resident problems are essential. The consultant needs to interpret negative and hostile behavior of poorly socialized adolescents as institutionally ingrained and not personally specific. The consultant can work with staff members to make their role descriptions as clear as possible. If staff roles are vague, under such adverse conditions problems of morale and motivation increase.[15]

The consultant needs to work to build natural positive reinforcement mechanisms within the staff group. Staff members need to be alerted to avoid manipulation by residents. Through consistent application of house rules, resident-induced dissension can be minimized. Staff members should be encouraged to meet frequently on their own to share and to find solutions to problems. The consultant should have direct contact with outside fee-for-service providers and encourage them to have periodic direct involvement with the staff to bridge the role-relationship gap.

Staff/Resident Relationships

Staff/resident interactions are often characterized as conflict laden, and a small staff dealing with a large group of residents may become weary and defeated. Staff members can be encouraged to use positive sanctions rather than negative denials in interaction to avoid conflict. For example, when a resident who is given medication every four hours approaches a staff member two hours early, instead of saying, "No, you had medicine two hours ago," the staff member can avoid denial by stating, "In two hours you can have more medication." This simple technique frequently prevents a conflict situation from occurring. Also, when denial of a request is necessary, staff members can avoid confrontation by stating their reasons in a clear, concise manner. Residents often accuse staff members of making decisions without providing adequate explanations and this often does happen. Many staff decisions are made for reasons that have nothing to do with residents' behavior, but any unexplained decision or restriction of activity in the home is interpreted by residents as punishment.

Residents frequently engage in verbal abuse of staff members and accuse them of not doing their jobs. In many instances the underlying message is, "We are not going to let you do your job." Profanity and accusations need to be explored openly. Inadequately socialized residents see staff members as objects. Profanity directed at staff members is commonly justified on the basis that the staff gets paid for this and therefore should willingly accept derogatory comments. Staff members can be helped to express their feelings when verbally abused. When both staff members and residents openly share their feelings in these areas, accusations and profanity in general decrease. Staff members and residents need help in identifying and sharing their personal feelings about emotionally powerful situations. The number of ways of appropriately responding to emotionally charged encounters is not infinite, and repeated efforts to explore adequate responses to these situations are needed.

Deviant behavior within the house, such as drinking, theft, marijuana usage, and sexual activity, is viewed by staff as structurally threatening. Often such behavior occurs with more frequency within the house than outside. In some situations this may indicate that the residents trust the staff to deal with this behavior in a more rational manner than do such outside institutions as the police, courts, and schools. Staff members need assistance in making every effort to recognize this trust and to use a rational problem-solving process rather than dismissal of the resident. If dismissal becomes the primary problem-solving mechanism, some residents will use a deviant act manipulatively to avoid involvement in the rehabilitative efforts. Staff members need to be helped to confront deviance with helpful concern. Angry confrontation leads residents to conclude that staff members are interested only in discovering and punishing deviant behavior instead of caring about the well-being of residents.[16]

CONCLUSION

With the increased use of group homes as structural means of rehabilitating acting-out adolescents, social workers are being called on to provide consultative services to these nontraditional settings. The role of consultant can be enhanced through using appropriate degrees of role-distancing and an interpersonal role model conception as opposed to a conventional role model. Consultation can be organized effectively through use of role theory based on an interactional focus of (1) residents' interpersonal relationships, (2) staff relationships, and (3) staff/resident relationships.

NOTES AND REFERENCES

1. **Ellen Handler,** "Residential Treatment Programs for Juvenile Delinquents," *Social Work,* 20 (May 1975), p. 217.

2. **William L. Rohde,** "Urban Homes for Youths," *Social Work,* 20 (July 1975), pp. 324–325.

3. *See,* for example, **Theodore Levine,** "Community-Based Treatment for Adolescents: Myths and Realities," *Social Work,* 22 (March 1977), pp. 144–147.

4. **Ronald I. Weiner,** "The Criminal Justice System at the Breaking Point," *Social Work,* 20 (November 1975), pp. 439–440.

5. *See* **John P. Hewitt,** *Self and Society: A Symbolic Interactionist Social Psychology* (Boston: Allyn & Bacon, 1976), pp. 144–146.

6. The issue of authority is an especially significant and a highly charged matter in all criminal justice agencies. *See* **Weiner,** op. cit., pp. 440–441. Also, for a discussion of control related to the confusion of supervision and consultation, *see* **Yona Cohen,** "Staff Supervision in Probation," *Federal Probation,* 40 (September 1976), pp. 17–23.

7. **Handler,** op. cit., p. 221.

8. *See* **Leslie Button,** *Discovery and Experience: A New Approach to Training, Group Work, and Teaching* (London: Oxford University Press, 1971), pp. 69–70.

9. **Erving Goffman,** "Role Distance," in Dennis Brisset and Charles Edgley, eds., *Life as Theatre: A Dramaturgical Sourcebook* (Chicago: Aldine, 1975), pp. 123–132.

10. For a detailed discussion of language and dress in professional interaction, *see* **Margaret Schubert,** *Interviewing in Social Work Practice: An Introduction* (New York: Council on Social Work Education, 1971).

11. **Paul Halmos,** *The Faith of the Counsellors* (New York: Schocken Books, 1970), p. 91.

12. **Richard C. Tessler and Norman A. Polansky**, "Perceived Similarity: A Paradox in Interviewing," *Social Work*, 20 (September 1975), pp. 359–363.

13. **Ronald A. Feldman**, "Modes of Integration and Conformity Behavior: Implications for Social Group Work Intervention," in **Paul Glasser**, et al., *Individual Change Through Small Groups* (New York: Free Press, 1974), pp. 153–154.

14. **Alvin L. Bertrand**, *Social Organization: A General Systems and Role Theory Perspective* (Philadelphia: F. A. Davis, 1972), pp. 49–93.

15. *See* **Willard C. Richan**, "Indigenous Paraprofessional Staff," in **Florence Kaslow**, ed., *Issues in Human Services* (San Francisco: Jossey Bass, 1972), pp. 62–67.

16. For specific techniques related to this orientation, *see* **Fritz Redl and David Wineman**, *Controls from Within: Techniques for the Treatment of the Aggressive Child* (New York: Free Press, 1965).

Education Laws: The Silent Revolution

E. VIRGINIA SHEPPARD LAPHAM AND JOYCE DE CHRISTOPHER

The silent revolution occurring in this decade by and on behalf of handicapped persons and their families has resulted in a plethora of legislation, a knowledge of which is essential for social workers in nearly any setting.[1] Thus far, the arenas have been the courtroom, the U.S. Congress, state legislatures, and increasingly the local education agencies now mandated to provide a free appropriate education and related services to the eight million handicapped children in the United States.[2] Information about and effects of the new education laws—in particular Public Law 94-142, the Education of All Handicapped Children Act of 1975—are the specific focus of this paper.[3]

Education is and has been the vocation of children in America since compulsory school attendance laws were enacted in most states in the early part of this century. Yet in 1975, the Congress of the United States found that more than one million children of school age were out of school.[4] These one million children, and the seven million other children labeled as handicapped, have now been declared by Congress to have a right to education at no cost to their parents or guardians.[5] The due process rights of parents to participate in where and how their children will be educated is also spelled out in P.L. 94-142, which took effect October 1, 1977, and which will become fully implemented over a five-year period.[6] While declared by its Senate author, Harrison Williams (Dem.—N.J.), to be "the most significant development in our national elementary and secondary education program" in more than a decade, P.L. 94-142 is not without problems in its implementation.[7]

The changes that have resulted from passage of this law are producing significant stresses in individuals, families, schools, and other agencies, providing new challenges and new dilemmas for social workers. Before dealing with these challenges and dilemmas, let us briefly review the problems that this federal legislation has sought to remedy, how the new education laws came about, and what they include.

NEW EDUCATION LAWS

"Will my child be able to go to school?" has in recent decades been the question, spoken or unspoken, of nearly every American parent with a handicapped child. This does not imply that school is a panacea for handicapped children (or for nonhandicapped children), but it is true that denial of schooling has significant consequences both for the child and for its parents. The latter have traditionally had to provide or hire child care services during school hours and to become teacher as well as parent.

In the past, handicapped children accepted by local education agencies were often bused long distances, were placed in classes held in less attractive and more isolated surroundings than those for nonhandicapped children, and had frequent changes of program with little cooperative planning between teachers and parents. Some handicapped children have been placed in private schools, with fees being the responsibility of the parents. Education, although hardly the only or the most crucial problem faced by parents of a handicapped child, can still be seen to be a problem having a considerable impact.

In the past, many parents simply accepted the denial of the right to an education for their handicapped children. This situation changed only recently with a raise in parents' consciousness that resulted from the black civil rights movement of the 1960s and the women's movement that followed. A few parents filed suits asserting their children's right to an education. The first significant case, heard in a federal district court in Pennsylvania (*Pennsylvania Association for Retarded Children* vs. *Commonwealth of Pennsylvania,* 1971), resulted in a decision that all retarded children had a right to attend school. A second case, decided in federal court in Washington, D.C., the following year (*Mills* vs. *Board of Education of the District of Columbia,* 1972), had broader implications affirming the right of all handicapped children to attend school.[8] The U.S. Constitution does not guarantee anyone a right to an education, but since the individual states do provide and mandate education for children, the equal protection and due process provisions of the Fifth and Fourteenth Amendments to the Constitution formed the bases for these judicial rulings.[9]

During the same period of time when parents and advocacy groups were taking their cause to the judicial system, they were also applying pressure to the executive and legislative branches of the federal government.

The tactics used—adapted from the earlier civil rights movement—included wheelchair marches on Washington, protests at state capitals and at the White House Conferences on Employment of the Handicapped, organized letter-writing campaigns, and visits to legislative bodies. However, until the demonstrations over the Section 504 Regulations of the Rehabilitation Act of 1973 (P.L. 93-112), there was little media coverage or public reaction to the activities of the handicapped minority and their families.[10]

Lack of public awareness of—and therefore possible public opposition to—this latest civil rights movement has enabled the implementation of legislative reform without much opposition. For instance, P.L. 94-142 was passed by both Houses of Congress with a total of only seven opposing votes in each House. On November 29, 1975, when a reluctant President Ford signed P.L. 94-142 into law, he cautioned that "this bill promises more than the federal government can deliver "and is falsely raising the expectations of the groups affected. . . ."[11] Whether these words prove to be reactionary or prophetic depend on the actions of the nonhandicapped majority to implement or thwart the new legislation and its intent.

> Public policy determines the degree to which minorities, in this case the handicapped, will be treated inequitably by the controlling majority. It is almost axiomatic that those with power to distribute resources and benefits will not allocate those resources and benefits equitably to all who may have interests. Thus minorities and civil rights proponents seek from the controlling majority equal treatment for the minority.[12]

Provisions of P.L. 94-142

To assure that all handicapped children have available to them "a free appropriate education which emphasizes special education and related services designed to meet their unique needs," P.L. 94-142 includes the following requirement for state education agencies:

■To make extensive efforts to locate children not currently in education programs.

■To have in effect a policy that assures all handicapped children the right to a free appropriate education at no cost to parents or guardians and a timetable for implementing this policy.

■To maintain records on numbers and classifications of handicapped children and to guarantee the confidentiality of data and information.

■To establish procedural safeguards regarding educating handicapped children in the least restrictive environment, and to provide that testing and evaluation materials not be culturally or racially discriminatory.

■To assume responsibility for assuring that all educational programs for handicapped children meet education standards of the state education agency.

■To provide that the state have an advisory committee to advise on unmet needs of handicapped children, comment on proposed rules and regulations, and assist the state in developing and reporting data and evaluations.

■To establish procedural safeguards or due process provisions for handicapped children and their families, such as the following:

1. Providing opportunities for parents or guardians to examine and copy all relevant records of the child pertaining to identification, evaluation, and educational placement.

2. Appointing a surrogate parent when the parents or guardians are not known or are unavailable.

3. Providing written notice to the parents or guardians in their native language when there is reason to believe that a handicapping condition exists or a change in placement is being considered for their child.

4. Providing opportunities for parents to present complaints relating to the identification, evaluation, or educational placement of the child.

5. Appointing an impartial hearing officer to conduct an impartial due process hearing when parents disagree with a decision of the local education agency.

6. Advising the parents of their right to appeal a decision of the impartial hearing officer to the state education agency if they disagree.

7. Advising the parents of their rights to go into the courts of the judicial system if they do not agree with the decisions of the education system, all the way to the U.S. Supreme Court if they so desire.

8. Leaving the child in his or her current educational placement during the time appeal procedures are pending or in a public school class if the child has never been in a special education program.

■To provide each handicapped child with an individualized education program each year developed in consultation with the parent or guardian.

■To carry out the legal requirements in consultation with handicapped individuals and parents or guardians of handicapped children and to hold public hearings and provide opportunities for comment prior to adopting policies, programs, and procedures regarding the education of handicapped children.

■To write and submit a state plan each year that sets forth the policies and procedures that demonstrate how the state had or will carry out the provisions of the federal act.[13]

Primary responsibility for assuring the full, effective implementation of P.L. 94-142 has been assigned to the Bureau for the Education of the Handicapped.[14]

INFORMING PARENTS AND EDUCATORS

P.L. 94-142 mandates that parents of handicapped children be informed of the education rights of their children and of the due process procedures through which parents may exercise these rights. Pamphlets and brochures explaining these rights have been written by state education department officials and distributed widely. Spot announcements have been made over radio and television stations, giving telephone numbers parents can call to get more information. New items and feature articles have appeared in newspapers around the country as a public service and in response to increased public interest in this latest consumer movement. Local school districts have sponsored meetings on legislation and sent out letters to parents advising them of their legal rights. Parent groups representing children with various kinds of handicapping conditions are becoming better informed about the new education laws and are in turn sharing their information with others. Yet in spite of all of these efforts, large numbers of parents have not heard about the new rights accorded to them under P.L. 94-142, while others who *have* heard about the laws may be unsure of how they apply to their child or themselves, or may be fearful of taking advantage of them.

Getting Information

Providing information to parents of handicapped children seen by social workers in clinics, hospitals, institutions, rehabilitation centers, family or social service agencies, and private practice requires at a minimum the knowledge that these legal rights now exist and the names of places to which parents can write for additional information.[15]

Social workers who work primarily or exclusively with parents of handicapped children should themselves become fully informed about the education laws.

Sharing Information with Parents

The method by which information on legislation is provided to individual parents of handicapped children seen by social workers will be determined by the extent of the social workers' knowledge of the legislation and the understanding of the parents. Distribution of brochures and pamphlets on parent rights may be all that is needed. For groups of parents not already informed by other means and methods, organizing parent workshops or a series of meetings with persons knowledgeable and articulate about the legislation may be a helpful social work task. Ways in which the authors shared information included writing a column for a monthly newsletter, speaking at parent and community meetings and on a local radio call-in program, and preparation of a handbook for parents on federal and New

York State education laws.[16] The handbook was an attempt to weave together the social worker's understanding of parents' problems with a knowledge of the legislation and its significance.

Enabling Parents to Use Information

Parents who have had one or more negative experiences with their local school districts may now be reluctant to accept the assistance offered by the school district as a result of the federal mandate. Parents' mistrust may lead them to ignore letters sent by the school district offering educational placements for their children. The benefits to parents of cooperating with the local schools need to be strongly emphasized. Parents should also be advised that they now have the right to disagree with and to appeal decisions without jeopardizing their child's education. Social workers should facilitate the sharing among parents of positive experiences with the public schools.

Another important activity for social workers is to give as much direct support as possible to parents attending evaluations, reviews, or hearings regarding their child, since these, when unfamiliar, can be intimidating. Clarifying the kind of support that is needed—an educator who knows the special education needs of the child to accompany the parents, a legislative specialist or attorney familiar with education laws to be consulted, or ego support that can be supplied by the social worker, a friend, or relative— is also helpful. Excessive concerns about meeting with school officials may need to be dealt with through use of other kinds of interventive techniques to determine with the parents whether they are reacting to negative experiences with the schools or to something else.

One of the greatest dilemmas faced by one of the authors was in counseling the parents of a handicapped child being recommended for termination from educational placement. The issue was whether the parents had any alternative to the termination decision that had been made about their daughter, since they agreed with neither the recommendation nor the reasons given for the recommendation. Having been apprised of their legal rights by the social worker, the parents used this information to insist that the child remain in her current placement, contrary to the staff's desire and possibly to the best interests of the child. Although in this case the decision made may not have been the best, the action taken by these parents had a positive effect on the agency involved. The policy change resulting from the appeal made by these parents assured that no other children would be terminated without due process procedures being implemented.

Sharing Information with Educators

The other group of persons most affected by the new education laws are the educators, who may also need information, assistance in understanding and implementing the laws, and support when they feel threatened by change. The individual teacher or other staff member does not usually perceive of himself or herself as a member of a power structure against which parents need to use their due process rights. School staff may have anxiety about their own rights. This is an ongoing issue that will emerge whenever a parent disagrees with a school staff member. Frequent clarification and staff support will be needed.[17]

IMPLEMENTING THE NEW EDUCATION LAWS

Currently school social workers are plagued by implementing "the elaborate requirements governing each step" of P.L. 94-142.[18] Handicapped children are only a small percentage of the student population in the public schools, but because of the new laws, a disproportionate amount of time must be spent on their identification, evaluation, and placement. Interviewing the family of the child, writing a social history, preparing the family for meetings at which classification or placement of the child will be decided, advising the parents of their due process rights if they disagree with the decision of the school committee, attending meetings on the child, following through on recommendations for placement if this is to be outside the school district, and coordinating services with other agencies are all part of the annual work required for each handicapped child in the school system. Some of these requirements are illustrated in the following case:

Ricky P

Ricky, age 13, was referred to the social worker because of his contention that he was being neglected by his mother. It was learned in the initial interview that Ricky had just returned from placement in a residential treatment center.

A complete evaluation of Ricky was made, including a social history taken from many contacts with Mrs. P. Ricky's behavior deteriorated significantly as the school year progressed, becoming at times abusive and bizarre. His attendance at school worsened, he became delinquent in the community, and he was suspended from school many times. Mrs. P became angry with the school because she believed the suspensions were causing Ricky to act out even more in the community. Ricky was indeed acting out more. Eventually he became a youthful offender and was assigned a probation officer. Furthermore, Mrs. P, who was on public assistance, told her caseworker and the school social worker that she was going to kill Ricky and herself. Thus a referral was made to protective services by both workers.

Ricky was eventually exempted from school attendance and referred to the Committee on the Handicapped for classification and placement.[18] The school social worker again met with Mrs. P, who at the time was angry and resistant to any help offered. However, it was explained to Mrs. P that the public school could not appropriately educate Ricky. It was also explained to Mrs. P that Ricky's case would be reviewed by the Committee on the Handicapped in order to take the necessary steps for making a more successful placement for him. The school social worker encouraged Mrs. P to attend the meeting on Ricky in order to express her feelings about what had happened to him, as well as to express what she believed would be the best placement for him. At that time, Mrs. P indicated that her pediatrician did not believe Ricky needed a residential placement. Mrs. P was encouraged by the school social worker to obtain a statement from the pediatrician as to his recommendations for presentation to the committee. She was also encouraged to bring the protective services worker to the meeting as her and Ricky's advocate.

The committee met on Ricky, classified him as handicapped for emotional reasons, and recommended a day treatment center. Mrs. P brought the letter from the pediatrician and her worker to the meeting. She was satisfied with the classification and recommendation. However, she was informed by the school social worker that if she later objected to the decisions, she should write a letter indicating her disapproval to the appropriate school official within ten days. Mrs. P signed two release forms, enabling the school social worker to refer Ricky to the day treatment programs.

Both agencies rejected Ricky in early June. One agency had schooling only for its residents, and the other program considered Ricky "too sick" for their program. Another committee meeting could not be held before the end of the school year. The school social worker, protective services worker, and pediatrician met to discuss Ricky's situation. All agreed that Ricky really needed a residential placement, but additionally that the placement needed to be made through the probation department to prevent Mrs. P from taking Ricky out of the program prematurely, as she had with the last placement. This meant that probation would select the placement, and their approved placements are not the same placements as those approved by the state education department for reimbursement to the local school district. Thus, Ricky remains unplaced.

The specific problem this case exemplifies—difficulties in placement because of interagency conflict—will be discussed later in this article.

EMERGING ISSUES

Emerging issues that are of special interest to social workers include issues of children's and parents' rights, issues surrounding the operations of the local education agency, and the community practitioner's responsibilities. These will be discussed in detail.

Children's and Parents' Rights

The confidentiality of records and rights of privacy granted to handicapped persons and their families in the Freedom of Information Law (September 1, 1974) and the Family Rights and Privacy Act of 1974, also known as the Buckley Amendment, are in some conflict with P.L. 94–142 as interpreted by New York State.[20] For example, in New York, the Committee on the Handicapped, which is responsible for reviewing, classifying, and recommending placement for all handicapped children within its district, is required to have as a core member a parent of a handicapped child residing in the school district. This raises the question of how confidentiality of the records of that parent's child can be maintained. Reynolds discusses some of the conflicts in several institutions that threaten confidentiality.[21] These concerns are now applicable to the public schools as well.

Questions have also been raised regarding the parents' rights versus the child's rights. For example, at what point in due process and by whom is it determined that a parent is incompetent to represent his or her own child? Who represents the foster child, and how is this decided? Who appoints a surrogate parent? What is considered an appropriate education?[22] How do local education agencies resolve these issues without court and/or agency intervention?

Child advocates are needed to implement P.L. 94–142. Yet many agency clinicians, educators, and members of the committees on the handicapped known to one of the authors have questioned the use of advocates. They have raised questions as to how the advocate is selected and whether use of an advocate represents a usurpation of parental rights. It is extremely difficult for employees of a local education agency to be advocates. As Carr-Saunders notes:

> Social workers and teachers . . . have a dual responsibility to the employer as well as the client. But the employer lays down the limits to the service which can be rendered and to some extent determines its kind and quality. As a result a social worker . . . is far from free to treat a person committed to his charge in a manner indicated by his professional training and experience.[23]

A volunteer or lay advocate might better safeguard the rights of children and parents. Social workers have the skills to assume an advocacy role in addition to acting as impartial hearing officers provided they function outside their own local education agency and there is no conflict of interest.[24]

The Local Education Agency

The local education agency is a bureaucracy with all of the innate qualities of such. Social workers may regard it from that sociological point of view, being cognizant at what point the pathology of the system exacerbatesthe problems of the handicapped child. Specifically, the functioning of such groups as the Committee on the Handicapped (which perform case reviews, decide the classification of a child's handicapping condition, and prescribe the child's educational program) must be thoroughly understood by the school social worker.[25]

A second area of concern that is well stated and documented by Weatherley and Lipsky in their study of special education reform in Massachusetts is that the new legal "requirements presented school personnel with an enormous increase in their workload in several ways" and "in some respects, . . . the implementation . . . actually resulted in a reduction of services, at least during the first year."[26]

A third problem is the severe deficit in funding for the special services needed to carry out the mandate of P.L. 94–142. Even the increasing amounts of money to be available over the five-year period of implementation are only recommendations and must be approved in the budget each year by Congress and the President.

Fourth, when needed services exist, there are often other legalities, regulations, and structures of community agencies providing noneducational as well as educational services that prevent the successful use of these resources by the clients or the school. This was exemplified in the case of Ricky P. cited earlier. A social work task may be to assume some responsibility for assessing and communicating the noneducational needs of the school-age population in the community and to help to determine where the responsibility of the local education agency ends and the other community agencies' responsibilities begin. Many potentially successful placements of handicapped children have been delayed and in some cases denied because of interagency conflict regarding responsibility.

Although much has been said about the classification and labeling of the school-age handicapped child, little has been said about the purpose of such classification. Should the classification be clinical or should it be functional for the child's education? Should the classification be merely a tool for obtaining needed services or funding? Does the classification make for differences in the individualized prescribed educational methods and techniques to be used with the child?

Many questions arise as to the adequacy of current individualized educational planning for the handicapped child. Three questions seem most prevalent: (1) Do current laws and regulations feed into the tendency to plan on a short-term basis? (2) Should such planning for the school-aged handicapped child include ancillary services both within and outside the local education agencies? (3) How are the gaps in community services to be closed for the child leaving the school and entering the community upon completion of schooling?

The Community Practitioner's Responsibilities

The roles played by social, mental health, medical, and recreational agencies, as well as by private practitioners, are an important part of the delivery of services under P.L. 94–142. Community practitioners' knowledge of both the ascribed and assumed roles of the local education agencies is important. Social workers in the community will be called upon to provide both information and advocacy for both parents and children. They need to be familiar with the legalities governing their clients' educational and due process rights.

It is imperative that community practitioners be knowledgeable about federal, state, and local laws and regulations. However, equally important, they must be knowledgeable as to local school organization, lines of authority, and specific job functions of the various school employees who affect evaluation, review, and placement of handicapped children. Without such knowledge of the education system, community practitioners will be essentially immobilized in trying to work through the system for the benefit of their clients. This implies a need for the practitioners in the community to form working relationships with school personnel both within and outside the pupil personnel departments.

A NEW SET OF PROBLEMS

The implementation of P.L. 94–142 requires a new perspective on program policies, administration, and delivery of related social, medical, and rehabilitative services as well as special education for handicapped children. School social workers may have to reset priorities in providing services to meet the legal requirements of P.L. 94–142 satisfactorily. For example, state interpretations of the federal laws impose time periods, such as no more than 30 days from the time of referring a child for an evaluation to the time the Committee on the Handicapped must meet to recommend a classification and placement. In the past, making appointments for evaluation, evaluating the child, and getting results have often taken months. This may make it difficult or impossible to follow such basic social work tenets as "starting where the client is" or "traveling at the client's pace."

We may need to take a hard look at any inequity in services offered to nonhandicapped children that may result from the amount of services and the cost of educating handicapped children. Parent groups representing nonhandicapped children, particularly those concerned with education of gifted children, as well as school administrators, are already questioning this inequity, which may produce a negative backlash. The backlash effect must not be allowed to obscure the original inequities the federal legislation was intended to correct before handicapped children are included in the educational system. Graduate-level training for social workers may need to include information in the allied fields of education, law, and child advocacy. As Senna has written:

> Social work practitioners and other professionals who are in the field of human services and who are providing the services ought to be aware of the extent of judicial intervention which is occurring increasingly when basic human rights are violated. Also, judicial solutions to human service problems have an impact on overall agency administration, types of programs, and eligibility requirements, as well as professional education.[27]

SUMMARY

A review of the new federal education laws reveals that they are the result of a civil rights movement by and on behalf of handicapped persons and their families. From this movement has come social reform that many social workers consider long overdue.

Implementing the specifics of the legislation is not without problems, however. At times the legislation seems to contradict its original intent of providing legal assurance to every handicapped child of the right to an appropriate education and to every parent or guardian of a handicapped child of the right to be involved in the identification, assessment, and educational placement of the child.

School social workers have a central role to play in implementing the provisions of P.L. 94–142, The Education of All Handicapped Children Act of 1975. Social workers in practice settings involved in any way with services to handicapped children and/or their families may also be instrumental in providing and interpreting information about the laws to parents, referring parents for additional information or assistance regarding their legal rights, organizing workshops or classes on legislation for parents and school staff, counseling parents to enable them to use their rights, or becoming advocates for handicapped children and/or their parents. A few social workers will want to join in coalitions and activities to continue implementing legislative reform for handicapped persons at the state and local levels. The potential for being a part of systemic change to benefit the handicapped minority and their families is now open to social workers and others with a social conscience.

NOTES AND REFERENCES

1. Other writers have referred to this period as a quiet revolution. *See,* for example, **P. R. Diamond**, "The Constitutional Right to Education: The Quiet Revolution," The *Hastings Law Journal,* 24 (1973), pp. 1087–1127; and **Frederick J. Weintraub and Alan Abeson**, *Public Policy and the Education of Exceptional Children* (Reston, Va.: The Council for Exceptional Children, 1976), p. 7.

2. 94th Congress, P.L. 94–142, S. 6, November 29, 1975. In the "Statement of Findings and Purpose," *see* 3(b) "The Congress finds that (1) there are more than eight million handicapped children in the United States today."

3. Many of the provisions of P.L. 94–142 were included in a section of P.L. 93–380, passed more than a year earlier. U.S., Congress, 93rd Congress, P.L. 93–380, August 1974.

4. For additional information on the ages and categories of children not in school, *see Children Out of School in America,* a report by the Children's Defense Fund of the Washington Research Project, Inc. (Cambridge, Mass.: Children's Defense Fund, October 1974).

5. *Handicap* is defined as "a generic term that is considered synonymous with a limiting impairment of bodily form or function, or with a circumstance in the environment that limits or makes a particular activity or function impossible." *See* **William A. Spencer, MD., and Maurine B. Mitchell**, "Disability and Physical Handicap," *Encyclopedia of Social Work,* 16th ed., Vol. 1 (New York: National Association of Social Workers, 1971), p. 204. Handicapped children include those who are deaf or hearing impaired, blind or visually impaired, orthopedically handicapped, neurologically impaired or brain damaged, speech impaired, emotionally disturbed, mentally retarded, and the multiply handicapped—those with more than one handicapping condition.

6. For a fuller discussion of due process, *see* **Alan Abeson, Nancy Bolick, and Jayne Hass**, eds., *A Primer on Due Process: Education Decisions for Handicapped Children* (Reston, Va.: Council for Exceptional Children, 1975).

7. "Handicapped Act: Biggest Program since Title 1," *Washington Monitor,* December 8, 1975, p. 89.

8. **Abeson, Bolick, and Hass**, op. cit., p. 3.

9. **Tom O'Donnell**, "Sources of Law: Right to an Equal Educational Opportunity," *Amicus,* 2 (April 1977), pp. 22–26.

10. The regulations for P.L. 93–112 were signed by Secretary of Health, Education, and Welfare Joseph A. Califano, Jr., on April 29, 1977.

11. "President Ford Signs S.6," *The Exceptional Parent,* 5 (December 1975), p. 12.

12. **Weintraub and Abeson**, op. cit., p. 7.

13. The Council for Exceptional Children has produced a series of three film strip-cassettes to provide a review of P.L. 94–142 for parents, professionals, and administrators. Copies are available for purchase from the Council for Exceptional Children, 1920 Association Drive, Reston, Virginia.

14. P.L. 94–142, op. cit., Sec. 3 (c). For a discussion of implementation of P.L. 94–142, *see* Tom Irvin, "Implementation of Public Law 94–142," *Exceptional Children,* 43 (November 1976), pp. 135–137.

15. For copies of federal laws, such as P.L. 94–142, write to House or Senate Document Room, U.S. Capitol, Washington, D.C. 20510; Library of Congress, Division for the Blind and Physically Handicapped, 1291 Taylor Street, N.W., Washington, D.C. 20542; Bureau of Education for the Handicapped, U.S. Office of Education, 400 Maryland Avenue, S.W., Washington, D.C. 20202; U.S. Department of Health, Education, and Welfare, Office for Handicapped Individuals, Washington, D.C. 20201; National Information Center for the Handicapped, Box 1492, Washington, D.C. 20013 (newsletter, *Closer Look,* sent free upon request); The National Center for Law and the Handicapped, 1235 North Eddy Street, South Bend, Ind. 46617 (newsletter, *Amicus,* sent free upon request); Council for Exceptional Children, 1920 Association Drive, Reston, Va. 22091 (newsletter, *Insight,* subscription $20 a year). A comprehensive handbook that includes a section on education laws is President's Committee on Employment of the Handicapped, *A Handbook on the Legal Rights of Handicapped People* (Washington, D.C.: U.S. Government Printing Office, 1977). For copies of state laws and regulations, write your state education department.

16. **E. Virginia Lapham**, *Education Laws: Your Child and You, A Legislative Handbook for Parents* (Bronx, N.Y.: New York Institute for the Education of the Blind, April 1977).

17. For a discussion of teachers' rights, *see* Weintraub and Abeson, op. cit., Sec. V, pp. 331–378; and *The Rights of Teachers,* an American Civil Liberties Union Handbook (New York: Avon Books, 1971).

18. **Richard Weatherley and Michael Lipsky**, "Street-Level Bureaucrats and Institutional Innovation: Implementing Special-Education Reform," *Harvard Educational Review,* 47 (May 1977), p. 180.

19. In the state of New York, each local education agency must have a Committee on the Handicapped to review, evaluate, and recommend placement for each child thought to have a handicapping condition as well as to review annually the placements of children in special education programs. The committee must consist of a psychologist, teacher or supervisor of special education, physician, parent of a

handicapped child living in the school district, and other persons appointed by the chief school officer.

20. The Family Rights and Privacy Act of 1974 is contained in P.L. 93–380.

21. **Mildred M. Reynolds**, "Threats to Confidentiality," *Social Work,* 21 (March 1976), pp. 108–113.

22. Chapter 853 of the New York State Education Law, passed July 1976, requires only that each child with a handicapping condition be provided with a suitable placement. Whether this conforms to the federal law of most appropriate placement may well be challenged at some point.

23. **Alexander Carr-Saunders**, "Metropolitan Conditions and Traditional Professional Relations, in **Robert M. Fischer**, ed., *The Metropolis in Modern Life* (Garden City, N.Y.: Doubleday & Co., 1955), p. 283.

24. For a discussion of advocacy, *see* **Max R. Addison, Dennis E. Haggerty, and Marie Moore**, "Advocates on Advocacy: Defining Three Approaches," *Amicus,* 1 (May 1976), pp. 9–16.

25. **Joyce De Christopher**, "The Committee on the Handicapped," *The School Social Worker and The Education of the Emotionally Handicapped Child* (Glen Falls, N.Y.: University of the State of New York, November 1973), pp. 56–60.

26. Op. cit., pp. 181 and 190.

27. **Joseph J. Senna**, "The Trend Toward Wider Use of Due Process," *Social Work,* 19 (May 1974), p. 319.